T0301572

Management, labour and industrial politics in
modern Europe

Management, labour and industrial politics in modern Europe

The quest for productivity growth during the Twentieth Century

Edited by

Joseph Melling,
University of Exeter, UK

and

Alan McKinlay,
University of Stirling, UK

Edward Elgar
Cheltenham, UK and Brookfield, US

Published by
Edward Elgar Publishing Limited
8 Lansdown Place
Cheltenham
Glos GL50 2HU
UK

Edward Elgar Publishing Company
Old Post Road
Brookfield
Vermont 05036
US

British Library Cataloguing in Publication Data
Melling, Joseph
    Management, labour and industrial politics in modern Europe:
    the quest for productivity and growth during the twentieth
    century
    1. Labor economics – Europe. 2. Industrial policy – Europe
    3. Development economics – Europe
    I. Title II. McKinlay, Alan, 1957–
    331'.094

Library of Congress Cataloguing in Publication Data
Management, labour, and industrial politics in modern Europe: the
    quest for productivity growth during the twentieth century / edited
    by Joseph Melling and Alan McKinlay
        Papers presented at a conference held at the University of Glasgow
    in 1992.
        Includes index.
        1. Labour productivity—Europe—Case studies—Congresses. 2. Labor
    policy—Europe—Case studies—Congresses. 3. Industrial management-
    -Europe—Case Studies—Congresses. 4. Industrial relations—Europe-
    -Case studies—Congresses. 5. Labor productivity—Great Britain-
    -History—20th century—Congresses. 6. Labor productivity—Germany-
    -History—20th century—Congresses. 7. Labor productivity—Sweden-
    -History—20th century—Congresses. I. Melling, Joseph.
    II. McKinlay, Alan, 1957–
    HC240.9.I52M36 1996   95–49464
    331.11'094—dc20   CIP

ISBN 1 85898 016 X

Printed and bound in Great Britain by
Biddles Limited, Guildford and King's Lynn

Contents

Figures

List of Contributors

Werner Abelshauser is Professor of Economic and Social History at the University of Bielefeld University. His many publications include studies of industrialisation, the welfare state and the economic history of West Germany since 1945.

Alan Booth is Senior Lecturer in Economic History at the University of Exeter. He has written extensively on economic policy-making in the UK, including studies of the Keynesian revolution, unemployment legislation, and post-war economic development.

Christoph Dartmann is Lecturer in History at the University of Aberdeen. His research thesis was devoted to an examination of post-war productivity politics in West Germany and he is currently researching the growth of business welfare programmes.

Lars Ekdahl is a Senior Researcher at the Fellow at the Arbetslivinstituut, Stockholm, and has published on printing workers in Sweden. He has researched Swedish labour relations extensively and is currently researching a life of Rudolf Meidner and the formation of the Rehn-Meidner model.

Alf Johansson is a Reader at the Department of Economic History, Uppsala University and has published widely in Swedish labour history, having led a major research project on the history of work in Sweden. He is currently researching the economic history of the post-war period and comparative labour politics in Scandinavia.

Alan McKinlay is Professor of Management and Organisational Behaviour at the University of Stirling. He has researched and written on a variety of subjects including the history of labour relations in the engineering industry, Ford and Fordism in Europe, and the regional development of west Scotland.

Joseph Melling is Senior Lecturer in Economic and Social History at the University of Exeter. His publications include studies of business welfare and the welfare state, supervisory management, and the comparative labour politics of Britain and Scandinavia.

Jim Tomlinson is Reader in Economic History at Brunel University, and author of a number of books and articles on twentieth century British economic policy, including *Democratic Socialism and economic policy: the Attlee years* to be published by Cambridge University Press (1996).

Jonathan Winterton is Senior Lecturer in Management at the University of Bradford. He has published extensively on the history and politics of the British coalmining industry and the comparative history of mining in the UK and abroad.

Ruth Winterton is an experienced Researcher who has worked with Jonathan Winterton on a variety of research projects and consultancies in the UK and Europe.

Preface

The contributions to this volume of essays began life as papers at the conference on 'Work and authority in modern Europe', held at the University of Glasgow in 1992 and hosted by the Centre for Business History in Scotland. Alan McKinlay jointly organised the original conference. Professor McKinlay and I are grateful to Professor Tony Slaven for his help and hospitality at the time of the conference, including the funding of many conference expenses. Versions of many of the papers have been presented at the workshops attended by Alan Booth and myself as part of the network on European productivity organised by Werner Abelshauser at the University of Florence. The Universities of Exeter and Glasgow made a contribution to defraying the costs of publication.

Following the original conference I assumed the primary role in editing the papers, liaising with the authors, and preparing the essays for publication. In my editing tasks I received encouragement and valuable advice from members of the European research network on productivity politics as well as the separate network on productivity growth in the post-War period coordinated by Nick Crafts and Steve Broadberry. Alan Booth has been particularly generous with his time and criticisms as co-researcher on an Economic and Social Research Council project examining some of these questions in the British context. Chris Wrigley offered useful suggestions as a reader for the publishers, for which I am grateful. In preparing the text for publication I received valuable assistance from Ray Burnley and Kate Tyler at the Social Studies Data Processing Unit at the University of Exeter. Their help was particularly useful when I was compiling the Index. Edward Elgar, Dymphna Evans and especially Julie Leppard at Edward Elgar were unfailingly positive in their advice and direction. Kjersti Bosdotter of Svenska Metall in Stockholm searched the archives for suitable cover photographs, for which I'm grateful. Finally, I wish to thank the contributors for tolerating my editorial edicts with such a good grace, and my son Ross for giving me so many moments of light relief in the, occasionally laborious, task of editing these essays.

Joseph Melling
University of Exeter

1. Management, labour and the politics of productivity: strategies and struggles in Britain, Germany and Sweden *

Joseph Melling

These essays are primarily concerned with the ways in which labour management became the subject of political interest during the middle decades of the twentieth century. Industrial production features, necessarily, in the power and authority structures of modern societies. Industrialisation has been encouraged, if not orchestrated, by states seeking to modernise their production systems and increase their economic and military resources. During the 1930s new forms of state management and economic regulation were devised which subjected large areas of industry to political scrutiny and debate. The politics of industry were no longer driven merely by the explosive confrontations of capital and labour, or the threats of national strikes. Various forms of state regulation were evolved to promote output and harmony, or to protect the public interest. Labour management was itself developed in this changing political environment, as the comparative experience of Britain, Germany and Sweden demonstrate. Many of the contributions in this volume examine the formative period of European reconstruction between the defeat of fascism and the onset of structural crisis in older European industries at the end of the 1960s. The collection includes surveys of industrial policy-making alongside more detailed examinations of mining and metalworking. Each study is grounded on primary research as well as a review of recent secondary literature.

The early chapters outline the strategies pursued by peak organisations of employers, labour and political parties as they wrestled to define the scope and limits of state intervention in the national economy. Later essays consider the dynamics of production, innovation and bargaining in coal and engineering. These case studies suggest that the public debates on productivity growth in post-war Europe formed only the most visible expression of production politics which were formed and defined at the workplace and in industrial society, as well as in the corridors of the nation state. The surveys of particular industries also reveal the complex material conditions in which workplace politics evolved and the different levels of political activity which can be identified in sectors such as

1

coalmining. Such areas of production possessed not only the powerful physical and regional characteristics which were embodied in the structure of the industry, but also the distinctive layers of authority and power relations which defined the bargaining nexus between capital, labour and the state.

The contributions share an assumption that industrial management is a product not merely of the technical capacities of production and organisation but also of the wider social and political environment in which it is practised. After both the First and the Second World War, the Continent saw not only the creation of a new political state system and the rebuilding of the European economies, but also the creation of new forms of bargaining relations between capital and labour, involving the formation of fresh management structures and strategies to deal with changes in the environment of production. These reforms in the arrangement and management of production were deeply contested and remained a battleground in countries even where a strong consensus was reached on political and civic ethics after 1945. An important feature of the growing stability of bargaining relations during the 1950s was the gradual recognition of such consensual values and social goals as a basis for centralised agreements on wages and conditions of labour in a number of European countries. Social Democratic and Christian Democratic parties were closely associated with such projects and with the ideology of 'welfare capitalism' which emerged particularly clearly in Scandinavia and Germany. Social democrats in Britain had held power for a relatively short period after the war, though centre-left intellectuals in the UK also contributed to the enduring myth of evolutionary socialism via collective ownership and consumption.

Much of the debate on the relative merits of public and private management models in post-war Europe has revolved around the growth of corporatism in the capitalist economies. Contemporary socialists were divided between those who recognised centralised bargaining between producers and the state as a refinement of organised capitalism, and those (like Walter Korpi) who hailed the advent of 'welfare capitalism' as a significant step on the road to economic and social democracy.[1] Similar differences of perspective can be found in the parallel literature on the growth of the European welfare states, which formed such a significant feature of the post-war settlement and the terms in which the European labour market was organised after 1945.[2] The role of collective consumption and the economic welfare effects of central bargaining is a key theme in recent discussions of economic performance in corporatist and free market economies, stimulated by the work of Calmfors and Driffill.[3] Debates continue amongst those seeking an efficient form of 'market socialism' as well as those engaged in a sustained assault on the principle of collective regulation.[4]

Yet it was the social democratic models of regulation which were subjected to the most powerful and effective criticisms as the Keynesian forms of fiscal management were discredited in the 1970s and the radical right seized the initiative in the 1980s, defeating social democratic parties in Britain, Germany and Sweden where their grip on power had been considerable. Many writers have followed Mancur Olson in emphasising the deleterious impact which organised interests (and particularly those of labour unions) had on the moderate performance of many European economies in the post-war era.[5] The post-war era is seen not only as a golden age of capitalism but also the zenith of European corporatism. These producers' interests are embodied in the institutional structures of capital, labour and the state which appear to dominate the politics of post-war Europe. To sociologists such as Lash and Urry this period marked the high point of organised capitalism before the mode of 'disorganised capitalism' emerged after the international crises of the 1970s.[6] There is much less agreement with Olson's central claim that producers' organisations cemented the distributional coalitions which appropriated the fruits of output, distorting the efficient play of the market and impeding output growth. These effects were most marked (argued Olson) in those countries where there had been a long period of political stability and institutional growth, where sectional groups of producers had been most successful in inserting themselves into the existing order and promoting their claims until restrained by free market forces.[7]

This climate of critical appraisal has provoked a wide-ranging appraisal of the whole social democratic project, including its intellectual coherence and the historical significance of social democrats to the formation of welfare states and the impact of such social reforms on the economic vitality of the countries engaged in building welfare programmes.[8] Scholars such as Barnett have figured prominently in the attacks on post-war welfare and corporatist collusion, though the criticism of co-operative arrangements and collectivist experiments (particularly in the case of Britain) has become part of the mainstream literature on the post-war economy.[9] Even though such reforms were often supported by Christian Democratic and agrarian interests concerned to protect their own position in post-war Europe, it was Europe's parliamentary socialists who became closely identified with the models of central bargaining, corporatist representation and welfare expenditure. Intellectual legitimacy for 'welfare capitalism' in post-war Europe was provided by socialist intellectuals such as Walter Korpi, linking the mobilisation of the working class to the growth of social citizenship and economic democracy in such countries as Sweden.[10] Such pathways to modernity appear less secure in the aftermath of the collapse of centralised bargaining in Sweden, as the essay by Ekdahl and Johansson indicates.[11]

Even though the ethics of consensus politics and labour market protection have been progressively stripped away by radical neo-liberals, weakening or demolishing many of the institutional supports erected in the post-war era, it is clear that European capitalism continues to be supported by institutional structures that derive from collaborative practices as well as market forces.[12] In studies of post-war Britain, it is widely recognised that institutional developments (rather than class relations or the social environment) has been the defining feature of economic and political relations, strengthening older institutionalist interpretations which had dominated the disciplines of labour history and industrial relations before the rise of radical and new Marxist accounts of production struggles.[13] Institutionalist accounts emphasise the importance of formal bargaining structures, usually focusing on the specific historical conditions in which sectional representation developed and the relationship between organised employers, labour and the state rather than the wider social and cultural environment in which producers established their identities as members of a class or fraternity.[14]

In such studies the vital context for the practice of labour management are the technical and market conditions which prevailed in particular industries, coupled to the 'institutional dispositions' of the parties in collective bargaining and the specific strategies pursued by employers, labour and the state over a significant period of time.[15] In their survey of employers' labour strategies in different countries, Tolliday and Zeitlin provide an explanation of variations in labour management which draws heavily on the institutionalist perspectives of industrial relations, economics and business history.[16] Whilst stressing the fundamental importance of institutional 'interaction between the strategic choices of employers, trade unions and the state', as the framework for the management of labour, such writers largely discount the relevance of class, social, national or cultural identities in the explanation of national diversities.[17]

There is little doubt that the institutionalist approach to labour relations provides important insights into the dynamics of collective bargaining and has drawn attention to the fundamental role of formal organisations in defining the nexus between management and organised labour. From this vantage point, the politics of the European labour movements and the industrial milieus in which European management was reconstructed in the post-war period appears considerably more complex than an heroic account of class struggle would allow.[18] Earlier interpretations of post-war reconstruction which stressed the importance of popular mobilisation and radical sentiments in the politics of the 1940s have also been weakened by recent research on the period, which underlines the degree to which established elites, state bureaucracies and business leaders were able to shape events even in periods of social democratic success.[19] Even in the former fascist regimes, there now appear significant continuities between the wartime and post-war politics of organised business in occupied Europe.[20] 'Radical' Reconstruction may be viewed as the legacy of existing power elites at least as much as the product of popular mobilisation against the fascist authorities.[21] Such reappraisals differ from earlier Marxist criticisms of the limits of the post-war settlements as recent revisionist accounts question the coherence of class politics and class interests even in the early period of reconstruction, as questions are raised about the depth and weight of the radical challenge to existing institutions of governance. Older Marxist explanations of the functions of the state in capitalist societies have been subjected to intense criticism in new interpretations of the state-building and the interests of those who serve and manage the state.[22]

The enormous emphasis which has been placed on the role of institutions in economic development and the relations between capitalist management and labour has also contributed to the increased recognition of the role of the state in the rebuilding of the post-war European economies, including Marquand's celebrated discussion of the success of the 'developmental state' in countries such as Germany and the failure of British elites to undertake a similar task of economic transformation in the modern period.[23] Writing from a conservative rather than social democratic perspective, Barnett has recently restated his thesis that the post-war social democrats made the fundamental error of engaging in costly welfare programmes at the expense of economic renovation and thereby missed a golden opportunity to seize a competitive advantage in Europe.[24] Numerous other writers have attributed the problems which the British economy has experienced in comparison with its more successful European neighbours, to the inadequacies and distortions of its institutional structures - from the legacy of family capitalism to the politics of stalemate which infected its governmental structures.[25]

The brief survey given above merely illuminates some salient features of a rich and complex range of work, though it is clear that there are points of convergence in these studies which suggest that the institutional framework of post-war Europe provided the critical context for the development of labour management in the western capitalist democracies. There are also unresolved issues within the institutionalist literature which have implications for our understanding of management-labour relations. If we define institutions as a set of rules and constraints on behaviour then it follows that actors are not governed simply by market signals or rational calculations of their immediate needs and interests. The rational appreciation of these needs and interests must itself be constructed in terms of the expectations or perceptions defined by the institution for its members. Yet the work of scholars such as Mancur Olson appears to be grounded on the assumption that institutions defend the self-evident sectional interests of diverse social groups, whilst generating conflicts between the leaders of the organisation and its members.[26] Such a reading of institutional behaviour assumes reasonably constant preferences amongst the leaders and members, for continued power, more consumer goods, avoidance of the welfare consequences of their pursuit of self-interest, and so on. This approach enables ready comparison of institutional strategies across time and space, though it exaggerates the extent of institutional coherence and scope whilst understating the degree to which the functions of institutions are defined by the social, political and cultural relationships that surround and permeate them. It is arguable that bargaining institutions, in common with other bodies of rules, not only prescribe the terms of engagement with the opposing party but also reflect a wider distribution of power in society. The capacity of institutions to exercise power is dependent on possessing the intellectual and cultural resources to provide the members with a coherent understanding of their interests and how these may be politically mobilised. Essays by Abelshauser, Booth and Ekdahl and Johansson in this volume indicate how laboriously were the interests of capital and labour constructed and reconstructed by different groups of employers, workers and politicians in post-war European countries. Regional and confessional as well as sectional loyalties had to be overcome as new alliances were formed in economy and politics.

Most of the essays in this volume share an assumption that the economic structures of each country and the patterns of employment found in industry have an important bearing on the relationships which underpin institutional power. In contrast to much of the revisionist literature of recent years, most contributors emphasise the tensions in management-labour relations and the political significance of workplace conflicts in post-war Europe, including the detailed account of conflicts over technology provided in the Wintertons' analysis of new technologies in the British coal industry. The institutional developments in labour relations and the environment of labour management becomes more comprehensible when we recall the fundamental features of European economic development in the middle decades of the twentieth century.

It is possible to identify three broad trends in the changing structure of the European labour market during the during the middle decades of the twentieth century which shaped the context of management-labour relations. The first general characteristic of European labour in this period is the remarkable significance of primary extractive industries (particularly coalmining) and metalworking sectors in the years between the rearmament recovery of the 1930s and the onset of structural crises in the late 1960s. Not only were coal, iron and steel the basic constituents of the first economic community across European states, but they were a substantial proportion of output in the old industrial society of Britain and in some of the industrialising peripheral economies of Europe.[27] The strategic importance of coal and metal industries to European output in these years underpinned the rapid growth of the economies of both west and east Europe after the war, giving the highly unionised labour force a leading role in the industrial and political struggles of this period. Workers in the energy sectors were able to extend their position in the earnings league during the oil crises of the early 1970s, though as Abelhauser's essay on the Ruhr and the Wintertons' on British coal indicate, the balance of advantage was already shifting away from the coalminers of west Europe at the end of the 1960s. McKinlay's study of post-war engineering and the essay on Sweden's historic compromise as well as Dartmann's survey of German industrial politics suggests the enormous influence which metal unions could exercise in the years when solidaristic politics were being pursued by social democrats. Whether we see the past two decades in terms of the birth of disorganised capitalism and flexible specialisation, or as the triumph of regulated capitalism on a Germanic and

Japanese model, there is little doubt that the strategic position occupied by the miners and metalworkers in European heavy industry has been severely weakened by the collapse or contraction of the traditional industrial base in Europe. Very different skills are now required of labour managers even in the mass production metalworking factories which spread so rapidly in the post-war era.

A second fundamental trend shaping the fortunes of European workers during much of the twentieth century has been the rapid growth of private and public service employment, generating increased demand particularly for female labour but affecting every aspect of production in the mid-century decades. Kocka has pointed out how the state bureaucracy in nineteenth century Prussia provided a model of organisation which the business community assimilated in building industrial enterprises during the industrialisation of Germany, though it is arguable that the key function of the state was to promote the knowledge base which enabled German industry to develop a technical superiority in key branches of production by the beginning of the twentieth century.[28] The Germanic model of technical education certainly assisted the scientific, professional and management 'white collar' grades to acquire the status and cultural resources to associate as a distinct group of salaried staff, occupying a quite separate position from that of organised labour in countries such as Germany.[29] Whilst Sweden and France provided technical education and promoted scientific methods in industry on lines similar to those found in Germany, it has often been noted that Britain retain an artisanal and practical knowledge base in many key sectors of production and did not create the educational system which would have provided students with high technical and scientific abilities to proceed to industrial management.[30] Even where the state specified a rigorous standard of training and qualification for hazardous industries, there was little evidence that technical instruction was developed as part of a scientific culture which strengthened the knowledge base of British management. As the essay on safety in the coal industry demonstrate, the technical knowledge of the mining deputy and his safety obligations to the state became a battleground between employers, supervisors and workers engaged in production struggles before and after the Second World War.

These deficiencies have led some writers to argue that insufficient attention was paid to the productive needs of British industry after 1945 and too many resources were devoted to expensive programmes of social welfare by an unscientific and unworldly state elite.[31] It is difficult to sustain a case that the United Kingdom was at all exceptional in the proportion of domestic product which was dedicated to welfare expenditure in the post-war period, and on some calculations it was well below competitors such as France, Germany and Sweden.[32] Nor can it be assumed that public expenditure on welfare programmes was necessarily an alternative to investment in industry or human capital, as the example of technical education noted above indicates. For a third key structural feature of the post-war European labour market (both east and west) has been the remarkable growth in the employment of women. One of the most powerful stimuli for and response to the growth of welfare expenditure was this rising tide of female employment throughout Europe in the post-war period, with the heaviest participation rates in the 23-45 years age range, when women were most in need of family support.[33] Even if women were often directed into lower status and lesser paid employment in industry and services, there is little doubt that they represented the most significant addition to the European labour force in the post-war years and that welfare amenities to assist maternity and family care were an important part of the politics of household maintenance in this period.[34] The addition of females to the European workforce also represented a challenge for management seeking to respond to the demands of women workers whilst devising various methods of control for the growing numbers of white collar staff in a wide range of service sectors.

The expansion of services and female employment was to a significant extent generated by state expenditure and involved public sector investment as well as the explosive growth of private sector services. The social as well as economic consequences of public sector employment should not be underestimated. Nationalisation of whole sectors of industry was relatively unusual in the western capitalist democracies, though public ownership rather than state regulation was adopted by social democrats most noticeably in the UK in 1945-51. It is interesting that nationalisation in Britain should have come in such male-dominated industries as coal, steel and railways, and that the state was not merely responding to lengthy campaigns by male workers to protect their jobs but also retained the heavily masculinist character of employment and working methods thereafter. This may be contrasted with the preponderance of female labour in many of the booming private and public services at this period. The essays by Abelshauser, the Wintertons, and myself confirm the point that, in historical practice, the existence of state property rights was usually less important than the forms of corporate management adopted and the scope for the participation of employees in the executive decisions of the enterprise. In Germany and Sweden there was much greater access by leading unions to the instruments of strategic planning, though the political costs of engaging in decision-making at moments of structural crisis were as apparent in those countries as in the UK during the 1970s. It should also be remembered that it was the threat to capitalist control of the Swedish economy in the radical wages-fund campaign of the 1970s which precipitated a crisis in the consensual order and prompted the emergence of a radical conservative opposition, advocated by the business community. Property rights clearly matter, though they do not necessarily imply the enlargement of positive rights or active control for citizens.

To explain the limited success of public sector employment in generating new forms of labour management and workforce empowerment we need to examine not only the dynamics of European growth and the politics of the Cold War during and after the Marshall Plan era, but also the particular conditions which prevailed in the nation states of the post-war world. Such assessments reveal not only the value but also the limits of institutionalist accounts which understate the importance of different modes of intellectual, cultural and social production in the making of labour relations and labour management. Even in the high politics of economic planning and corporate discussions, where the interactions between the formal organisations of capital, labour and the state appear most visible and substantive, it is evident that these relations were part of a complex process in which interests and loyalties were being re-defined after the turmoil of the war years. One of the most significant features in the process of social reassessment was the engagement of middle class and agrarian interests with the risks they shared in common with working class groups and the support for the welfare state project in the 1940s.[35] The growth of solidaristic politics and popular support for the principle of central wage regulation and distribution bargaining, appear to have had deepest roots in countries like Sweden, where a collective culture was actively nurtured by social democrats in the interwar period and where (as in Germany) the right of the state to define national economic goals was widely accepted. It is widely argued that the terms of the post-war settlement in Britain seriously hindered the development of effective management in large sections of production, contributing directly to the comparatively modest rates of productivity growth recorded before the 1980s.[36] Yet there *were* opportunities for similar reforms in the United Kingdom after 1945, and it is worth briefly considering the fate of various radical initiatives as a means of assessing the contribution of different institutional and non-institutional forces to the determination of state-industry relations and the formation of the peacetime bargaining environment.

The making of the British disorder: post-war production debates

The institutionalist bias of British historical scholarship is evident in recent studies of the development of bargaining arrangements and production politics in the 1940s, with much of the current literature devoted to an examination of strategies devised by national organisations of employers and labour. Their relationship with the state and what we might term the 'high politics' of economic development and collective bargaining has been the principal focus of recent research. Thus Clegg's magisterial study of trade unions in the 1940s inevitably devotes a large space to the consideration of Government policy, from wages to nationalisation.[37] Although the period of the post-war Labour Government has attracted a number of impressive research studies, writers have usually addressed one of two key problems: firstly, the degree to which the social democrats in Britain achieved a fundamental shift in the balance of power and opportunity by social and economic reforms; and secondly, the impact of the Labour programme and its post-war settlement on the longer term economic prospects and performance of the British economy. Barnett has again restated his thesis that gains and benefits in the area of social citizenship resulted in a substantial cost to Britain in the neglect of its production base.[38] Hinton offers a contrasting interpretation of the 1940s as a period when the promise of new citizenship via democratic control over production withered in the hands of the Labour Government, in marked contrast to planning experiments in contemporary France.[39] In their detailed investigation of productivity initiatives during the Attlee years, Tomlinson and Tiratsoo argue that British industrialists were able to effectively sabotage progress towards industrial renovation by exploiting the vacillation of Labour at key periods of potential reform.[40]

Such debates are a valuable resource for research on post-war labour management though they have been largely concerned with establishing the moral responsibility for the failures of political intervention and the institutional barriers to reform rather than the changing context of industrial politics in wider society. Many of the structural features of the European economy and society can be seen in specific forms in the British case, though the institutional arrangements which existed in Britain embodied the peculiar relationships and cultural identities of the UK. Close examination of the initiatives taken by the post-war Labour Government suggest that there were indeed opportunities for fashioning a new kind of productionist alliance between business, labour and the state in the 1940s, though the ultimate failure of such initiatives have to be traced to the limitations of political imagination within the ranks of the employers, organised labour, and the state itself rather than to the iniquities of one group of producers. This intellectual poverty was as apparent as the institutional rigidities which it fostered and drew upon.

On assuming office in 1945, Britain's social democrats had an unprecedented opportunity for implementing radical economic and social reform. One of the main concerns of the incoming Attlee Government was to secure the revival of overseas trade as a means of restoring the balance of payments and dealing with the American deficit. Shortages of investment capital, skilled labour and raw materials restricted the scope for output growth and pointed to the need to raise the productivity of labour by more effective management of existing manpower, as the essays by Booth and Tomlinson show. Difficulties with the balance of payments remained throughout the 1940s and provided the background to the vague experiments with new forms of economic and labour management at this period. The transformation of labour relations and the creation of a centralised system of bargaining and consultation was certainly one means by which a social democratic government might promote 'productivity coalition' between capital and labour similar to those devised in Sweden and Germany. There were other alternatives available to a political party which had the confidence to undertake a sweeping programme of nationalisation in key sectors of the British economy.

The first possible strategy by which Labour might transform bargaining relations and develop fresh models of labour management was in the newly 'socialised' (i.e. nationalised) sectors of industry directly under state control. Labour did not have to deal with intransigent employers in such industries as coalmining, gas, electricity, railways and steelmaking. Amongst social democrats there was some consensus on the advantages of extending consultation with the workforce after nationalisation.[41] British civil servants recognised the value of exploiting the commitment of miners and railway workers to public ownership, which would be lost if workers and their managers felt that they 'were simply working for a fresh set of employers'.[42] Yet the bureaucrats who considered the practical measures which could be adopted to achieve workers' assistance in the management of public corporations, emphasised from the outset the basic autonomy of the Boards responsible for each industry, and the first duty of their trade unions to represent employees.[43] The minister commonly recognised as the British architect of the public corporation, Herbert Morrison, underlined the distinction between the interests of trade union representatives and the qualifications needed of those appointed to serve the industry.[44] An official Memorandum on the question made the fundamental point: the gains in efficiency and psychological benefits from consultation with the workforce would most properly take place at factory or workshop level via the Joint Production Committees (which had been in place since 1942 in many plants), whilst the right of consultation should be reserved to established trade unions rather than any 'unofficial movements'.[45] The principle was one of consultation rather than participation or co-determination and the state officials were anxious that even limited consultation should not provide an opportunity for shop floor radicals to politicise the issue of consultation as a route to industrial democracy. Britain's Trades Union Congress (TUC) and its union leaders were ready to support moves to consultation whilst themselves expressing anxiety about challenges from radical activists in sectors such as engineering and shipbuilding.[46]

Not only were Labour politicians and their civil servants concerned to limit the functions of the trade unions to the representation of a sectional interest within society, but they were quickly committed to the goals of labour efficiency and high output as the main criteria of success in the new public corporations. Morrison advised the Minister of Labour (Isaacs) in 1948 that the Government was committed to the removal of restrictive practices - a view shared by Harold Wilson who argued that in eradicating outdated customs 'public industry ought to give a lead to private and not to lag behind it'.[47] By defining the problem of labour co-operation in terms of removing customary restrictions and in terms of improving health and safety, social democratic ministers effectively sanitised the difficult questions of responsibility for management innovations but also ensured a suspicious response from union members. This mentality is apparent as early as 1945 in the report of a Working Party Squad set up by Bevin as Minister of Labour to enquire into double shift working. Reviewing the statutory provisions for the holding of ballots before the introduction of such working, the Squad objected to the continuation of this formal consultation not because of any evidence that ballots resulted in adverse votes but rather than the mere holding of a ballot implied that shift working was an exceptional arrangement to which workers might reasonably object and therefore 'tends to the formulation of doubts and fears which might otherwise remain latent ...'.[48] Such conclusions give little ground for confidence that the British civil service was predisposed to see a radical shift in the scope of workplace consultation in the post-war years.

If there are few signs of social democrats and bureaucrats using the new public corporations as a model of innovative labour management, there was considerable interest in the first decade of the peace in the professional status of management and the improvement of the technical and personnel skills of production managers. This interest had been stimulated by the wartime debates on managerial control and the technical needs of modern industry.[49] In 1946 a Production Efficiency Service (PES) was set up to extend the wartime advisory function of the state, whilst the Tizard Committee considered the application of technical and human research to improve industrial efficiency.[50] Whilst virtually every interested group agreed on the principle of improving professional management in UK industry, the struggles around the appointment to such bodies revealed not only serious divisions within the ranks of industry but also within the civil service as the Board of Trade mandarins struggled to contain the scope and influence of the (Tizard) Committee on Industrial Productivity and ensure its direct influence on policy was minimal.[51] Such officials had an exaggerated fear that the British Institute of Management (BIM) would claim direct representation on the Committee and through it on all similar bodies. Civil servants were appalled at the possible political implications for the British state's traditional role in relation to industrial consultation and dramatised the constitutional implications, with one Memorandum noting, that:

> In fact, every two-side body might well become triangular in future, and the role of the independent or Government member to ensure that the work got done with the maximum reconciliation of interests of employers and trade unionists would tend to disappear in the claim of the non-elected manager to speak in effect for the public interest in efficiency. This would be the 'managerial revolution' with a vengeance.[52]

The significance of such episodes is not that the BIM posed a serious threat to the existing machinery of formal consultation but that it represented a limited effort by some industrialists and managers to promote the ideal of professional management. The anxious response of the civil servants indicates, once again, the resistance of the post-war bureaucracy to serious shifts in the traditional procedures of consultation and recognition of interests. In contrast to Germany, Sweden and a number of other European countries, post-war Britain signally failed to promote the technical, professional and political basis for a strong independent grade of industrial managers, still less the technocracy capable of engineering the new era envisaged in Burnham's *Managerial Revolution*. It is not surprising that managers, supervisors, technical and scientific grades should have given expression to their aspirations as strongly in the new white-collar unions of the 1950s as in the professional associations attached to different occupations.

The reluctance of politicians and bureaucrats to promote a technical and managerial elite in British industry did not rule out the possibility of post-war governments overhauling the tripartite machinery of industrial policy-making and consultation. Here was the third possible strategy by which a 'developmental state' could have been fashioned out of the institutional matrix of the war years. A significant opportunity came with the passing of legislation to set up Development Councils in 1946-7, even though the opposition of British employers and competition between government ministries slowed the introduction of the scheme.[53] The Councils opened the door to joint discussions between employers and labour on production questions that were usually claimed as the respective provinces of 'management prerogatives' and workshop custom and practice.[54] It was this threat to the ingrained, if contradictory, assumptions that employers possessed an absolute authority to manage production and their employees had a historic right to defend past or present customs, which prompted strong opposition from the Federation of British Industry (FBI), representing industrial opinion together with the British Employers' Confederation (BEC). The FBI argued that production matters belonged to the domain of management rather than that of collective bargaining.[55] Such resistance from organised business prevented the Councils from establishing themselves in key sectors of the British economy or from developing a strategy for modernisation in the few industries where they were introduced.[56]

Similar difficulties arose when the Ministry of Labour and Board of Trade attempted to extend the consultative activities of their respective Advisory Councils in the post-war years.[57] The FBI initially favoured a merging of the two bodies into one Council capable of discussing 'major questions of industrial policy', whilst the unions argued for the retention of the existing dual structure.[58] This apparently radical proposal from the FBI was quickly reappraised when the Minister of Economic Affairs, later Chancellor, Stafford Cripps assumed control of NPACI and all enthusiasm amongst employers for a merger faded.[59] Competition between the two key ministries concerned again enabled such resistance to developmental initiatives and effective consultation to prosper. The essays by Booth and Tomlinson indicate the resistance of British industrialists to state-sponsored initiatives to raise industrial efficiency in this period, as does the earlier work of Tiratsoo and Tomlinson.[60] There is also evidence that the British civil service opposed reforms which in their view disturbed the proper relationship between the sovereignty of the state and the interests of producers' organisations. Ministerial staff even joined forces to oppose the fusion of the Advisory Councils,[61] whilst the TUC attacked such a merger from a fear of facing more powerful employer representation on a larger body.[62] On those few occasions when pro-interventionist employers gained ascendancy and moved towards a corporatist vision of economic management, civil servants anxiously advised their ministers that such a conception of a 'Parliament for Industry', raised a fundamental issue 'of profound political and constitutional importance'.[63]

The difficulties experienced by the advocates of economic modernisation in the immediate post-war years illustrate the impact which institutional arrangements inside and outside the British state had on reform initiatives. Relations between the peak organisations of employers, organised labour and the state appear to dominate the political agenda in this period. Yet the essays in this volume suggest the continuing importance of workplace and local struggles in the post-war years, including political factors which appeared in the bargaining environment at workplace and district levels.   These conflicts and accommodations in industry and society were part of a process which encompassed, but did not solely consist of, formal institutional relations and exchanges at the peaks of British political life. Much of the existing literature on British workplace struggles in the 1940s presents the politics of the workforce almost exclusively in terms of factional strife between Labour Party and Communist Party (CPGB) supporters.[64] Such an approach can be easily justified from the archives relating to the metalworking and engineering industries in the 1940s, as McKinlay's essay on Glasgow clearly shows.   The controversy surrounding the CPGB's attempts to affiliate to the Labour Party after 1944 sent ripples throughout the branches of the main engineering union.[65] The General Council of the TUC fought the Communist-influenced National Shop Stewards' Movement in the post-war years, as the Director of the Engineering Employers' Federation told his fellow industrialists in 1947, noting that they,

> had taken a very strong line not only against the Shop Stewards but against the Communist Party. As far as the Unions were concerned they were doing what they could to refuse to recognise the informal Shop Stewards' Movement and to keep it in place as far as they were able.[66]

The Communists saw in the Joint Production Committees and workplace consultation the instruments for a continuing politicisation of production questions inside and outside the individual plant.[67]   McKinlay's essay on Clydeside illustrates the strategic activities of the Communists in specific regions of the UK.

Without denying the influence of the Communist Party in the workplace during the years following the Nazi invasion of the Soviet Union, we can read such shifts in popular support for Communist activists in the context of a wider transformation of the labour force and of workplace attitudes at this period. The addition of millions of female, youth and unskilled male workers to large sections of the metalworking industries not only introduced these groups to a new industrial politics but also forced skilled male unionists to confront the aspirations of these groups. The Male engineers appear to have slowly moved from the exclusive attitudes of the craft fraternity to a more open style of recruitment and organisation, including the discussion at national and district levels of such issues as welfare provisions for women at work and in wider society. The provision of nurseries for female workers was endorsed by Labour ministers such as Bevin during the war itself, and reflects a widespread recognition of the importance of women to industrial output.[68] When the Glasgow Communists identified issues of factory welfare and equal pay for women along with full employment and production questions as mobilising issues in 1946, they were striving to rekindle the political spark which had ignited wartime campaigns amongst female as well as male workers.[69] Even the Amalgamated Engineering Union (AEU) sought to hold the line on the dilution of skilled labour and defending craft privileges, whilst calling for equal pay for female workers, a minimum wage, state welfare programmes and assistance to the unemployed in 1944-46. The leadership of such unions strove to promote policies which would shore up their own authority with core skilled groups whilst advocating a programme of industrial reconstruction and planning which could integrate the machinery of regional consultation and JPCs into a new Ministry of Production.[70] In advocating a strategy of high productivity through industrial reconstruction under state control, the AEU leadership tried to contain the radical opposition in its own ranks and to articulate an imaginative policy for securing high wages and averting mass unemployment.[71]

Such a policy was coupled to a formal commitment to equal pay for women and improved conditions for labourers in this skill-intensive industry. We can trace at least the beginnings of a solidaristic wages principle in the British metalworking industries, based on the assumption of continued state regulation and collective welfare provisions. Union leaders explicitly endorsed the commitment to high productivity growth and were apparently ready to consider the removal of customary practices in return for assurances on wages and employment. Similar undertakings had delivered wage restraint and deskilling during the war years when workers surrendered their bargaining power in return for various state controls on prices, food, taxation, and so on. In the absence of firm agreements on industrial reconstruction and as central consultation yielded poor fruits, voluntary bargaining was being reasserted in such sectors as the Coventry automobile industry, where shop stewards soon made deals that contravened the AEU's official commitment to equal pay for equal work. As a defence, the shop floor negotiators pointed out that such policies had to be pursued at national level before they could be enforced in the workplace.[72] Similarly, the strong union commitment to full employment and protection for those without jobs visibly withered as engineering exports surged ahead in the post-war years and firms were able to rapidly expand production and searched desperately for skilled labour.[73] Employers soon conceded substantial wage claims against the strong advice of their district associations.[74] By the early 1950s output gains were the subject of widespread negotiation at district and enterprise levels over piecework and incentive pay, as firms tried to extend their control over the workplace and to buy out the allowances which had accumulated during the 1940s.[75]

The political alignments which resulted from such struggles and from factional contests within the metalworking unions were more complex than a contest between Communists and their opponents. Certainly the Communists sought to use the fear of both unemployment and victimisation of activists by employers as a means of mobilising support for the unofficial shop stewards movement in 1944-45,[76] though there appears to have been a much more widespread and profound politicisation of the district and regional organisations of such trade unions in the war years which the (pro-Communist) leadership of the AEU sought to contain.[77] As in the First World War, controversies over dilution, female work and the employment of apprentices were amongst the issues which galvanised the membership into rather wider discussions of trade rights and also a serious consideration of the particular needs of women in the workplace. In this sense, it is probably a mistake to see welfare questions as non-radical or a means by which management eased workers away from discussions of sensitive production matters. Just as discussions on wartime and post-war unemployment stimulated interest in state policies, so questions of workplace welfare allowed the unions to engage in a more comprehensive critique of employers' labour strategies in the war and reconstruction years.[78] It is significant that so little was achieved on women's pay and welfare in the 1940s, at a time when the welfare state was being created by Labour, and that by the beginning of the next decade British employers appear to have effectively captured the initiative on workplace welfare and working conditions as an emblem of enlightened capitalism. As the question of female wages re-surfaced in the bargaining conferences of the early 1950s, the leadership of the Engineering Federation defended the employers in the domestic market industries (including the motor industry and consumer durables sectors) for adopting some progressive employment and welfare policies. Equally remarkable was the willingness of the AEU to accept such arguments on the quality of business welfare programmes as a particular necessity where women were employed.[79] The capture of the 'human factor' agenda was part of a process of depoliticising workplace issues that British industrialists skilfully undertook in the post-war years, confirming the capacity of industry to provide working conditions without political regulation.

Conclusions

The essays in this collection show that the management of labour in modern Europe has developed in relation to a complex set of historical conditions which varied significantly in Germany, Sweden and the United Kingdom. Yet the politics of reconstruction in Britain during the 1940s can be interpreted as a response to the forces transforming the European economy in the middle decades of the twentieth century, as much as they were an expression of the peculiar cultural and institutional formation of an ageing industrial society. The development of all three countries suggest that the management of labour was defined by a particular phase of European economic and social development, in which the mining and metalworking industries occupied a strategic position in the expansion of output as the energy demands of the basic industries continued to depend heavily on coal production and metalworkers provided the best-paid and most highly organised sectors of the workforce in much of Europe. The coming of mass production techniques had swelled the ranks of the labour force but did not revolutionise the management of labour or the methods of bargaining across whole tracts of European industry, in the way which advocates of Taylorism and Fordism sometimes assumed. Even though the semi-skilled groups expanded in relation to both the traditional skills and the unskilled, the strong demand for workers during the war years and in the great post-war boom gave the miners and metalworkers a remarkable bargaining position which was eroded during the crises of the late 1960s but only decisively damaged after the energy crises of the 1970s as European industry adjusted to its changed competitive position in the world. The rapid contraction of the European mining, steel, shipbuilding and even heavy engineering industries, threw the trade unions on to the defensive and opened up divisions within the ranks of labour. In these conditions a new managerialism was created which forced through more flexible working regimes and broke with the centralised bargaining practices that had been promoted in the years of expansion and tight labour markets.

One of the major points of controversy within the labour movements of Sweden, Germany and Britain during the 1970s was the status and rewards of the mass of white collar workers, including the large public sector labour force, and the differentials which existed between them and employees in the private export-oriented industries. The growth of private and public services had transformed the European economies in the mid-twentieth century, with profound implications for the management and rights of the workforce. Much of the existing literature on European economic development has emphasised the degree to which the central state played a key role in the course of German industrialisation compared with that of Britain, and the model of 'Rhenish capitalism' is still advocated by those who look to the developmental state as the agent of successful modernisation in Europe. There seems little doubt that the state was a major influence in the spread of bureaucratic models of management and administration in modern Europe, though it is arguable that the basis of its power and its capacity for transforming civil society lay in the accumulation and promotion of particular forms of *knowledge*. The efficiency and prestige of German and Swedish industrial management was founded on a technical and professional expertise that the state education system and training programmes fostered much more effectively than did the government in Britain. Production management in much of British industry derived more from the shared, practical culture of the industrial artisan rather than the technical qualifications of a polytechnic or college graduate. Even in industries, such as coalmining, where statutory provisions were made for the appointment of supervisors and managers, the expertise of the manager became a battleground for control over production and personnel rather than a model for professional competence in the rest of British industry.

The preference for empiricist, industry-specific and even amateur methods of management in the UK should be recognised as the responsibility of the state as well as of private enterprise and organised labour. Employers and workers colluded in depriving managers and supervisors the status and autonomy which would have enabled an effective enforcement of managerial prerogatives in post-war production. It is noticeable that Labour ministers wanted to use the newly nationalised industries as a showcase of efficient production and to exploit workers' goodwill in raising output, yet there was very little discussion of how professional standards of management could be secured or the participation of workers achieved. Social democrats and liberal politicians in Germany introduced more far-reaching forms of co-determination in private firms that were regulated by the state than did the socialised corporations of the UK. When Labour ministers and their civil servants faced the prospect of professional managers being represented on central consultative bodies, along with employers and unions, they drew back in some alarm. British governments appear to have consistently placed the need to preserve equilibrium in the tripartite relationship of employers, labour and the state above their inclination to push through measures of economic modernisation. One consequence was the growth of white collar unionism amongst managers, supervisors and technical staff that were squeezed by the conflicting pressures of workplace control and bargaining demands.

Some conservative critics of the welfare state have argued that the growth of public services, and particularly social services, in the post-war years marked a serious policy mistake, drawing essential investment away from industrial reconstruction. This argument can be challenged on a number of points. Most obviously, Britain was only part of a broad European movement in building a welfare state in the 1940s and spent less per head on its social services than many of her industrial competitors in the post-war period. Moreover, these provisions facilitated the expansion of female participation in both the private and public sector labour market, which can itself be seen as a third key structural feature of the European labour market after 1939. A more persuasive argument *can* be made that welfare reforms in the UK did not contribute to the building of a corporatist settlement or productivity coalition on lines seen in Sweden and Germany.

The potential for such a production politics based on welfare consumption and a social wage can be read into the industrial campaigns to secure equal rights for women and workplace welfare during the 1940s, as well as the demands of the trade unions for radical social reform to protect workers against unemployment and sickness. The persistence of voluntaryist bargaining in the UK was not a foregone conclusion or the inevitable outcome of institutional preferences. The essays in this volume suggest that it was the complex politics of the labour movement as well as the reluctance of the state to take a grip on production planning in the face of employers' hostility which allowed labour market bargaining to acquire a powerful momentum in 1946-47. These failures were clearly the consequence of cultural and political preferences as well as institutional factors. We can see the failure of the British state to create an integrated bargaining system comparable to Sweden and Germany as the result of intellectual and administrative barriers within the state as well as resistance from powerful groups in civil society. In the debates on full employment there appears to have been a shared assumption that job security was to be purchased by moderation on wage demands and the removal of some customary practices by the unions. There is evidence that organised workers were at least open to the proposal that collective goods, including welfare services, should figure in the national bargaining strategies of the unions.

The failure of such schemes cannot be adequately explained by exposing the undoubted resistance of organised employers to state initiatives, nor by documenting the conservative inclinations of many civil servants in the post-war years. Centralist bargaining arrangements were able to take root in Sweden and Germany in part because of the historical precedents of state intervention in economic life, but also as a result of the political cultures which had been fostered by the social democrats in those countries. In Sweden and Germany the achievement of positive liberties through the state was an established discipline which enabled the state to assume a regulatory role in bargaining, though it was the political culture of consensus which was consciously fostered by social democrats in Sweden during the 1930s-40s and Germany in the 1940s-50s which underpinned the ethics of central bargaining and solidaristic wages. Whereas a political tradition was nurtured at local level as well as in the national arena by the Swedish SAP, Germany's SPD was engaged with the liberals and Christian Democrats in the rebuilding of national consensus at a time when German industrialists were facing the break-up of the cartels and willing to cooperate in a national reconstruction programme. The British union leaders as well as employers and the state retained their suspicions of central regulation, whilst also seeking to contain those workplace and regional movements which threatened their control of the organisations they governed.

The result was that problems of production management and collective bargaining were often left in the hands of those who had few resources and even less inclination to address the structural problems which beset their industries and which left them vulnerable to crisis when the long post-war boom finally ended. At that point familiar weaknesses in the process of decision making emerged as the nation state sought to modernise a labour market and labour management systems which remained firmly anchored in the particularistic bargaining practices of the post-war years. As the essays gathered here indicate, there remain important issues of debate and discussion in seeking to explain the strengths and weaknesses of the social democratic project, including the degree to which power was effectively shifted to organised labour in the European democracies. These studies are offered as a contribution to that debate and the wider reassessment of European politics in the aftermath of the Cold War.

Notes

* This essay forms part of a contribution to a continuing research network on European productivity. The research project jointly directed by Alan Booth and myself has been funded by the Economic and Social Research Council, the Centre for Economic Policy Research, and the University of Exeter. I am grateful to Alan Booth for useful criticisms of this introductory survey.

1. W. Korpi, *The working class and welfare capitalism*, Routledge (1978) London. This debate is discussed extensively in the essay by Ekdahl and Johansson below. See also J. Fulcher, 'On the explanation of industrial relations diversity: labour movements, employers and the state in Britain and Sweden' *British Journal of Industrial Relations* 26 (1988), pp246-74.
2. J. Melling, 'Industrial capitalism and the welfare of the state: the role of employers in the comparative development of welfare states' *Sociology* 25 (1991), pp219-39, provides a critical survey.
3. L. Calmfors and J. Driffill, 'Bargaining structures, corporatism and macroeconomic performance' *Economic Policy* (1988, April), pp13-61; M. Pohjola, 'Corporatism and labour market performance' in J. Pekkarinen, M. Pohjola and B. Rowthorn, *Social Corporatism: a superior economic system?* Oxford University Press (1992), pp44-81.
4. D. Marquand, *The Unprincipled Society: new demands and old politics* Fontana (1988), pp175-202 and passim for an attack on governing institutions in the UK from a social democratic perspective; C. Barnett, *The Audit of War: the illusion and reality of Britain as a great nation* Macmillan (1986), pp201-233 for similar criticisms of the institutions and culture of ruling elites from a radical Tory view; and *The Lost Victory: British dreams, British realities 1945-1950* Macmillan (1995), pp123-32, 183-93, for parallel criticisms of old elites, Fabians and New Jerusalem prophets.
5. M. Olson, *The logic of collective action: public goods and the theory of groups* Harvard University Press (1971), Cambridge, Massachusetts, and *The rise and decline of nations: economic growth, stagflation and social rigidities* Yale University Press (1982) Yale, Connecticut. See also Olson's 'The political economy of comparative growth rates' in D.C. Mueller (ed.), *The political economy of growth* Yale University Press (1983) New Haven, Conneticutt, pp7-52.
6. S. Lash and J. Urry, *The end of Organised Capitalism* (1987), and S. Lash, 'The end of neo-corporatism? the breakdown of centralised bargaining in Sweden' *British Journal of Industrial Relations* 23 (1985), pp215-39. See also P. Armstrong, A. Glyn and J. Harrison, *Capitalism since 1945* Blackwell (1991), pp136-150, for discussion of 'managed capitalism' including the welfare state and German co-determination.
7. Olson, *The rise and decline*, pp75-101; A. Booth, C. Dartmann and J. Melling, 'Institutions and economic growth: trade unions and the politics of productivity in West Germany, Sweden and the UK, 1945-55', (1995, forthcoming), provide a critical survey of the literature.
8. M. Shalev, 'The social democratic model and beyond: two generations of comparative research on the welfare state' *Comparative Social Research* 6 (1983), particularly pp319-23; C. Offe, 'Democracy against the welfare state? Structural foundations of neo-conservative political opportunities' *Political*

Theory 15 (1987), pp501-37; P. Baldwin, *The Politics of Social Solidarity: class bases of the European welfare state 1875-1975* Cambridge University Press (1990), pp10-31 and passim.

9. Barnett, *Audit,* pp263-75, and *Lost victory,* pp194-211, 212-27. Barnett sways between criticism of policies of 'tinkering' and complaints of inaction, which could be read as a powerful case for the imposition of corporatist planning on the UK, and attacks on nationalisation and public ownership.

10. Korpi, *Working class.* For critical assessment see E. Lundberg, 'The rise and fall of the Swedish Model' *Journal of Economic Literature* 23 (1985), pp1-36; also A. Johansson and J. Melling, 'The roots of consensus: bargaining attitudes and political commitment among Swedish and British workers, 1920-1950' *Economic and Industrial Democracy* 16 (1995), pp353-97.

11. See Ekdahl and Johansson below. G.M. Olsen, *The struggle for economic democracy in Sweden* Avebury (1992) Aldershot.

12. Colin Crouch and David Marquand, 'Introduction' in *Ethics and Markets* Blackwell (1993), pp1-5 for a discussion of Rhenism versus Anglo-American models of capitalist regeneration; Crouch, 'Co-operation and competition in an institutionalised economy: the case of Germany' in Crouch and Marquand, *Ethics,* particularly pp90-92 for labour market and institutional legacies. J.G. March and P. Olsen, 'The new institutionalism: organisational factors in political life' *American Political Science Review* 78 (1984), pp734-49.

13. A. Fox, *History and Heritage: the social origins of the British industrial relations system* Allen & Unwin (1985) London, for a brilliant synthesis; H.A. Clegg, *The changing system of industrial relations in Great Britain* Blackwell (1979) Oxford, pp1-5, 53-61, and *A history of British trade unions since 1889: volume III, 1934-1951* Oxford University Press (1994). J. Melling, 'In search of the British Model' *Economic and Industrial Democracy* 16 (1995), pp291-99, assesses the institutionalists.

14. G.S. Bain, *The growth of white collar unionism,* Oxford (1970), provided a seminal critique of Weberian sociological methodology, particularly D. Lockwood's *The black-coated worker: a study in class consciousness* Unwin (1958) London.

15. H.A. Clegg, *Comparative study,* pp.1-3 for rules and historical development; Fox, *History and Heritage,* xii-xiii, for 'institutional dispositions'; c.f. R. Hyman, 'Pluralism, procedural consensus and collective bargaining', *British Journal of Industrial Relations* 16 (1978), pp23-25, and passim for a Marxist critique of the pluralist philosophy underpinning these texts.

16. S. Tolliday and J. Zeitlin, 'National models and international variations in labour management and employer organisation' in *The power to manage? Employers and industrial relations in comparative-historical perspective* Routledge (1991) London, pp279-82, 310-11, 324 and passim. Tolliday and Zeitlin make considerable claims for their comparative institutionalist model and firmly reject any sociological or cultural reading of institutional relations. See also Zeitlin, 'From labour history to the history of industrial relations' *Economic History Review* 40 (1987), p159-61 and passim.

17. Tolliday and Zeitlin, *The power,* pp310-11, and Zeitlin, 'The internal politics of employer organisation. The Engineering Employers' Federation 1896-1939', in *The power,* pp52-80.

18. W. Kendall, *The Labour Movement in Europe* Allen Lane (1975) London, pp24-34, 308-32, for a New Left assessment; D. Geary (ed.), *Labour and Socialist Movements in Europe before 1914* Berg (1989) Oxford, 'Introduction' emphasises the impact of industrialisation, state intervention, and party strategies in the formation of socialist movements.

19. H. Mercer, N. Rollings and J.D. Tomlinson (eds.), *Labour Governments and private industry: the experience of 1945-51* Edinburgh University Press (1992), Edinburgh; H. Mercer, 'Labour and private industry, 1945-51' in N. Tiratsoo (ed.), *The Attlee years* Pinter (1991) Leicester. This literature is critically reviewed in J. Hinton, *Shop Floor Citizens: engineering democracy in 1940s Britain* Elgar (1994) Aldershot, pp1-8. Hinton, like Barnett, emphasises the state's neglect of British aircraft production, Hinton stressing the benefits of French planning on industrial production.

20. R. Vinen, *The politics of French business, 1936-1945* Cambridge University Press (1991) Cambridge, pp202-29.

21. A. Carew, *Labour under the Marshall Plan: the politics of productivity and the marketing of management science* Manchester University Press (1987). See Dartmann essay for a contrasting approach.

22. See contributions to Tiratsoo (ed.), *Attlee years*. Much wider debates on the state are reviewed in Marquand, *Unprincipled Society* and K. Middlemas, *Power, competition and the state: the end of the post-war era. Britain since 1974* Macmillan (1991) London. J.D. Smith, *The Attlee and Churchill administrations and industrial unrest 1945-55: a study in consensus* Pinter (1990), London, provides a good summary of events.

23. Marquand, *Unprincipled Society*, pp144-74 and passim for a summary.

24. Barnett, *Lost* Victory, pp371-79 for UK's inferior use of Marshall Aid compared with France and Germany, for example.

25. The literature is enormous but see N.R.F. Crafts, 'Economic growth' in Crafts and N. Woodward (eds.), *The British economy since 1945* Oxford University Press (1991), pp261-90; and 'Productivity growth reconsidered' *Economic Policy* (1992), pp388-426; and 'Reversing relative economic decline? The 1980s in historical perspective' *Oxford Review of Economic Policy* 7 (1991), pp81-98; and c.f. B. Elbaum and W. Lazonick, 'An institutional perspective on British decline' in *The decline of the British economy* Oxford University Press (1986), pp1-17, for two distinct but influential perspectives. M.W. Kirby, 'Institutional rigidities and economic decline: reflections on the British experience' *Economic History Review* 45 (1992), pp637-660, for a survey.

26. Olson, *Logic*, pp66-97; c.f. K. Choi, 'A statistical test of Olson's model' in Mueller (ed.), *Political economy of growth*, pp57-78. See also B. Strath, *Organisation of labour markets: modernity, culture and governance in Germany, Sweden, Britain and Japan* Routledge (1995) London, for a radical alternative to rational-interest models of bargaining institutions.

27. S. Pollard, *Peaceful Conquest: the industrialisation of Europe 1760-1970* Oxford University Press (1981), pp316-321; F.B. Tipton and R. Aldrich, *An economic and social history of Europe from 1939 to the present* Macmillan (1987), pp89-94.

28. J. Kocka, 'Capitalism and bureaucracy in German industrialisation before 1914' *Economic History Review* XXXIV, 3 (1981), pp453-57, 467-68.

29. J. Kocka, *White collar workers in America 1890-1940: a social-political history in international perspective* Sage (1980) London, pp251-84, for comparative survey. Also Kocka, 'The European pattern and the German case' in Kocka and A. Mitchell (eds.), *Bourgeois Society in nineteenth-century Europe* Berg (1993), pp30-32 and passim for professionalisation. Strath, *Organisation of labour markets* draws on Kocka and Torstendahl.

30. M. Sanderson, *The missing stratum: technical school education in England, 1900-1990s* Athlone (1994), pp155-75 and passim; H.F. Gospel (ed.), *Industrial training and technological innovation: a comparative and historical study* Routledge (1991) London, including essay by Gospel and Okayama; Barnett, *Audit*, pp229-33.

31. Barnett, *Lost Victory,* pp147-59. A contrasting view of the civil service to that given by Barnett is R. Davidson and R. Lowe, 'Bureaucracy and innovation in British welfare policy 1875-1945' in W.J. Mommsen and W. Bock (eds.), *The emergence of the Welfare State in Britain and Germany, 1850-1950* Croom Helm (1981) London, pp263-95.

32. P. Flora and J. Alber, 'Modernisation, democratisation and the development of Welfare States in Western Europe' in Flora and A.J. Heidenheimer (eds.), *The development of Welfare States in Europe and America* Transaction (1981) New Brunswick; Andrea Boltho (ed.), *The European Economy: growth and crisis* Oxford University Press (1982), p191-92, Tables 7.1-7.2; G. Ambrosius and W.H. Hubbard, *A social and economic history of twentieth-century Europe* Harvard University Press (1989), p258, Figure 4.5, after Flora.

33. Ambrosius and Hubbard, *Twentieth-century Europe*, p51, Figure 2.2.

34. G. Bock and P. Thane (eds.), *Maternity and gender politics: women and the rise of the European Welfare States, 1880s-1950s* Routledge (1991) London, pp9-15. The contributions stress the complex social politics of maternity provision from fascist Italty to Norwegian family allowances. Also S. Perdersen, *Family, dependence and the origins of the Welfare State: Britain and France 1914-1945* Cambridge University Press (1993) Cambridge, pp354-56 for complex gender politics of state welfare.

35. Baldwin, *Politics of Social Solidarity*; also A. de Swaan, *In care of the State: health care, education and welfare in Europe and the USA in the modern period* Polity (1988) Cambridge. Melling, 'Industrial capitalism', an assessment.

36. N.R.F. Crafts, 'The assessment: British economic growth over the long run' *Oxford Review of Economic Policy* 4 (1988), pxiii, Crafts, 'Productivity growth reconsidered', p407; S. Newton and D. Porter, *Modernisation frustrated: the politics of industrial decline in Britain since 1900* ... (1988); E.H. Phelps Brown, 'What is the British predicament?' *Three Banks Review* 116 (1977), pp3-29.
37. Clegg, *British Trade Unions*, chapters 4-5.
38. Barnett, *Lost victory*, pp330-43 for failure of misguided regional development policy, for example.
39. Hinton, *Shop Floor Citizens*, pp150-61. Hinton appears to share with Barnett an exaggerated view of the possibilities of formal state intervention in a liberal capitalist society.
40. N. Tiratsoo and J. Tomlinson, *Industrial efficiency and state intervention: Labour 1939-51* Routledge (1993) London, pp95-110.
41. Official Committee on the Socialisation Industries, 'Workers' assistance in the management of socialised industries', notes of meeting of 10.10.1946 in Public Record Office (PRO) BT64/2416, p1.
42. Minute on 'Workers' Assistance in the Management of socialised industries', 10.7.1946, BT64/2416.
43. 'Workers' Assistance', 10.7.1946. The document also stressed the need to protect Ministers from accepting political responsibility for the consultative arrangements actually made.
44. H. Morrison letter to J.A. Sparks, 20.6.1949 [? 1946?], BT64/2416.
45. Memorandum by the Official Committee on the Socialisation Industries, 'Workers' assistance in the management of socialised industries', BT64/2416, paras 1, 8 (d).
46. Clegg, *A history of British trade unions*, pp342-43.
47. Morrison to Isaacs 5.5.48, 3.6.48, BT64/2352; H. Wilson to N. Edwards 25.6.1948, BT64/2352.
48. Report of Working Party Squad on double shifts, 'Double day shift working WPS', 1949, BT64/2226, p2.
49. J. Burnham, *The Managerial Revolution* Putnam (1942), London pp68-72, 132-44.
50. File on PES in BT64/2403 including clipping from *News Review* on the resignation of Frank Chappell as Director after complaining bitterly of the bureaucratic regimen and red tape which crippled his efforts in 1946-47.
51. S.A. Dakin's Memorandum, 'Committee on Industrial Productivity', 31.12.1947, in BT64/2360: 'The great danger is, of course, that the Committee may insensibly spread its energies to the formation of policy ... the greatest care must be taken [to ensure] that the policy-making function of departments should not be encroached on.'
52. S.A. Dakin Note, 18.5.1948 summarising Objections to BIM representation on the CIP and also Nowell's supportive comments, in BT64/2360.
53. 'Industrial Organisation Bill: outstanding points for decision. Scope and Functions of Development Councils', BT64/2226.
54. Paper by C.B. Reynolds, 10.1.1947, pp1-2. BT64/2226.
55. Letter of N. Kipping of FBI to Nowell at Board of Trade, 7.1.1947. BT64/2226.
56. 'Brief for President's Meeting with the TUC Economic Committee on October 8 [1947]', in BT64/2329.
57. H.J. Hutchinson, Minute notes, 15.9.1947 in BT62/2352.
58. Tewson of the TUC argued that the FBI demands reflected their rivalry with the BEC and the latter's position on the NJAC whilst the FBI worked with NPACI and felt it was being marginalised.
59. Notes of W. Hughes, 23.3.48, 22.6.48; Note of G. Parker, 29.7.48 in BT62/2352.
60. N. Tiratsoo and J. Tomlinson, *Industrial Efficiency*, pp166-67 and passim.
61. 'Relationship between NJAC and NCPACI: Note of a meeting held in the Cabinet Offices...', 9.12.1947, pp2-3, 6-7, where the officials decide that a formal joint meeting of civil servants would be 'pointless as well as unnecessary' if their Ministers were advised and decided that a merging of the bodies raised difficult and controversial questions! BT62/2352
62. Note of meeting of Tewson and Hutchinson at Board of Trade, 15.9.1947 in BT62/2352.
63. Hutchinson note of 3.9.47 of FBI visit to Board of Trade, 3.9.47 in BT62/2352.
64. Hinton, *Shop floor citizens*, for example.
65. R. Croucher, *Engineers at War* Merlin (1982) London, p65. Croucher is discussed in McKinlay.
66. Modern Records Centre (MRC), Engineering Employers' Federation (EEF) records, Policy Committee Minutes, 17.9.1947.

67. PRO, Ministry of Labour, copies of documents from Scottish Labour Party and the Glasgow district branch of the Communist Party, May 1946, in LAB10/591.
68. A. Bullock, *The life and times of Ernest Bevin* Heinemann (1960), I, pp652-53; Croucher, *Engineers*, p17.
69. Glasgow Communist Party Organiser's report, May 1946, in LAB10/591, where the 'question of youth in Industry' and Youth Committees was mentioned alongside that of women's pay and opportunities.
70. National Engineering Joint Trades Movement, *Memorandum on Post-War Reconstruction in the Engineering Industry.* TUC Library, TUC HD9678.6, 'Engineering Labour' box, p9.
71. Labour Research Department, *Engineers and Reconstruction*, Introduction by Jack Tanner. Copy in TUC HD9678, 'Engineering General to 1951'.
72. Coventry City Archives (CCA), AEU, District Committee Minutes, 25.8.47-8.9.47.
73. CCA, AEU Minutes, 5.9.50 for example of Standards.
74. E. Wigham, *The power to manage* Macmillan (1973) London, pp162-68.
75. CCA, Pontypool District Committee, Minutes, 13.12.1951, for example.
76. MRC, AEU Executive Council (EC), Minutes, 23.5.1944-31.7.1944, for example.
77. MRC, AEU EC Minutes, 21.9.1944, Openshaw's letter.
78. MRC, AEU EC Minutes, Political Sub-Committee, 2.10.1944, consideration of unemployment resolutions for Labour Party Conference; Meeting with Ministry of Labour, 4.10.1944 and Memorandum 'Redundancy and Dilution'; Resolutions considered by EC (and National Committee of AEU) for Women's National Conference, 1944, including one demanding the implementation of the 1943 Resolution on Health and Welfare.
79. MRC 237/1/series: EEF Conference, 13.1.1950 for discussion of Lucas, Hoover and others.

2. Productivity, joint consultation and human relations in post-war Britain: the Attlee Government and the workplace

Jim Tomlinson

Introduction

The Attlee Government's economic policy agenda was dominated by two issues. On the one hand was the balance of payments problem, leading to macroeconomic policies of containing domestic demand and channelling resources into exports and investment. This is the focus of attention of Cairncross's major work.[1] On the other hand the economy was clearly suffering from problems of supply falling short of demand, and this led to a range of policies aimed at raising output and productivity.[2] It was in the context of the latter objective that the Labour Government was drawn into attempts to reform the workplace, those reforms covering almost every aspect of enterprise practices from industrial design to wage systems. But this paper focuses on one major part of that reform effort, the attempt to build up systems of joint consultation at factory level. These efforts are of particular interest in relation to Labour's overall political stance. Above all, they relate to the question why, unlike other Western European social democratic parties in power at this time,[3] the Attlee Governments did so little to reform workplace politics in the direction of greater industrial democracy. In answering this very large question the emphasis is placed on the *ideas* that dominated Labour policy-making in this period, in the belief that too little emphasis is usually placed on this perspective, and too much on the clash of 'interest groups' whose objectives, and the ideas that underlie them, remain under-explored.[4] Also, it should be noted, the primary focus is on the Labour Party and Government rather than the trade unions.

Public and Private Sectors

The Attlee government is well known for its extension of the public sector to embrace about 20 per cent of total output.   But the particular form of nationalisation in Britain, the 'Morrisonian corporation' excluded any direct role for worker representatives in the management of the new corporations.   Joint consultation was enshrined in the statutes of the newly nationalised industries, (except the Bank of England), with varying success.   But the question of *direct* representation of workers was regarded by the Government and the majority of trade union leaderships as having been settled by the debates in the Labour Party and TUC in the early 1930s, and attempts to re-open the issue in the 1940s were successfully resisted.[5]   Other aspects of the status and role of the worker in the enterprise remained very much open to debate, joint consultation being a term of great ambiguity, but it plainly did *not* mean 'workers control' or a direct role in corporate management.   The debate about the public sector is well covered in the literature,[6] and here the focus is on the private sector, which even after the nationalisations of 1945-51, still embraced 80 per cent of employment and output.

Doctrinally, it is clear that a vacuum existed in the Labour government's attitude to the private sector of industry.   Labour's election manifesto of 1945, *Let us Face the Future*, had referred only to the need for a tough anti-monopoly policy and the general expectation on the Parliamentary Left was that the private sector would become residual and not therefore worthy of serious policy consideration.[7]   The debates around syndicalism and guild socialism of the earlier part of the century found rather little echo outside the discussion of nationalisation.[8]   However, despite this doctrinal vacuum on the Left, a very substantial and significant extension of industrial democracy had taken place in the war period.   Joint Production Committees, Pit, Yard and Site Committees had proliferated in much of British industry (hereafter JPCs).   Probably never before or since has there been such an extensive role of workers and trade unions in production decisions at factory level.[9]   Above this there was, of course, a highly elaborate set of bipartite or tripartite bodies involving unions in production and other decisions.[10]

Much of this structure fell into disuse at the end of the war, and for a period there was no clear sense of direction in policy.   In addition, demobilisation in 1945/6 created a fluidity in the labour market which only began to 'settle down' in 1947.   This paper will therefore focus on the attempt at reviving JPCs in the private sector which was pursued from 1947;[11] the reasons why it was not pursued more effectively, and therefore why its achievements were so limited.   The first section reviews the wartime developments as a necessary background to events after 1945.

Joint consultation in Wartime

Much of the wartime history of JPCs from the 'official' point of view is well
known.[12] More recent work has looked at their functioning from the workers'
and union side.[13] Taking this material together a number of points seem clear.
First a considerable part of the initiative for such committees came from the
Ministry of Labour, in alliance with trade union leaders.[14] Initially this met with
little enthusiasm from shop stewards or rank and file workers - or managers.[15]
But by late 1941 the situation altered sharply. The Soviet Union entered the war,
and the Communist Party (CPGB), previously anti-war, shifted to being its most
enthusiastic supporters. While the direct role of the CPGB was uneven, it
spearheaded a movement in militant trade unionism away from the traditional
focus on wages and conditions, and a distrust of any production responsibility,
towards an emphasis on raising production *against* managerial inefficiency and
incompetence.[16]

In October 1941 a decisive move towards the spreading of JPCs was made
when the unofficial but powerful Engineering and Allied Trades Shop Stewards
National Council called a well-publicised conference in London to press for the
extension of JPCs. Pressure was also being exerted by the tripartite Midlands
Regional Board for Industry, on which unions were strongly represented, and
which was campaigning for JPCs in its area. The TUC was concerned that these
unofficial trade union pressures were enhancing the role of shop stewards in
general and the Communist Party in particular, and pressed the Ministry of
Labour to urge the Engineering Employers' Federation (EEF) to agree to JPCs to
allow official trade unionism to reassert itself.[17]

Employers were divided on the benefits of JPCs. Like most trade unionists,
they had been initially hostile, and the EEF., the crucial employers' organisation,
initially resisted Amalgamated Engineering Union pressure for JPCs in early
1941 - the AEU having just changed its own mind on the issue. This opposition
was primarily based on the fear of loss of managerial prerogative. The EEF
eventually agreed to the general establishment of JPCs under substantial pressure,
but only as long as the new bodies did not impinge on their right to manage and
as an alternative to having such structures imposed by the government.[18] 'They
were forced by political circumstance to accept the Committees as a necessary
evil'.[19] Employers' views on JPCs remained uncertain. Some saw them as a
possible way of inculcating in shop stewards 'responsible' attitudes and detaching
them from their rank and file support.[20] Others may have seen the need for
involving the unions in the disciplining of workers, given the shift in the balance
of power in the factories under wartime tight labour markets' and the restrictions
on labour mobility imposed by Essential Works Orders.[21]

Both employers and official unionism were, for their various reasons,
eventually drawn into the popular enthusiasm for 'productionism' which

probably has no parallel in British history. In February 1942 the Ministry of Supply and the unions concerned agreed to set up JPCs in the Royal Ordnance Factories. In the following month the EEF and the AEU signed an agreement, providing for JPCs where alternative consultative machinery did not exist. Neither this nor other parallel agreements made JPCs compulsory though the TUC had mooted such compulsion.[22] But the supply Ministries came close to a form of contract compliance, in urging factories they dealt with to set up JPCs. Precise quantification of the number of JPCs is difficult. In July 1943 the Board of Trade estimated that 65-70 per cent of all firms in engineering and allied industries had JPCs, varying from 35 per cent in Scotland to 92 per cent in London and the South East. This regional pattern has been plausibly linked to the degree of craft organisation in different areas.[23] The peak period was probably October/November 1944, although no substantial decline was recorded before the war's end.[24]

The Engineering Agreement was broadly typical of the wartime agreements in stating the purpose of JPCs to be 'to consult and advise on matters relating to production ... in order that maximum output may be obtained from the factory'.[25] Whilst it does seem to have been the case that production dominated the JPCs discussions, the latter also covered welfare and wage issues, though wages had been explicitly excluded from the agreement. Employers were generally keen to emphasise that JPCs were a purely 'domestic' concern, and were hostile to the TUC's efforts to form District Production Committees to co-ordinate the union side. They were also unenthusiastic about reference of difficulties at factory level to the Regional Board, though this was formally established as the channel in late 1942.

The result of JPCs existence is very difficult to assess. They were rarely looked on with enthusiasm by managers, (especially junior managers or foremen). This was linked to an ambiguity over their function. Formally purely advisory, the distinction between advice and execution was both in principle and practice difficult to sustain and the source of recurrent conflict. In some cases the JPCs seem to have done little, whilst in others they became the focus of an enthusiastic pursuit of production without parallel. Stafford Cripps, President of the Board of Trade, and later, Chancellor of the Exchequer, judged that they made 'a significant contribution to the war's effort', and this seems a reasonable conclusion.[26] The spread of JPCs also resulted from a conjunction of highly particular circumstances. These were, first, the political pressure on employers arising from an alliance of militant groups of workers, unions, and Ministers, each with their rather different objectives coupled with the general commitment to raise production for the war effort. There was also the realisation by employers that in the full employment context of the war new difficulties had to be faced. In the words of the Ministry of Labour's *Industrial Relations Handbook*:

In peace time many difficulties do not come to a head because the worker leaves the employer. During the war freedom to discharge and freedom to seek other employment are necessarily restricted and there is a greater need than ever for full collaboration between employers and workpeople.[27]

In modern jargon, 'voice' displaced 'exit'. From the workers' side, the undoubted enthusiasm for production to aid the war effort was encouraged by the CPGB and other trade union militants.[28] Official trade unionism took up this enthusiasm, whilst attempting to prevent it from undercutting normal trade union channels and giving excess powers to shop stewards.

The Ministry of Labour and the Supply Ministries gave production goals priority over traditional rights and procedures, although the former Ministry was concerned not to go beyond what could be agreed by employers and unions and what could be seen as promoting peaceful good industrial relations. Compulsion was not applied, but a great deal of exhortation and arm-twisting occurred, creating circumstances in which employers found it very difficult to resist.

The decline of JPCs

In a letter to its constituent associations in 1947, the Engineering Employers' Federation argued that notwithstanding national government and trade union support, workers' interest in JPCs had started to fade before the peace, and a number of committees had already by that time fallen into disuse. 'Again notwithstanding the efforts of the TUC and the new Labour government to revive interest in these committees, the changeover from wartime to peacetime production rather accelerated this process of decline'.[29] In fact in the first period of the Labour government the attempts to revive interest in JPCs were extremely limited, and this was only reversed from 1947. However, it was undoubtedly true that the transition from war to peace accentuated a decline which had already begun.

In the engineering and munitions industries where JPCs had been most significant there was of course a rapid switch in the composition of both output and employment at the war's end. The switch of output from war to peace production led to widespread redundancies, even though many of those made redundant quickly found new jobs. Coupled with this many women and other 'dilutees' left these sectors, and some were replaced by demobilised servicemen. The AEU, the dominant union in the sector, did not fight a battle against these redundancies, nor did it, of course, fight the change in the composition of the labour force - it had been the strongest proponent of the need to return to pre-war labour-use norms.[30] Hence the end of the war radically undermined the organisational basis for JPCs in many factories. Also the dominant goal of much of the labour movement was not to defend these institutions, but to ensure the election of a Labour government and the maintenance of full employment, whilst assuming these would not be incompatible with a revival of traditional voluntary collective bargaining. The TUC and most unions were committed in principle to the continuation of JPCs into peacetime, but to a striking degree towards the end of the war union activity was focused away from shop floor activity and on to the election and the sustenance of a Labour government.[31]   This posture was true even of the Communist Party for the first couple of years after 1945.

At the ministerial level, there was substantial scepticism expressed about the value of JPCs within the Ministry of Labour. A senior official, M.A. Bevan, argued in February 1945 that JPCs had tended to institutionalise the 'two sides' of industry, that employers were sceptical of union objectives pursued via JPCs and that their scope was in any event very much limited to the engineering industries.[32]   Shortly after the end of the European war the Ministry of Production conducted a survey amongst the Regional Boards of Industry on JPCs. They found general, if low key support for them in most areas, but also a stress on the desirability of their remaining voluntary. However at this stage there was no question of compulsion. The Ministry survey did not portend an initiative on the matter, but simply a desire for information for answering questions. The new Minister of Labour, George Isaacs, stressed in response to such questions that the matter was one for workers and employers, although endorsing the need for more co-operation at factory level.[33]   The EEF hoped that at the end of the war the 1942 agreement on joint consultation would lapse.   But they were wary of showing open hostility in case the government legislated on the issue. So when the AEU asked for a removal of the agreement in 1946, this was agreed to.[34]

For all these reasons JPCs undoubtedly declined between 1944 and 1947, though exact quantification is impossible. Their revival re-emerged as an issue only with the onset of the economic crisis of 1947. This crisis evoked a sustained campaign in favour of increases in production and productivity which is the broad context in which the debates over JPCs were to take place in the succeeding years.

Productivity and the revival of JPCs

This production and productivity campaign has been examined in detail in some recent treatments of the Labour government, and even though Cairncross stresses the macroeconomic aspect of government policy, he does provide data showing the success of the Labour government in diverting resources into investment and raising industrial output.[35]   The broad basis of this new feature of economic policy is clear enough. By 1947 it was evident that for the foreseeable future that the problem was not to be one of a return of mass unemployment, but shortages of labour.[36]   Hence a rise in living standards and the increased production of exports could only come from increased production from a static labour force - increased productivity. It should be emphasised that in this area, as in others, the data available to government was minimal - only in 1947 did Rostas' work at the Board of Trade on productivity begin to give some statistical basis to assess fears of declining/stagnant productivity in the post-war years. The general impact of Rostas' work was that some of the fears were exaggerated, but that in comparison with the USA especially Britain's position was poor, and so this quantitative work helped to justify the increasing focus on promoting higher productivity as a policy objective from 1947 onwards. Rostas also stressed that productivity could most easily be measured by labour productivity (output per man hour) which gave a particular if unintended bias in productivity discussions towards 'labour' issues.[37]

The drive to increase productivity seems to have been mainly initiated by Cripps. From early 1947, with Herbert Morrison, previously 'overlord' of economic issues, ill, Cripps came to the fore alongside the Chancellor, Dalton in economic policy- making. In September 1947 Cripps moved from President of the Board of Trade to Minister of Economic Affairs, and in November to Chancellor of the Exchequer. From his central position in economic-policy making Cripps directed increasing attention to this issue, and from late 1948 this is reflected in the focus of the government's economic propaganda.[38] Whilst this ministerial initiative was very significant, it needs to be considered alongside a feature of the machinery of policy-making. After the war the Regional Boards of Industry, set up under the various wartime supply Ministries, had been brought under the Board of Trade with a diminished and less precise role. Tripartite in character, in some cases, notably the Midlands, these bodies seem to have taken their own initiative in attempting to encourage JPCs as part of the production drive.[39]

Such a policy accorded with TUC and much official trade union policy. The TUC, in late 1946, even before the growth of interest at Ministerial or other levels, had proposed to the Joint Consultative Committee (a tripartite slimmed-down version of the National Joint Advisory Committee, a wartime advisory body to the Ministry of Labour) a policy of encouragement of JPCs. The paper on which this was based effectively sums up for all its vagueness what we may call the social democratic case for joint consultation in the late 1940s. Significantly the document was headed *Production under Full Employment'*. The key paragraph read:

The real problem is to find a substitute for the lingering fear of unemployment and to create confidence that full employment can be maintained. The General Council have definitely come to the conclusion that there is no alternative except the creation of an atmosphere of mutual confidence throughout the factories and workshops of the country. During the war period, this country took the lead in the formation of JPCs and, although their history is very uneven, there is little doubt that when they were worked with enthusiasm by both management and labour they produced excellent results.

They therefore proposed that the trade unions and employers should approach the Ministry of Labour on a joint basis to encourage JPCs.[40] In May 1947 the NJAC (reconstituted and enlarged the previous year) recommended to unions and employers that they should set up JPCs 'for the regular exchange of views between employers and workers on production questions'. This was subject to three qualifications: that the machinery would be purely voluntary and advisory in character, would not deal with terms and conditions of employment, and that it would be for each industry to decide the form of machinery. Whilst employers thereby agreed to the encouragement of JPCs their enthusiasm was limited. Typical was the comment of Sir Alex Ramsay of the British Employers Confederation who responded to the TUC view that JPCs were fundamental to productivity increase by saying that they were 'valuable', but we 'could not agree that they were fundamental and that their general adoption would solve the problem of the productivity of labour'.[41]

Over the remaining period of the Labour government there was persistent lamentation at a slow progress of the spread of JPCs. There were also periodic calls for them to be made compulsory - in the House of Commons, by the TUC and by the Labour Party Conference. But the public records suggest that this never came close to happening.

The role of JPCs

The reasons for this absence of compulsion were partly embedded in a division in Ministerial responsibilities which mirrored and reinforced a difference in view about the significance of joint consultation. As already noted, the wartime JPCs had largely been the children of the Supply Ministries, mostly working through the Regional Boards for Industry. These boards had been continued in the post-war period and were the main regional sites of the production drive. They had encouraged JPCs as part of that drive, and seemed to have gained a new lease of life from that function from 1947 onwards. In this they were encouraged by Cripps as the 'supremo' of the production drive. On the other hand, the Ministry of Labour always regarded joint consultation as really their pigeon. Whilst there are some suggestions that they got caught up in the initial enthusiasm for linking JPCs with production and productivity, they soon came to put forward a characteristically Ministry of Labour view that JPCs should be seen as part of a long-term programme for improving industrial relations rather than part of a short-term drive for increased production.[42]

This divergence of view about JPCs meant that Cripps's role was very important. He was the Minister most concerned with the production drive, and could probably have overridden the rather weak Minister of Labour - though it should be noted that the Ministry of Labour had a much greater role in general economic policy-making at least in the early years of the Labour government, than subsequently became the case, because of the importance of manpower planning during the war.[43] Cripps's view on JPCs were complex. He at one stage publicly emphasised the lack of managerial competence amongst workers, and the role of JPCs in stimulating such competence.[44] But he predominantly stressed their role as a means of increasing productivity. Now such a link between joint consultation and productivity can in principle be forged in a number of ways. For example, it could be done by emphasising the capacity of workers to force efficiency on ignorant or reluctant managers - as was common in the foundation of many early wartime JPCs. Alternatively, the linkage has been made by suggesting that the conferring of democratic rights on workers will give a new legitimacy to management - as in the Bullock Report of the 1970s.[45]

But the linkage Cripps made between productivity and JPCs was explicitly on a *psychological* basis. He seems to have been attracted to the kinds of research being undertaken by the Tavistock Clinic (which in 1946 gave birth to the Tavistock Institute for Human Relations), which in turn stemmed from both the pre-war work in the US human relations school (notably the Hawthorne experiments and work of Elton Mayo) and the perceived success of the use of psychological techniques in the forces during the war. This emphasised the importance of inter-personal and especially inter-group relationships as the basis for trust in the workplace, and the need to build institutions both to reflect and develop this trust.[46]

This psychological emphasis, one can note, did not conflict with a widely prevalent ideology of industrial *democracy* within the labour movement, though this term was coming into use by the late 1940s. Whilst the TUC and the Labour Party did argue for JPCs this was mainly based, as noted above on a very vague notion of such institutions as 'confidence-building' agencies. There was no elaborated doctrine of the significance of the JPCs, no forceful rhetoric to link them to traditional trade union of socialist thinking and activity. This is in marked contrast to the period after World War One, when significant links were made between the 'practical' pursuit of guilds, for example in building, and an elaborate doctrine of guild socialism.[47] Into this ideological vacuum came psychology and psychoanalysis. Such notions, a long way from traditional socialist ideas about the enterprise, did fit in with a growing belief on the part of Labour in 'progressive' managerialism. Cripps himself, a Christian socialist with a strongly ethical attitude to economic issues, saw 'humanised' management as part and parcel of the 'tripartism', the co-operation of Government, employers and workers, which is the core of what he meant by 'economic planning'.[48]

One outcome of this psychological emphasis was that the officially sponsored research on the 'human factors in productivity' was entirely psychological in character. When a committee with this title (under the aegis of a broader committee on industrial productivity) was set up in 1947, it looked to the new Tavistock Institute and the National Institute for Industrial Psychology (NIIP) as likely sources of expertise. In the event it was the NIIP which carried out the research on joint consultation by the 'human factors committee'. Whether this derived from a preference for the more individual basis of the NIIP over the more group-oriented work of the Tavistock is unclear, though this distinction was recognised by the Committee.[49]

Some rather optimistic expectations about the capacity of psychological changes to affect productivity were entertained at the beginning of the official enquiries in the area. Indeed the setting up of the Committee on Industrial Productivity separate from the Advisory Council on Scientific Policy, and the establishment of the 'Human Factors' research under the former was explicitly because of hopes of short-term productivity gains from such work. In announcing the setting up of the main committee, Herbert Morrison commented,

> I am advised that a major contribution to industrial productivity cannot be expected in the short-run from current research in the natural sciences, but there are considerable possibilities of increased returns, first, from the more widespread application of research already carried out in the natural sciences and technology, and, secondly, from current research in the social science field.[50]

Such a view did not long survive work by the Human Factors Panel. By October 1948, in a memo to the Lord President and the Chancellor of the Exchequer, the chairman of the main productivity committee was emphasising that human factors research was essentially long-term, would not have the hoped for short-term effects on productivity and should be conducted by the Medical Research Council. This memo it may be noted, echoed what may be called an economist's view of low productivity - that it is mainly a matter of 'obsolete equipment and out-of-date methods of operation' - a view that found echo in the Economic Section the major source of economic advice to the government.[51]

This emphasis on the psychological basis for joint consultation affected policy in two vital ways. It played some part in displacing the ideology of JPCs as a forum for the exposure and correction of managerial efficiency. This wartime posture was very much resisted by the Ministry of Labour in particular. In the name of good industrial relations, Lloyd Roberts wanted to emphasise the importance of discouraging these charges of managerial inefficiency of which so much capital is made by the extremists. However this point should not be overstated, because such a view of JPCs was conditional upon an enthusiasm for production which was never revived on its wartime scale in the late 1940s.[52] Secondly, the psychological focus undercut any short-term links between joint consultation and productivity - for if the crucial element was changing habits of mind, this was clearly a long-run programme. In the same manner it ruled out any compulsion. If the whole rationale of the committees was mutual adaptation and trust then it clearly made little sense to impose them on unwilling workers or employers.[53]

This was accepted by Cripps, and if there had ever been any chance of his pushing for compulsion, by August 1948 he was following the Ministry of Labour line in rejecting any such policy, and emphasising the need for consent on both sides. Cripps nevertheless pushed quite hard for encouragement of JPCs and emphasised the role of the Regional Boards as well as the officials of the Ministry of Labour. This dual emphasis seems to have been because of the recognition of the very uneven activity of the Regional Boards in this area. The Chancellor put pressure on the Ministry of Labour to appoint a senior official to oversee the encouragement of joint consultation. This was done in 1948 and the man appointed was Lloyd Roberts, in the Ministry of Production during the war and about to retire from ICI. There was little reluctance on the part of the Ministry of Labour to make such an appointment, partly because of their desire to emphasise their distinct vision of joint consultation. A Ministry of Labour memo of September 1948 argued that employers' hesitancy over JPCs was encouraged by the fact that

the campaign is primarily sponsored by the Chancellor of the Exchequer of whose views and intentions as to the future control of industry they have some suspicion. It would have a beneficial effect on this aspect if gradually the Ministry of Labour came to be recognised as the sponsoring Ministry, and if, simultaneously, the emphasis in the campaign were put on the industrial relations value of joint consultation rather than on its contribution to increased productivity as a direct objective.[54]

This strategy was not unproblematic with regard to employers. Lloyd Roberts's emphasis on making joint consultation part of the personnel management service of the Ministry of Labour (he was an immediate past president of the Institute of Personnel Management) was recognised to be anathema to the British Employers Confederation, as 'an attempt to teach employers their business'.[55] This led to playing down the personnel management rhetoric, but this mechanism was still used for pushing joint consultation.

Employers generally seem to have been unhappy with the Ministry of Labour enlarging its role in this area.[56] They tended to see it as a production issue, albeit a fairly marginal one of largely domestic concern. They resisted any *initiative* by the Ministry of Labour, and in this they were supported by the TUC - despite the pressure from TUC Conference for more radical measures. Here, as elsewhere, the TUC was reluctant to allow enthusiasm for production to erode too far the autonomy of unions and their rights to bargain collectively without excessive Government intervention.[57] The most that could be agreed at the National Joint Advisory Council was that the Regional Industrial Relations Officers of the

Ministry of Labour could be approached by firms interested in JPCs as long as there already existed a national agreement covering the relevant industry.[58]

The Ministry of Labour used the NJAC agreement, and the employers and TUC positions it embodied, to resist pressure at the 1948 Labour Party Conference for compulsion. At this stage the Ministry, for obvious political reasons, emphasised the production aspect of joint consultation. But Lloyd Roberts over the next couple of years placed more and more emphasis on the 'industrial relations' rather than the production side of joint consultation.[59] Through 1948 to 1950 both (some) Regional Boards of Industry and the Ministry of Labour propagandised for the extension of joint consultation. This seems to have yielded results as measured by the setting-up of new JPCs. But lamentations as to slow progress continued, and pressure was exerted on the NJAC to allow room for more initiative by the Ministry of Labour. But the basis of this enhanced role, at least as viewed from inside the Ministry, was the improvement of industrial relations, not the increase of production. In consequence the Ministry wanted to play down the role of the Regional Boards.

> Regional Boards had been asked to take special action in connection with the drive for greater industrial productivity, and in the main they regarded joint consultation as one of the measures by which the desired results could be obtained. The Ministry of Labour doctrine, however, was to regard joint consultation as an end in itself and sought the acceptance of joint consultation as a permanent feature and essential part of good industrial relations.

Lloyd Roberts thought it would be disastrous if joint consultation came to be regarded as a temporary expedient directed to any particular short-term objective, although he accepted that increased productivity was one of the long run benefits which would ensue from good industrial relations. This view was accepted by Isaacs, the Minister of Labour.[60]

The evidence presented to the Ministry of Labour suggested that the slow growth of joint consultation was partly based on employer resistance, a resistance facilitated by the confusions and hesitations of both unions and Governments about what such consultation involved. Trade unions were generally supportive, though rank and file enthusiasm was unusual, and employers were quite happy to take advantage of this. Employers were resistant because of a common feeling that shop steward enthusiasm for joint consultation represented the thin end of the wedge of pressure for workers' control. The little support they did give seems to have mainly been aimed at undermining the case for compulsion.[61]

The likelihood of such compulsion was affected by the general pattern of government-industry relations. Up to the middle of 1948 general industry-government relations had been relatively cordial. But two issues worsened relations from then on. At the Labour Party Conference of May 1948 the government had announced its determination to proceed with steel nationalisation. Secondly, the decision was made that summer to press on with the setting up of some industrial development councils without the support of the employers in the industries. This latter, with its potential for conflict between the private sector and the government, clearly worried the government..[62] Thus, despite high level Ministerial emphasis on the need to raise productivity, and although the link of this to joint consultation continued, and indeed gained new impetus during the crisis of 1949, compulsion never got on the Cabinet agenda. Efforts to proselytise for joint consultation continued into the period of Conservative government, but the chance of establishing a new regime in the factories as part of the post-war settlement had passed.[63]

Conclusions

This paper has suggested the highly specific circumstances in which joint consultation became a policy issue in this period and how these circumstances exacerbated rather than mitigated the failure of Labour to do more on the industrial democracy front. The conclusion will draw together and elaborate on these elements. At the level of doctrine, Labour's broad doctrinal and policy position had been set in the late 1930s. This focused on nationalisation, full employment and the welfare state. There was little clear idea on what to do about the private sector beyond changing its ownership. These positions were surprisingly unmodified by the war period, and in particular by the growth of new structures in the private sector. Industrial democracy was not a phrase that occurred in the programmes or pronouncements of the Labour Party at this time.

This altered during Labour's tenure of office. By 1949, *Labour Believes in Britain*, in emphasising the need for more production, celebrated the advance of industrial democracy, represented both by Development Councils and factory level committees. Equally prominent however was the celebration of Labour's partnership with (most of) the private sector, and these aspects as we have seen were not easily combined given employer hostility to industrial democracy's advance. Doctrinally, by the end of the 1940s industrial democracy had revived on the Left - but too late to have much impact on policy. In the 1949 document, and also in the Manifesto for the 1950 General Election, these claims of industrial democracy were clearly seen as part of the campaign to raise output. I venture no comment on the plausibility of such a link, either in general or in the particular circumstances of the late 1940s.[64] But posing the issue this way had serious consequences. For one thing the enthusiasm for production which had undoubtedly underpinned the growth of output during the war could not be evoked in peace-time - despite unprecedented propaganda efforts.[65] The norms of worker/employer suspicion for the most part defeated the official union attempts to make increased production part of the political task of support for a Labour government. This support was all the more difficult to obtain when production in the late 1940s was often obviously constrained by shortages of raw materials. Ludicrous situations arose where workers were being exhorted to work harder when some were laid-off through lack of material inputs.

Secondly, whilst most employers didn't resist the production/joint consultation link in principle, they were strongly resistant to the view that productivity was largely a function of such structures, and worried by the potential such a link had for challenging managerial prerogatives. Thirdly, the link between productivity and joint consultation was inherently difficult to demonstrate, and often relied on psychological arguments about which there was widespread suspicion. One consequence was that it was very difficult to challenge anybody [notably the Ministry of Labour] which had an alternative and relatively elaborated conception of the role of joint consultation. The Ministry's view, whilst detaching such consultation from its problematic links to productivity, at the same time made it hard to view consultation as something that could be extended on a compulsory basis. The essence of the Ministry of Labour view was that good industrial relations techniques, such as joint consultation, should only be advanced by agreement, without undercutting traditional management and union prerogatives, and without undermining traditional forms of collective bargaining. Here the Ministry's views were exactly parallel with their attitude to incomes policies.[66] Going too fast on either joint consultation or compulsory incomes policies threatened the notion of a stable and de-politicised industrial relations system, in which the Ministry and government generally should play an emollient rather than an initiating role.

This line chimed in well with that of the TUC and much official trade unionism. Whilst there was union pressure for compulsion and expansion beyond the area of joint agreement, the TUC General Council resisted this and agreed with the employers that any reforms of worker-owner relationships should be subordinate to the traditional national collective bargaining frameworks. The TUC was undoubtedly keener on joint consultation than most employers. It wanted both to support the government's production drive and to keep the pressure for shop steward involvement in factories under official control. But it would not allow these considerations to cut across its traditional concern to keep factory level structures within the ambit of recognised agreements whose main concern was wage bargaining.

Finally, at the Ministerial level, policy was constrained by the desire not to antagonise employers, given the other areas of dispute emerging from 1948; by the psychologistic framework within which much of the discussion was undertaken, so that even if the political dangers of compulsion had been faced, such a strategy would have made no logical sense; and by the role of the Ministry of Labour as an equivocal agency for the policy. JPCs and the whole emphasis on human relations in this period were all part of an emergent 'politics of productivity' which had reverberations from Cabinet level down to the shop floor. This politics can be represented in a number of ways. One view is that in this period government and unions agreed a 'cosy deal' whereby in exchange for limiting wage pressure, unions gained from the government an agreement not to attack restrictive practices. In this way, low wage inflation had as its price low productivity growth.[67]

This approach seems to derive more from an economist's *a priori* model than from the historical record. In fact, the unions were constantly under governmental pressure in this period to accept that the securing of full employment required union support for productivity enhancing measures, and to a striking extent unions, especially at the leadership level, accepted this.[68] On the other hand, the government did allow the employers to pursue the issue of restrictive labour practices - but employers could not, when it came to the issue, find much evidence of the existence of such practices on the wide scale commonly alleged.[69] Hence the 'cosy deal' story seems much exaggerated.

In the broadest terms, the failure of Labour to press harder on the industrial democracy front shaped an important feature of the post-war settlement in Britain. This settlement largely left intact the 'voluntarist' tradition of industrial relations which has been such an important feature of post-war industrial and economic arrangements. Despite the maintenance of compulsory arbitration, and the incomes policy of 1948-50, the 1945 government never seriously challenged that tradition. Indeed it was strikingly unadventurous in this area, its main legislation being simply a repeal of the 1927 Trades Disputes Act and a restitution of the *status quo ante*. Sustained pursuit of JPCs as instruments not of improved 'human relations' but of industrial democracy would have cut across this voluntarist tradition with incalculable consequences.

Again, however, it is important to look at the survival of this voluntarism in some detail. Commonly it has been seen as an example of the excessive power of unions to defeat government proposals for improvements in British industrial relations.[70] However the evidence suggests that, when debated in the 1940s, the 'wage planning' versus free collective bargaining issue was not a government versus unions problem. The tradition of voluntarism was not just about union's view of this role, but also about the danger *for government* of governmental involvement in wage determination. Hence many Ministers were wary of such involvement even if they were not notably sympathetic to trade unions. Often the debate was one of Left versus Right rather than government versus unions. The proponents of wage planning saw it as a necessary and logical corollary of economic planning more generally. The Right saw it as likely to get government held responsible for decisions over which their effective control would be limited, and they knew enough statecraft to reject any such move to responsibility without power.[71]

The commitment to voluntarism provided an uncongenial atmosphere for JPCs. Without legislative backing they faded away in the 1950s in the face of competition from shop stewards committees.[72] By contrast in France and

Germany the attempts at such 'industrial democracy' were embedded in a legal framework which meant they were much less subject to the ebb and flow brought about by changes in the immediate industrial relations context.[73]   Whilst the impact of the French Ordinance on Comite d'entreprise of February 1945, and the various laws passed in the Federal Republic in the early 1950s should not be exaggerated, they did mark a shift in the formal status of labour which was never secured in Britain.   Industrial democracy then had *no* legislative basis in Britain, outside the (ambiguous) commitments to consultation in the nationalisation statutes.   That legislative absence may, perhaps, be taken to symbolise the incoherence and weakness of Labour thinking in this area.   Circumstances strongly told against such legislation no doubt; but the inescapable element of intellectual failure should also be acknowledged.

Notes

1. A. Cairncross, *Years of Recovery: British Economic Policy 1945-51* Methuen (1985). For criticism of Cairncross's macroeconomic emphasis see E.A.G. Robinson 'The Economic Problems of the Transition from War to Peace', *Cambridge Journal of Economics* 10 (1986), pp165-85. For a survey of Labour's management of the economy see J. Tomlinson, 'Labour's Management of the National Ecoomy, 1945-51: Survey and Speculations', *Economy and Society* 18 (1989), p26. Older texts remain important, especially G.D.N. Worswick and P.H. Ady (eds.), The *British Economy 1945-50* Oxford University Press (1952) Oxford; J.C.R. Dow, *The Management of the British Economy 1945-60* Cambridge University Press (1965) Cambridge, chap. 2.
2. J. Tomlinson, 'Mr. Attlee's Supply Side Socialism', *Economic History Review* Vol. 46, 1993, pp1-22; J. Tomlinson, 'A Lost Opportunity?: Labour and the Productivity Problem 1945-51' in G. Jones and M. Kirby (eds.), *Competitiveness and the State in Twentieth Century Britain* Manchester University Press (1991) Machester, pp40-59; N. Tiratsoo and J. Tomlinson *State Intervention and Industrial Efficiency: The Experience of Labour 1939-51* Routldedge (1993).
3. For brief surveys, see Coventry and District Engineering Employers Association, *Worker Participation: the European Experience* EEF (1974) Coventry; E. Batstone and P.L. Davies *Industrial Democracy: The European Experience* Macmiillan (1976). See also note 73 below.
4. K. Middlemas, *Power, Competition and the State Vol. I. Britain in Search of Balance* Macmillan (1986), chaps. 4-6.
5. For one example, see R.V.O. Roberts and H. Sallis, 'Joint Consultation in the Electricity Supply Industry 1949-59', *Public Administration*, 37 (1959), pp115-33. Trade unions were far from simply accepting the Morrisonian public corporation model. For example the Union of Post Office Workers, long a supporter of workers control, passed motions at all its conferences in the late 1940s favouring such a structure for the Post Office. M. Moran, *The UPW: A Study in Political Sociology* Routledge (1974), pp27-30. Similarly with the railwaymen: P. Bagwell *The Railwaymen: The History of the National Union of Railwaymen* Allen and Unwin (1963), pp523-6. The issue was debated at the Ministerial level in the 1940s, notably in the Socialisation of Industries Committee, but the idea of workers control or direct representation was vigorously attacked, notably by Morrison and Gaitskell. See, for example, Public Record Office (PRO) PREM 8/1039, 20 October 1949. The Labour leadership was easily able to ignore Conference resolutions on this issue. 'Although there was yet to come the open contempt for conference decisions displayed by some leading members of the Parliamentary Labour Party, there was rigorous continuation of the long accepted principle that Labour governments must insist on their prior constitutional responsibility to Parliament. Party leaders must be free from conference dictation', A. Fox, *History and heritage: The social origins of the British industrial relations system* Macmillan (1985), p.365.

6. R. Dahl, 'Workers Control of Industry and the British Labour Party', *American Political Science Review* 41 (1946), pp108-146 and J. Tomlinson, *The unequal struggle? British socialism and the capitalist enterprise* Methuen (1982), chap. 4. On the origins of the 'Morrisonian' public corporation, see H. Morrison, *Socialism and transport* Macmillan (1933); J. Tomlinson, *Government and the Enterprise Since 1900: The changing problem of efficiency* Oxford University Press (1994) Oxford, chap. 8.

7. A. Rogow and P. Shore, *The Labour Government and British industry* Oxford University Press (1955) Oxford, p.73; H. Mercer 'The Labour Government and Private Industry' in N. Tiratsoo (ed.), *The Attlee years* (London 1991), pp90-105; H. Mercer, N. Rollings, J. Tomlinson (eds.), *Labour Governments and private industry: The Experience of 1945-51* Edinburgh University Press (1992) Edinburgh.

8. On the general doctrinal background to Labour Policy, see E. Durbin, *New Jerusalems* Routledge (1985) and B. Pimlott, *Labour and the Left in the 1930s* Cambridge University Press (1977) Cambridge.

9. For industries other than those where formal agreements were entered into, information is very short. PRO 'Worker Co-operation on Production Problems. Development of Ideas in Industries where no General Agreements or Arrangements have been made', August 1943, LAB 10/258.

10. International Labour Office (ILO), *Joint production machinery in British industry* ILO (1944) Geneva.

11. R. Price, *Labour in British society* Routledge (1986), p200 suggests that nothing happened on JPCs after 1947, but this seems to be based on the common assumption of an across the board change in Labour's policies after 1947, which seems exaggerated, for all that important changes took place in that year, especially in macroeconomic policy.

12. ILO, *Joint production machinery*; P. Inman *Labour in the munitions industries* HMSO (1957).

13. J. Hinton, 'Coventry Communism: A study of factory politics in the Second World War', *History Workshop Journal* 10 (1980), pp90-118; R. Croucher, *Engineers at war* Merlin (1982).

14. Ministry of Labour, *Industrial Relations Handbook* (London 1944); Inman, *Labour*.

15. E. Wigham, *Power to Manage: A History of the Engineering Employers Federation* Macmillan (1973), p157.

16. Hinton, Coventry Communism', p97.

17. PRO, 'Establishment of JPCs in the Engineering industry', 7 January 1942, LAB 10/213; Hinton, 'Coventry Communism'; Croucher, *Engineers at War*.

18. Wigham, *Power*, p157.

19. Inman, *Labour*, p379.

20. Inman, *Labour*, p378.

21. A. Exell, 'Morris Motors in the 1940s', *History Workshop Journal* 9 (1980), pp90-114; ILO *Joint Production*.

22. PRO, Bevan, 1 January 1943, BT168/171.

23. PRO, 'JPCs Regional Register', 7 November 1945, BT168/167; Price *Labour* plausibly links this pattern to that of strength of craft traditions. See also Croucher *Engineers*, pp168-9.

24. PRO, 'JPCs Regional Register', 5 October 1946, BT168/168.

25. Inman, *Labour*, p382.

26. PRO, Cripps (n.d. but June/July 1945), BT168/170.

27. Ministry of Labour, *Industrial Relations Handbook*, p116.

28. Hinton, 'Coventry Communism', pp96-7.

29. PRO, EEF, 29 September 1947, LAB 10/213.

30. Croucher, *Engineers*.

31. TUC, *Annual Report* 1945; Tolliday 'Government, Employers and Shop-Floor Bargaining in the British Motor Industry 1939-69' in S. Tolliday and J. Zeitlin (eds.), *Shop-Floor Bargaining and the State* Cambridge University Press (1985) Cambridge, pp108-47.

32. PRO, Bevan, 2 February 1945, BT168/169.

33. House of Commons, *Debates*, 9 October 1945; PRO 'Views of Regional Boards on JPCs' (n.d. but June/July 1945), BT168/170.

34. Wigham, *Power*, pp157-8.

35. Cairncross, *Years*, Conclusion.

36. J. Tomlinson, *Employment Policy:The Crucial Years 1939-55* Oxford University Press (1987) Oxford.

37. L. Rostas, 'Industrial Production, Productivity and Distribution in Britain, Germany and the USA', *Economic Journal* 53 (1943), pp39-54; PRO Nicholson, Memo, 5 July 1945, CAB 124/1139; PRO 'Changes in Productivity in British Industries', 4 June 1948, CAB 134/191; for discussion of Rostas see J. Tomlinson 'The Politics of Economic Measurement: The Rise of the Productivity Problem in the 1940s' in A. Hopwood and P. Miller (eds.), *Accounting as social and institutional practice* Cambridge University Press (1994).

38. S.W. Crofts, 'The Attlee Government's Economic Information Propaganda', *Journal of Contemporary History*, Vol. 21, (1986), pp.453-71. Cripps central role in the economic policy of the Labour government is apparent, but he surprisingly lacks a serious biography.

39. PRO, 'Future Use of the Regional Organisation', July 1947, CAB 124/350.

40. PRO, 'Production Under Full Employment', 5 November 1946, LAB 10/655.

41. PRO, Minutes of NJAC, 5 June 1947, LAB 10/652.

42. PRO, 'Machinery for Joint Consultation', 26 January 1949, LAB 10/721; PRO 'Joint Consultation in Industry', 25 January, LAB 10/722.

43. Cairncross, *Years of Recovery*, Chap. 2; Middlemas *Politics in Industrial Society*, p391.

44. E. Estorick, *Stafford Cripps* Heinemann (1949), pp347-9.

45. Report of the Committee on Industrial Democracy, (Bullock Report), Cmnd. 6706, Parl. Papers 1976/7, Vol. XVI.

46. PRO, 'Committee on Industrial Productivity', November 1947, CAB 124/1093; on the background see P. Miller 'Psychotherapy of Work and Unemployment' in P. Miller and N. Rose (eds.), *The Power of Psychiatry* Cambridge University Press (1986) Cambridge. For more extended discussion on 'human relations' and the Labour government, see Tiratsoo and Tomlinson, *State Intervention and Efficiency*, Ch. 6.

47. A. Wright, *G.D.H. Cole and Socialist Democracy* Oxford University Press (1979) Oxford, pp143-76, chaps. 5, 6.

48. J. Tomlinson, 'Planning Debate and Policy in the 1940s', *Twentieth Century British History*, 3 (1992), pp154-74.

49. PRO, 'Problems Affecting Industrial Morale and Productivity', 5 November 1947, CAB 124/1093.

50. PRO, Morrison Memo, 18 December 1947, CAB 124/1094.

51. PRO, Tizard Memo, September 1948, CAB 124/1096; PRO Meade Memo, June 1946, T230/98.

52. PRO, Lloyd Roberts Memo, 27 March 1947, LAB 10.213; H. Clegg and N. Chester: 'Joint Consultation' in H. Clegg and A. Flanders *The Structure of Industrial Relations in Great Britain* Oxford University Press (1964) Oxford, p344.

53. The focus on psychology led to worries that the policy involved 'psychoanalysing all the workers'. PRO 'Note for the Record', 9 December 1947, CAB 124/1094.

54. PRO, 'National Union of Bank Employees Proposal for Joint Efficiency Committees in Banks', 3 August 1948, LAB 10/811; PRO Lloyd Roberts Memo, 17 September 1948, LAB 10/722.

55. PRO, Lloyd Roberts Memo, 2 December 1949, LAB 10/722.

56. PRO 'Report on Joint Consultation in North West', 31 October 1949, LAB 10/725, for example.

57. TUC, *Annual Conference Report* 1947.

58. House of Commons: *Debates*, 18 November 1947.

59. PRO, 'Machinery for Joint Consultation', 26 January 1949, LAB 10/721.

60. PRO, Lloyd Roberts Memo, 5 January 1949, LAB 10/722; this view was echoed by the Minister: G. Eastwood *George Isaacs* Macmillan (1952), pp169-70.

61. PRO, 'Joint Consultation, Midlands Region', 27 June 1950, LAB 10/724; worker attitudes to JPCs were not uniformly those suggested by the election of a deaf mute to one such committee. NIIP, *Joint Consultation in British Industry* NIIP (1952), p134.

62. Rogow and Shore, *Labour Government*, pp139-40; PRO 'Minutes of Economic Policy Committee', 6 July 1948, CAB 134/216.

63. Joint consultation seems to have declined quite rapidly, at least from the late 1950s, as shop steward organisation grew rapidly, especially in the engineering industry. W.E.J. McCarthy *The role of shop stewards in British industrial relations*, Royal Commission on Trade Unions and Employers Associations, Research Paper No. 1 HMSO (1967).

64. But see G. Hodgson, *Democratic Economy* Penguin (1984), chap. 9; J. Tomlinson, *Monetarism: Is There An Alternative?* Blackwells (1986) Oxford 1986, pp111-13.

65. Crofts, 'Economic Propaganda'.

66. R. Jones, *Wages and Employment Policy 1936-1986* Allen and Unwin (1987).

67. S. Broadberry and N. Crafts, 'Implications of British Macroeconomic Policy in the 1930s for Long Run Growth Performance', *Rivista Di Storia Economica* 7, (1990) pp1-19; N. Crafts 'The Assessment: British Economic Growth Over the Long-Run', *Oxford Review of Economic Policy* 4(1), (1988), ppi-xxi.

68. J. Tomlinson, 'Labour and the Trade Unions' in N. Tiratsoo (ed.), *The Attlee Years* Pinter (1991).

69. N. Tiratsoo and J. Tomlinson, 'Restrictive Labour Practices in post-war Britain: Myth and Reality', *Business History* 33 (1994), pp82-92.

70. S. Beer, *Modern British Politics* Faber and Faber (1982), pp214-16.

71. Tomlinson, 'Labour and the Trade Unions'; J. Tomlinson 'The Iron Quadrilateral: Political Obstacles to Economic Reform Under the Attlee Government', *Journal of British Studies* 34 (1995), pp90-111.

72. McCarthy, *The Role of Shop Stewards in British Industrial Relations*.

73. Shennan, *Rethinking France* Oxford University Press (1989) Oxford, chap. 8. It is perhaps ironic that French enthusiasm for workers participation was partly inspired by wartime JPCs in Britain. V. Berghan and D. Karsten *Industrial Relations in West Germany* Berg (1987) Oxford, pp172-87; V. Berghan, *The Americanization of West German Industry 1945-1973* Berg (1986) Leamington Spa, pp207-230. In both countries the issue of workers participation seems to have been much higher on the agenda of the trade unions and Left generally than in Britain. In part this may reflect the recent experience of authoritarian, enterprise level industrial relations, not undergone in Britain.

3. Corporate politics and the quest for productivity: the British TUC and the politics of industrial productivity, 1947-1960 *

Alan Booth

Introduction

The British trade union movement emerged from the war in high public esteem for its part in organising and sustaining wartime industrial production, but criticisms of its role have multiplied since 1945.[1]   By the late 1980s, social scientists from different disciplines and divergent political and analytical perspectives seemed to agree that, first, institutions matter in the processes of post-war British economic development and, secondly, trade unions have retarded the British growth rate.[2]   Much of this work has emphasised labour control at the point of production, resulting in over-manning and the obstruction of new technology and work practices but comparatively little attention has been devoted to peak level discussions. Building on Olson's pioneering work on the dynamics of collective interest groups, Batstone has suggested reasons why British trade unions might limit the rate of productivity growth.[3]   Olson concluded that the longer a society enjoys political and social stability, the more likely it is to suffer 'institutional sclerosis', or a pattern of collective interest groups which slows the resource reallocations needed for fast growth. Batstone noted that Olson's 'sclerotic' tendencies arise in industrial relations not only as a result of long run social stability but also of the 'scope' and 'sophistication' of collective organisations. Those with narrow scope represent the interests of only small groups and will be more obstructive towards productivity growth than more inclusive organisations (i.e. with a broader scope) which would have to bear directly a much higher share of the costs of any growth-inhibiting actions. 'Sophistication' involves the ability of an organisation to represent and co-ordinate interests and implement strategies. In this context, Britain is a 'high sclerosis', 'narrow scope', 'low sophistication' industrial reactions system in

44

which trade unions are long-established and sectional and are free from constraint by the centre because the TUC is incapable of formulating and implementing policy.[4]

Recent research on national tripartite bargaining has not shared this rather negative view. Both Middlemas and Tomlinson have argued that in the 1940s bargaining at peak level was intimately concerned with productivity growth in ways which had real content and relevance for the conduct of the shop floor.[5] Both seem to suggest, albeit implicitly, that if the politics of productivity had worked out differently at the peak level, the performance of British industry since 1945 might have been more impressive. Not the least challenging aspect of this work is the very clear demonstration by both of an apparently strong TUC commitment to faster productivity growth.

There is, however, an alternative view. Barnett and others have argued that policy-makers of the 1940s gave too little priority to the lack of competitiveness of British industry and took much to the creation of a 'new Jerusalem' of social welfare policy.[6] An important element in the 'post-war settlement' was the incorporation of unions into policy-making, resulting in policies which inhibited the power of management to manage and slowed the spread of new technologies and work practices. These proverbial chickens came home to roost when international competition intensified in the 1960s. Only when the institutional matrix of policy-making was changed under Thatcherism could productivity growth be accelerated and competitiveness be regained. Thus, the power of unions on the shop floor derives from the peak-level incorporation of the TUC during the 1940s.

Thus peak level discussions could have been instrumental in creating the political conditions for slow productivity growth and, even if Batstone's view of the weakness of the central institutions of British trade unionism is accepted, it remains important to understand why the TUC's clear interest in productivity policy did not yield better results. Ideally, any examination of trade unions and productivity should examine both peak and shop floor levels and the ways in which the two might be related. This paper represents no more than a first step and presents necessarily tentative conclusions. The focus is mainly on TUC thinking and policies in a period which begins with plans for post-war reconstruction, embraces the economic and political crises of the late 1940s and continues into the years when the economy had to confront the competitive strengths of European and Japanese industry. The paper has three main themes. It examines first the evolution of the TUC's position on productivity. Secondly, it attempts to understand the content of the TUC view and, finally, there are some preliminary thoughts about the relevance of peak level discussions to shop floor practice.

The TUC's position

At the end of the war, policy-makers were confronted by enormous national and global shortages of every type of good. A return from the horrors of war to more normal, stable conditions depended upon quick recovery in industries supplying basic peacetime producer and consumer goods for both domestic and export markets. There was widespread agreement that the state would need to retain its controls at least for a long as these 'abnormal' conditions persisted but, as will be seen below, there were differences about precisely which controls were needed and for how long. The TUC's policy recommendations pivoted on the need to create a peacetime planned economy and to integrate the trade unions into planning. The TUC also called for more joint consultation at the workplace.[7] All shades of union opinion seem to have concluded from wartime experiences that managerial weakness and worker motivation were the keys to higher productivity and that both could be improved by greater work involvement in production decisions.[8] Trade unionists were confident that output and productivity would rise together. The 1946 annual congress called for higher productivity and asked the General Council to prepare reports on new methods, machinery, materials and power tools to aid worker representatives in joint production machinery.[9] This policy was certainly open to very radical interpretation. The AEU, for example, speculated that the task of running socialised industries and planning the private sector might need a new type of trade unionism:

> Full employment, and maximum output by the most modern mechanised industrial equipment, imply a different conception of trade union practice. In the past the unions ... constrained trade union executives and responsible officials to drive the hardest possible bargain with employers. It justified the unions imposing many restrictive measures to protect the workers' investment in industry ... Are such methods of trade union activity out of date? Restrictive practices stand in a different light when it is realised that the public interest, along with the workers' demands for improved standards of life, higher wages, more leisure, and the maintenance of full employment are bound up inseparably with the increase of production per unit of labour. ... The experience of our own union ... during the war years goes to fortify this point of view. It is incidentally one that received considerable attention in our Union Executive's Memorandum on the post-war reconstruction of the engineering industry. In the light of the clamant needs for engineering products to renovate and expand our own national economy and to meet the urgent demands of the whole world, we laid stress in that memorandum upon many of [the] questions which came from the Brighton Congress. The suspension of numerous workshop practices and customs to secure maximum output in the munitions trade during the war also supplies a guide to the future treatment of the related problems of full production and full employment.[10]

This extract has been quoted at length to illustrate not only the unreal expectations of the new government even as late as November 1946, but also the powerful belief that the wartime mobilisation of shop floor radical politics and discontent with private ownership could be recreated in peacetime. Hinton has demonstrated however that the objective conditions for an alliance between shop floor radicals and the state did not exist in the post-war years.[11] Radical expectations did not long outlast the publication of this editorial in the AEU *Journal,* as the fuel and then convertibility crises lowered perceptions of what was economically and politically possible.

As the sense of crisis grew during 1947-8, the focus on productivity became harsher and more direct. Tomlinson has demonstrated that higher productivity seemed the only logical answer to an economic problem in the late 1940s which comprised severe balance of payments problems (especially in the dollar account) with tight constraints on the capital stock and a domestic political commitment to full employment.[12] In this context, TUC leaders sought to mobilise support for measures to raise productivity by appealing to faith in the government and to fear of what the Conservatives might do. The classic statement of loyalty formed the coda to the General Council's statement on productivity policy: 'The living standards of *our* members, the social welfare of *our* Government and the emergence from *our* present difficulties are at stake' [original emphasis]. But there was more at issue than loyalty alone. As will be seen below, the TUC continued to emphasise the need for faster productivity growth under Conservative governments to which there were no debts of allegiance and with which there were considerable differences of view on fundamental issues. There were other reasons why the TUC advocated higher labour productivity and to understand them we must go back to the war.

In planning for the post-war world, TUC leaders strove above all to retain as much of the wartime structure of policy-making as possible while at the same time reversing the state's intrusion into industrial relations. The TUC was adamant that in peacetime wages should be fixed under free collective bargaining, or voluntarism, even if government could maintain full employment after the war.[13] Unfortunately the economic problems which forced it into a positive productivity policy also suggested that voluntarism might be an expensive luxury. The Labour Government was always at least as much concerned with 'production' and 'competitiveness' as with 'productivity'; the government wanted not only more output per unit of input but also more output of exportable goods. 'Exportable' in this sense meant goods which would sell in difficult dollar markets dominated by efficient US producers. Tomlinson has argued that productivity policy rose in political priority in successive editions of the annual *Economic Survey* after 1947, but the issue is not quite as clear cut.[14] The most consistent theme in successive *Economic Surveys* was for higher exports to the dollar area.[15] The configuration of economic problems faced by Britain in the late 1940s and beyond may have urged the need for productivity improvement, but it also required redistribution of the labour force and control of costs. With this broader base, it becomes possible to understand why the TUC leadership supported productivity policy so clearly, even when the Attlee Government had left office and why, to anticipate the discussion of the second section, the TUC's policy was preoccupied with exhortation.

Panitch, Jones and others have shown that the Cabinet conducted vigorous debates over the machinery of economic planning in the first months of the Attlee government.[16] The argument was extremely wide-ranging and involved ministerial and departmental responsibilities for the conduct of 'planning' and the role of labour controls in the machinery of economic policy. Cripps hoped to take responsibilities for economic policy away from central departments and turn the Board of Trade into a peacetime planning ministry, whilst the left believed that labour allocations were an essential part of socialist planning. The Crippsian 'Gosplan' was defeated by the Treasury and Cabinet Office, which hoped to retain their wartime responsibilities in economic policy and the advocates of labour controls ran aground on the combined resistance of Bevin, Isaacs, the TUC and Ministry of Labour to any compromise with the long term goal of restoring the voluntary system of industrial relations.[17] The TUC had won a short-term victory; restoration of voluntarism was now also the government's policy. But there was also a cost.

The government's economic problems mounted alarmingly in late 1946 and early 1947, as noted above. More than ever, the government needed levers to influence what was produced in the economy. One of its answers was a 'wages policy' to hold down wages in general (to increase competitiveness) but with flexibility to engineer limited rises in those sectors important to sustain the growth of output and exports. Ministers favoured a 'National Industrial Conference' in which national priorities could be introduced into pay negotiations, but the TUC blocked this as a threat to voluntary wage fixing.[18] In the event, the government merely expanded the terms of reference of one of the wartime tripartite bodies, the National Joint Advisory Council (NJAC) to make it the vehicle through which it disseminated 'the fullest understanding among both employers and trade unions of the new problems and responsibilities inherent in a policy of planned full employment'.[19]

It soon became clear what the government understood by 'responsibilities inherent in a policy of planned full employment'. The NJAC did not meet for the first year of the new government while the fate of labour controls was resolved, but as soon as business began Morrison, Dalton and Cripps all used the NJAC to urge on industry the need for wage restraint in the tight labour market. There followed long and tortuous discussions between the TUC and the government over wages policy beginning in late 1946 and reaching a climax with the publication of the government's second white paper on wages policy in February 1948.[20] Under free collective bargaining, the only way of influencing wage settlements appeared to be by shaping public opinion. The government pressed hard for a vigorous condemnation of wage rises without corresponding increases in production and began to attack workplace practices which curtailed fast growth of output. The TUC tried to avoid blame for upward pressure on wages and for the comparatively slow growth of productivity, but it knew that it was vulnerable. Union leaders accepted the government's main points that full employment depended on the ability to finance the required level of imports and that wages played an important part in competitiveness and the ability to export.[21] It co-operated fully with the 'voluntary' wage policy demanded by Cripps and Attlee but also began to complain that ministers were favouring the employers rather than their friends in the unions.[22] In part, the unions were losing ground with the politicians because they were meeting increasing opposition within Whitehall. The Ministry of Labour remained keen to promote orderly industrial relations, but criticism of the TUC's apparent inability to control wage demands was mounting in the Treasury, the Cabinet Offices and the Board of Trade.[23]

If its problems on wages and competitiveness were not bad enough, the TUC was also being squeezed by the government on union customs and practices. Employers were successful before 1948 in arguing on the NJAC that pre-war trade practices should not be restored because of the difficulties of the economic situation, but the government encouraged unions to believe that permanent legislation was threatened. In the debate on the Monopolies Bill, the opposition had complained that trade union restrictive practices were leading to wasteful use of labour in industry. Cripps appears to have shared this view and, not wanting to let the unions off the hook, referred the matter to the NJAC, where the BEC picked it up with some relish and greater surprise - it had no paper ready.[24]

The TUC should have drawn three conclusions from its experiences during 1947-8. First, despite rising output the economy appeared to be in a mess. The fuel and convertibility crises were bad enough, but there was no long term answer to the shortage of dollars. Although Marshall aid was announced in June 1947 it was not approved by the US Congress until July 1948 and did not begin to flow in any volume until 1949. In that interim the balance of payments with the dollar area was under great strain. Secondly, as the dollar account deteriorated, concern over competitiveness and wage inflation had mounted. A compulsory wage policy had been averted in early 1948, but if the financial position deteriorated further, the TUC could be sure that pressure for control of wages would return. Finally, the unions learned that they could deflect some of the pressure for control of wage increases by giving greater emphasis to raising labour productivity. In short, the TUC was being finessed by the Attlee government which threatened legislation if steps were not taken to help overcome Britain's problems on external account. This is not to deny the existence within the General Council of enthusiasm for faster productivity growth for its own sake or a genuine loyalty to the government and a readiness to help it overcome its problems.   But the TUC promoted faster productivity growth to defend voluntaristic pay bargaining and was on the defensive throughout the entire period of office of the Attlee government. The commitment to voluntarism also limited the General Council's dealings with member unions. It could not force autonomous unions to act in the way it wanted. It was caught between the government and voluntarism.

Very little changed with the arrival of the Conservatives in power in 1951. The new government found it equally easy to pressure the TUC into support for faster productivity growth, and the TUC found it equally difficult to push member unions to do what the government wanted. The Conservatives decided to retain the tripartite framework established by Labour and to use it to 'educate' the unions into 'responsible' behaviour. Churchill chose as Minister of Labour Walter Monckton, a lawyer with conciliatory views, and instructed him to reassure the TUC that the government planned neither penal sanctions nor industrial relations legislation.[25] If the unions were to be released from the fear of legislation, the pressure had to be maintained in other ways. The format of the NPACI and NJAC was changed to make them both channels through which ministers informed both sides of industry, but particularly the TUC, of economic problems, especially relating to inflation and the balance of payments.[26] Some pressure was less subtle. Monckton rejected twelve Wages Council recommendations for cost-of-living pay increases, to the huge annoyance of the TUC Economic Committee, and also floated the idea of linking wage rises to increases in productivity.[27]

The Economic Committee's response indicated both its continuing susceptibility to such pressures and its inability to lead where wages were concerned. It asked member unions to comply with the introduction of incentive payments, new machinery and methods, greater labour mobility and renewed efforts to raise industrial productivity.[28] However, this appeal was not published and the TUC refused an invitation from the Chancellor to find ways of linking pay to productivity.[29] The Cripps pay pause had failed in 1950 and the unions were unwilling to expose themselves to another erosion of their authority.

There were undoubtedly those on the General Council who wanted to go further. Leaders of large unions (GMWU, TGWU, USDAW, AEU) were heavily engaged in promoting faster productivity growth both within their own unions and on the national stage.[30] In May 1954, the Chancellor of the Exchequer, R.A. Butler, offered the prospect of higher growth if inflation could be controlled and work practices could be modernised more rapidly.[31] The unions did support a very similar mix of growth-oriented macroeconomic policies plus pay restraint and productivity bargaining in the 1960s. But in the mid-1950s the offer was declined. Middlemas has explained the TUC's trepidation in terms of a division between a moderate leadership and a militant shop floor, evident in the rise of domestic bargaining, the unofficial strike, shop floor control and shop stewards' power in the motor car, aircraft and electrical industries during the mid-1950s.[32] Such factors may have played a part, but they did not prevent the AEU, the union most obviously concerned in these sectors, from mounting a strong campaign for higher productivity.[33] If AEU leaders could face down their radical critics on the shop floor, there is no reason why the TUC should not have followed suit. It is equally plausible to argue that the General Council was more concerned to uphold the voluntarism which it had defended so stoutly in their dealings with ministers. 'Free' collective bargaining implied the absence of intervention by both government and the wider trade union movement in the agreements between specific unions and employers.[34] Each union should be left to formulate its own policy according to its own circumstances. At the centre, the role of the TUC was to try to shift the burden of blame for low productivity growth from the shoulders of trade unions; it continued to emphasise the need for higher investment to secure export markets, full employment and rising living standards.[35]

In early 1954 the TUC Economic Committee secretariat pointed out the strength of Japanese and German competition and the vulnerability of sterling area markets.[36] In April, the reports of Courts of Inquiry into disputes in engineering and shipbuilding warned of the danger to competitiveness of constantly rising costs driven by shop floor pressures. But the Economic Committee decided against a call for greater discipline and to oppose an official enquiry into the impact of rising production costs on British industry. It also came close to accepting that radical changes in industrial relations would be needed to restore the authority of formal union structures; but it did not grasp the nettle.[37] In the circumstances the Economic Committee, like the Production Committee before it, reverted to complaints about the rise in dividends which made wage restraint more difficult and retarded productivity-enhancing investment.[38] The TUC also failed to lead on automation in 1955-6, even though its Production Committee believed that there were greater dangers from technical change being introduced too slowly rather than too quickly.[39]

Union leaders were helped out of this defensive redoubt by the Treasury's economic policy errors in 1955-6. The controlled expansion which Butler had envisaged in 1954 turned instead to a boom with accelerating inflation, an exchange crisis and threats of devaluation. There was strong pressure from the Treasury and the Prime Minister's Office for a deal on wage restraint, but also a recognition that the TUC leadership was unwilling to place itself in such a vulnerable position.[40] As in 1946-8, the key economic departments tried to appeal to wage bargainers over the head of the leadership by shaping public opinion directly. A further parallel with the Cripps era was government support to the BEC to oppose union 'restrictive practices'.[41] Neither of these initiatives provided answers in 1955-6. The Treasury found that the only way to reduce inflation and restore foreign exchange equilibrium was to cut the pressure of demand, but the stop phase of policy had to be deeper and longer-lasting than originally anticipated, with cuts in public investment and a rise in unemployment.[42] The General Council found an issue around which it might campaign to restore both unity to and its own authority within the movement. Its pronouncements on automation, for example, were now framed within the context of making an expanding economy and full employment essential to accelerate the pace of technical change.[43] At last, here was an opportunity for the TUC to lead.

The aim thus far has been to show that the General Council concluded at a relatively early stage in the post-war period that various aspects of trade union behaviour were inimical to the national economic interest as defined by the government of the day. The evidence suggests that this attitude persisted at least until the mid-1950s. There were dissident voices, but they were marginalised.[44] The pro-productivity majority on the General Council also saw that faster productivity growth could not only help resolve some of these national economic problems but also help secure goals which were associated more narrowly with the trade union movement like full employment, higher wages, shorter hours and so on. However, the strength with which faster productivity growth in the broadest sense could be championed depended upon conjunctural factors; in effect, there *was* a 'high politics' of productivity. But it remains to be seen whether these debates had any impact beyond the proverbial smoke-filled corridors.

The details of productivity politics

Having looked at when the TUC emphasised the productivity issue, it is now appropriate to examine the details of that policy and what was done to put it into effect. The best place to begin is the 1944 *Interim Statement on Post-War Reconstruction* which continued to shape TUC thinking into the 1950s.[45] This is by now a very familiar document, but its concern with questions of productivity and efficiency have been underplayed. The key to greater efficiency, as to much else, was to develop the wartime system of controlling industry. At the core, economic planning would stretch down from the tripartite National Industrial Council, through Industrial Boards for the private sector and governing boards for nationalised industries (on which workers would be represented), down to Joint Production Committees (JPCs) and Works Councils at shop floor level. It was hoped that worker involvement at all levels of economic planning would raise productivity but, as the essay of Tomlinson shows clearly, there was no clear consensus on the precise function of the JPCs and their relationship to the higher levels of the planning machine.[46] Some parts of the private sector had been characterised in the interwar years by a long tail of inefficient firms. These industries were to be rationalised by the industrial boards. The *Interim Statement* also proposed a new National Investment Board, which would direct capital to both public and private sector industries, and would provide finance for the reorganisation of inefficient industries.[47] TUC leaders also considered the problems posed by established trade union structures and practices. Union evidence to Beveridge's employment policy inquiry, not only offered the prospect of wage constraint in return for long-term full employment, but also hinted at relaxing demarcation rules to promote greater labour flexibility.[48] The 1944 Congress also noted the difficulties which arose from the decentralised nature of British trade unionism, but proposed only amalgamation and federation and minor strengthening of TUC headquarters. There was no real need for more at this stage as the tide appeared to be running in favour of labour. The first reports from the working parties on old industries like pottery, textiles and iron founding (the government's answer to the industrial boards) seemed to vindicate the TUC's own analysis that in many of these industries there was a long tail of very inefficient firms with low investment levels and poor leadership.[49] But the machinery of industrial planning also demonstrated to union leaders that there were costs to workers from higher efficiency and greater competitiveness. The acute sensitivity over the wages question has already been noted, but there were also problems over production and productivity. At the second meeting of the NPACI, Cripps proposed to set up a Production Efficiency Service, a form of state run industrial consultancy.[50] The TUC responded defensively. It wanted no part of a policy which implied the use of the stopwatch and threatened intensification of work effort and would simultaneously raise the level of private profits and unemployment.[51] In the end, the TUC admitted the advantages of motion study (ergonomics could help to reduce worker fatigue and raise interest in the task) while seeking to limit the use of time study. The General Council endorsed the Production Campaign early in 1946, accepting that trade unionists must work harder, but remained happiest when drawing attention to the impact on production of the shortage of labour, particularly of skilled grades.[52] During 1946, the TUC was much happier to discuss efforts to raise production rather than productivity. But the government itself also gave much less thought to efficiency than to the volume of output during this early phase of conversion to peace.[53]

This rather comfortable situation was undermined by the crises of 1947 and the government's pressure on wages policy. Congress accepted, albeit for the duration of the emergency only, the government's case for greater effort and greater mobility of labour into the undermanned industries. In two months the union side of the NJAC agreed to accept fuller use of European Volunteer Workers and longer hours of work in the industries vital for recovery and exports, state encouragement of piecework systems, the re-introduction of the Control of Engagements Order and was prepared to discuss direction of labour if necessary.[54] The TUC also continued to press for more skilled workers. The *quid pro quo* was help from the government to establish the machinery of joint consultation, particularly JPCs, and full disclosure to the TUC of details of the economic situation.[55]

But in union eyes, lack of investment remained the key cause of low productivity. Lack of investment was not simply a question of finance. Steel and other constructional materials were in short supply, and the TUC wanted a say in how such scarce resources were allocated. The Labour government went some way towards this position with the creation of a tripartite Economic Planning Board (EPB) in 1947.[56] But the TUC also wanted to return to the wartime practice of detailed targets of production to be made on an industry-by-industry or, better, on a factory-by-factory basis, a persistent demand from Tewson on the NJAC and EPB. This was, of course, consistent with the call for more economic planning but union leaders also assumed that workers would strive by whatever means to do what their own Labour government asked (as long as the TUC endorsed the request and workers were involved in production questions).

If these proposals were designed to galvanise the shop floor, they also opened the way to greater central control. From the onset of the 'cold war' in 1947 the General Council began to view opposition to its policy as inspired by the Communist Party. Attempts began to silence the formidable communist opposition which had won an increasing number of posts in key unions such as the ETU, AEU, the Foundry Workers, the NUM and the TGWU. Middlemas has described anti-communism as 'the TUC's most vigorous political activity' from 1947 onwards.[57] The General Council's difficulties lay first in the fertile ground of wages policy which was far from popular on the shop floor, not least because dividends and profits began to rise despite employer commitments to restraint.[58] But the Communists also began to criticise the new-found enthusiasm for the production drive. To the General Council, such criticism was a breach of trust to a government which needed all the help and loyalty which could be mustered.

Congress might have been able to mobilise the shop floor and isolate its critics if it had been able to show to rank and file trade unionists that the labour view was being heard and accommodated in policy. But very few concrete gains could be identified. After 1947, the Labour government found itself conciliating employers in the face of enormous economic problems which could be solved only by increasing output and selling in highly competitive markets. Employers were able to support those parts of productivity policy which they believed were of benefit and exercise an effective veto against potential threats. The FBI encouraged the government to promote piecework payments systems. It believed that low levels of production and productivity would be overcome by greater incentives, especially if there were more consumption goods in the shops.[59] But industrialists were concerned by Cripps's support of the TUC's call for more extensive joint consultation, which seemed to the FBI and the BEC to be a backdoor route to workers' control. As other essays in this volume have pointed out, employers were very keen to divert the JPC idea from the potentially damaging area of assessing managerial competence to the more congenial area of the building of trust and confidence at the workplace. When the Anglo-American Council on Productivity (AACP) gave new opportunities for unions and government to criticise the quality of British industrial management, the FBI was again successful in protecting the managerial interest, even at the cost of an effective productivity policy.[60] Employers also lobbied to frustrate working party idea and rationalising the inefficient, old-established industries.[61]

The determination of employers to frustrate an effective productivity policy by drawing the teeth of any plan to scrutinise or criticise managers only underlines the weakness of both unions and the state. Hinton has pointed to the deep-seated antipathy of the British polity towards an interventionist state, even in the extreme difficulties of 1946-9.[62] Middlemas's overview of the broad canvas of economic policy-making also shows that Labour ministers believed that change in industry could be effected only by consent; force and direction would not work.[63] The government could apply pressure and seek to shape public opinion, but it believed that it could not tackle industrial problems head-on. However, the susceptibility of interest groups to government pressure and censure by public opinion was asymmetrical. From 1947, industrial labour was by some measure the most vulnerable interest group. Business could sense the tide of opinion running in its direction and the government, though battered, was far from broken as by-election results continued to attest.[64] But the TUC was worried about both the effect of wages on competitiveness and its relations with the government. After the crises of 1947, the union leadership began to act independently to promote productivity growth. Its efforts focused on the 'General Council side' of the NPACI. Before 1948, it had done little more than attend the full NPACI. During 1948, however, the 'General Council side' established itself as a 'Production Advisory Committee' (PAC) and began to assume a responsibility for faster productivity growth.

There was little difficulty in getting the large unions, except those with strong communist organisation, to fall in behind the drive for higher productivity and competitiveness, though different tactics were pursued. The TGWU, for example, tended to place great weight on the need for discipline on wages and the need to expel Communists. In the AEU, by contrast, Tanner was much less confrontational with the left and staked out very strongly, as did his successors, the case for a union obligation to raise productivity.[65] Driven by these two prominent leaders and by Tewson's determination to make the traditional relationship with the Labour party a success, the General Council could reach agreement on the broad outlines of what was needed to accelerate productivity growth. But smaller unions and those in key industries were a problem. The PAC called a conference of executives to enthuse union leaders who would, in turn, mobilise their members, in part by giving space in their journals to productivity matters.[66] The main hope to raise the productivity-consciousness of the shop floor was however the JPC. As Tewson argued:

> The crux of the whole question for us today and in the coming consultations is ... how can we make available on the floor of the workshop the facts which have convinced us that increased productivity is necessary, and the means by which it can be achieved? That has to be in the forefront of all our minds on this question, and, quite

frankly, I do not know how we are going to get it down on to the floor of the workshop
without something in the way of a Joint Production Committee. If the proposal means
anything then it does mean getting down to brass tacks with our own membership.[67]

Strictly speaking, of course, Tewson had no membership but if this strategy
strained trade union constitutional relationships, the follow-up meetings with
individual unions pushed it still further.[68] The unions interviewed by the PAC
found a range of practical problems and would not respond to peak level pressure
for change. The CSEU rejected time and motion study, the pottery workers were
reluctant to change traditional practices and the building unions continued to be
embroiled in demarcation disputes.[69] With so little return from its efforts to
manoeuvre union leaders, there was no alternative but to involve the mass
membership directly. In addition to promoting JPCs, the TUC won support from
the NJAC for 'know how' conferences to motivate workers:

In [the TUC] view an increase in production would be promoted by stimulating the
interest of the workers in their own particular job, particularly if their work was not
easily identified with the completed product in which it was incorporated. A vast
number of castings pass through our foundries each year, they are not very interesting,
and few workers know what use they will serve in industry. ... If a group from the
foundry in question could go to the flour mill, the pumping station, the motor car
works, or wherever it is that their products were being used, and could report back to
their fellow workers what they had seen and learned, it is anticipated that the results
would be beneficial to production.[70]

The General Council knew well by 1949 that union members were tired of
exhortation but hoped that even small gains in employee control over the
knowledge of production would increase motivation and productivity.[71] To this
extent, the TUC's ideas shared common ground with some aspects of the human
relations approach. This strategy was opposed to Taylorist mentalities and
authoritarian approaches to production which were commonplace in British
industry and which the FBI was struggling to defend.

However, after 1949 the TUC also took steps which *encouraged* the spread of
scientific management in British industry. The granting of Marshall aid to the
UK led directly to the creation of the AACP the main activity of which was to
send mixed teams of employers and works to observe US practices in their
industry and report back.[72] Although there is some dispute on the nature of these
reports, the TUC found in the first reports support for the view that managers
rather than workers were the problem:

The American members of the Anglo-American Council on Productivity agreed that,
somewhat to their surprise, British workers worked as hard as their American
colleagues. Their work was not so effective because of the bad 'lay-out' of plants,

lack of use of mechanical handling devices, poor production 'flow', and opposition to time and motion study.[73]

The poor quality of much of British management had been noted by most unions interviewed by the PAC and the TUC now concluded, as it had in 1941-2, that managerial inefficiency was the primary cause of low productivity. It campaigned for greater use of industrial consultants, and in particular for local union officials to be able to call Cripps's Production Efficiency Service into inefficient firms.[74] The PAC now began to present *time* and motion study as a route to better management practices, as long as there were safeguards (supplied by basic training in these methods for shop stewards and local union officers).[75] After an AACP visit of British trade unionists to study the way US unions used production experts, the TUC established its own Production Service. During the 1950s, union officers were given training in various management techniques.[76] Congress also instructed member unions that new technologies should be resisted by unionists neither on the ground of higher unemployment nor to preserve demarcation rules. The TUC was clearly aware that fear of redundancy had not disappeared (from textiles, for example) and that defensive practices were reappearing. In the context of veiled government threats that such behaviour was unacceptable under full employment, the PAC constantly emphasised the need for labour flexibility.[77]

The TUC was thrashing around in all directions for a viable productivity policy from 1947 to 1950. It gave support to almost any initiative. There was no coherence to its programme. It was driven by fear of and loyalty to the Labour government. Needing to participate in the tripartite machinery of economic policy-making, it found itself caught between government pressure for change of traditional union practices (which it had itself anticipated in 1944) and the logic of voluntarism. The PAC could not force autonomous trade unions to give up customs, practices and traditional attitudes of mind for the sake of a strained relationship with the Labour government. Precisely where the TUC placed itself within this network of conflicting forces depended essentially upon the quality of its leaders and the behaviour of other powerful interest groups involved in power bargaining.

After 1945, the union movement was poorly led, especially when contrasted with its successes during the war. It failed to capitalise on the favourable political climate in 1946 and was consistently outflanked by the FBI and BEC after 1947. The main irritant between organised labour and the government was the wages question, and here the TUC played its cards very badly. Cairncross's assessment of the post-war British economy has emphasised the restraint of wage bargainers during the whole reconstruction period.[78] However, until the Cripps pay pause the TUC failed completely to persuade any section of British opinion that the trade unionists were behaving with undue moderation. The handling of productivity policy was equally inept, and with little sign of central co-ordination, appraisal or strategic thinking. The leadership of the other economic interest groups was extremely successful by comparison. Employers emerged from the war in very low esteem.[79] The production crisis of 1941-2 had not been forgotten. However, the FBI skilfully exploited the opportunities afforded by the crises of 1947 and the export drive to improve its standing with the government.

The performance of the government is more difficult to assess. The government quickly saw the need to encourage private industry to produce at least cost the maximum supply of those goods which were most necessary to generate strong recovery and a sound balance of payments. But it did not devise ways of mobilising industry for faster productivity growth. The Board of Trade actively promoted shop floor involvement in planning as a means of raising productivity, only to be frustrated by the Ministry of Labour's determination to avoid compulsion in industrial relations.[80] The decisive force within Whitehall was almost certainly the goal of the Treasury and the economists in the Cabinet secretariat to hold down costs in those industries capable of selling in dollar markets. Accordingly the thrust of government dealings with employers and unions aimed to curb the growth of wages. The efforts to raise the rate of productivity growth were always much less direct, purposeful and sustained. There were opportunities to do more. Tiratsoo and Tomlinson have illustrated the failure of a series of initiatives on the rock of employers' resistance and the state's unwillingness to intervene in the internal workings or private industry.[81] The government was content to do no more than to maintain pressure for faster productivity growth, especially on the TUC.

The unions' position eased with the change of government in 1951, and the determination of the Conservatives to be seen as capable managers of social democracy. As noted above, the unions were still on the defensive but they were not squeezed as hard as they had been under Labour. There were also significant changes in the TUC leadership in the first half of the 1950s. Jack Tanner, who had taken such a prominent part in urging unions to champion productivity improvement, retired and there were soon important changes in the TGWU which reflected the rise of consumerist and wage issues. Union leaders were less ready to pronounce about productivity than they had been in the late 1940s. There was still a productivity policy, but its scope was much reduced. Much of the effort was channelled through the British Productivity Council, the body which succeeded the AACP at the end of 1952. All the members of the Production Committee served as council members of the BPC, except for the leader of the Boilermakers.[82] The BPC tried to create structures within industry which enabled shop floor workers to become involved in the problems of industry (local productivity committees) and to find out about new methods and machinery (productivity circuits - a form of inter-factory visits, not unlike the principle of the AACP). Outside its activities within the BPC, the TUC's public statements on productivity were designed to shift blame for slow productivity growth from workers to managers and governments. But at peak level, the TUC still found itself caught between the need to be involved in corporate bargaining and the requirements of voluntarism, but the tripartite structures were less powerful than before and the leadership was less inclined to give a lead to shop floor workers on customs, practices, and flexibility; these were issues for collective bargaining. This approach was complemented by Churchill's first Minister of Labour. Monckton tended to see all industrial relations questions as a matter of good human relations and he organised, through the NJAC, a number of conferences on the theme in the early 1950s.

Conclusions

This essay has shown that the TUC's programme for increasing the rate of productivity growth went through three phases before 1960. The first, lasting from the end of the war to the crises of 1947, saw higher productivity as an indirect benefit of policies which were desirable for other, more fundamental reasons. From 1947 until 1950, the TUC broadened its policy enormously to take in measures of which it had previously been most suspicious. Union leaders were willing to back almost any route to higher productivity, even those which could be to the detriment of the short term interests of ordinary workers. There was little consistency and no evidence of strategic vision. After 1950, and especially after Labour had left office, TUC leaders seem to have lost little of their collective belief in the desirability of faster productivity growth, but were much less willing to take the lead and much more concerned to try to shift blame for the shortcomings of British industry from workers to managers and policy-makers.

Although this productivity policy changed so much in a relatively short span, there was a consistent common core; it was believed that faster productivity growth would come from higher investment, above all in the material handling equipment which US industry deployed on such a lavish scale, professionalisation of British management and, significantly, greater effort from British workers. Although the TUC read the early reports of the AACP as evidence that effort levels were approximately the same on both sides of the Atlantic, the constant emphasis on mobilising, disciplining and motivating shop floor workers and the abandonment of defensive customs and practices indicates a conviction that more effort could be expended by British workers. This core was expanded when TUC leaders, still accustomed to wartime habits of strong direction, believed themselves under pressure on wages from a government to which they had strong ties of loyalty and trust. But even when the special economic and political conditions of 1947-50 abated and the leadership was faced by problems on which it was less inclined to lead, the TUC returned to its core position and plugged away at consensual approaches to faster productivity growth. It no longer tried to discipline and lead its members, but was a strong pillar of support for the BPC and, in the 1960s, came to support the Wilson government's planning initiative.

Nevertheless, the rate of productivity growth proved extremely resistant to change. The efforts to raise rates of growth of productivity and increase competitiveness failed unequivocally. When German and Japanese competition became a reality in the 1950s, markets were lost, Britain's share of world manufactured exports ebbed away and industrial casualties began to accumulate. British unions cannot escape some share of blame for this state of affairs, but the least compelling of the explanations of Britain's relative industrial decline with which we began is the new Right's prognosis of an obstructionist TUC which demanded pro-union policies from government. The TUC was consistently the weakest of the collective interest groups and was always boxed into a corner because, like the government and employers, it believed that rising wages threatened competitiveness if unaccompanied by productivity advance at a similar pace. After the war, union leaders gave highest priority to the recreation of the voluntary system of industrial relations. They could advise and mobilise member unions on wages policy only when the conditions were appropriate. They could campaign for all they were worth on the need for faster productivity growth, but voluntarism implied that they could not intervene in this area either.

In this light, the Batstone-Olson approach to the role of institutions appears more promising. What was distinctive about the TUC was its relative weakness. At the centre, sophistication was low. For much of the time the TUC had difficulty in devising an effective policy for faster productivity growth. When it did have such a policy (and much else besides) between 1947 and 1950, the programme could not be put into operation and the TUC had to reduce its ambitions. General Council leaders were happiest to allow individual unions to pursue their own productivity interests, revealing the narrow scope of British trade unionism. Employers' organisations were, of course, equally involved in this process and, again, the picture which emerges is of a strong desire from the membership for the restoration of managerial prerogatives and to distance industry from the state.[83] This picture tends to confirm the view of Tomlinson that the politics of productivity were the politics of stalemate.[84] However, this picture is also inadequate in some respects.

The Batstone-Olson view is that institutional behaviour is determined by structure and that structure is determined by history. Scholars within this tradition frequently point to the early development in Britain of sectional, craftist unionism with its strong attachment to the autonomy of individual unions, to voluntarism as a code of behaviour and to the preservation of jobs as the primary goal of organisation.[85] The industrial relations system is thus a prisoner of its past. The picture of the TUC which emerges from this study gives only equivocal support to this view. At various points in the 1940s union leaders were willing to consider structural change. That such steps were not put into effect may underline the power of history, but it is also significant that an industrial stalemate paralleled the political *impasse*. On the shop floor traditional defensive practices had already emerged by 1949 and there was very little evidence of employers having sought or found a new basis for giving workers additional responsibilities for running their enterprises. On many occasions, the TUC emphasised the importance of worker motivation to industrial performance but was unable to persuade the government to deliver any measures to help. No effective productivity coalition was built in British industry. Primary responsibility must lie with the state's unwillingness to confront employer insistence on managerial prerogatives. The Attlee Government successfully finessed the TUC into a position where it supported almost any proposal to raise the rate of productivity growth. But the TUC needed aid from the government and a radical bargain with employers to go further, and this almost certainly implied action by the government as power broker. Labour in office persistently refused to move beyond persuasion and on to the factory floor. The government's handling of the TUC was astute but its dealings with ordinary workers were less assured. For completeness, one might add that the nature of markets played a decisive impact on the course of productivity policy. Just as the specific nature of the British economic problem in 1948-9 placed particular emphasis on the need to raise productivity the emergence of boom conditions, especially in export markets (despite the loss of Britain's share of world trade) took off the heat. Prosperity both enabled the TUC Production and Economic Committees to withdraw into bland exhortation and raised issues which were more obviously for decentralised collective bargainers to resolve. If there was an opportunity for the 'high politics' of productivity to make a difference to methods of production on the shop floor, the window opened for a relatively short period in the late 1940s. Some part of the blame for the failure to achieve anything of value must lie with the policies and structure of the British trade union movement, but the primary responsibility lies elsewhere.

Notes

* This paper is the first step in a larger project on trade unions and industrial productivity since 1945. The project is jointly directed by Dr. Joseph Melling and has been financed by the Economic and Social Research Council, the Centre for Economic Policy Research, and the University of Exeter.

1. The range of literature in this tradition is voluminous, but good examples are: G.C. Allen, *The British disease: a short essay on the nature and causes of the nation's lagging wealth* IEA, 2nd edn. (1979); A. Kilpatrick and T. Lawson, 'On the nature of industrial decline in the UK' *Cambridge Journal of Economics* 4 (1980), pp85-102; E.H. Phelps Brown, 'What is the British predicament?' *Three Banks Review* 116 (1977), pp3-29; C.F. Pratten, *Labour productivity differentials within international companies* Cambridge University Press (1976) Cambridge. More recently, David Metcalf has sharpened the argument and applied it to the period since the mid-1970s: 'Water notes dry up: the impact of the Donovan reform proposals and Thatcherism at work on labour productivity in British manufacturing industry' *British Journal of Industrial Relations* 27 (1989), pp1-31. There have been persistent critiques of the theme, most notably T. Nichols, *The British worker question: a new look at workers and productivity in British industry* Routledge (1986).

2. See A. Booth and J. Melling, 'A cure for the British disease? Institutions, labour relations and the growth of British industrial productivity since 1945', mimeo.
3. E. Batstone, 'Labour and productivity' *Oxford Review of Economic Policy* 2 (1986), pp32-43. Mancur Olson, *The rise and decline of nations* Yale University Press (1982) New Haven.
4. It is worth noting that the ability of Batstone's structural factors to explain comparative rates of productivity growth is very good before 1973 but is weak thereafter.
5. R.K. Middlemas, *Power, competition and the state: volume I: Britain in search of balance* Macmillan (1986); J. Tomlinson, 'The failure of the Anglo-American Council on Productivity' *Business History* 33 (1991), pp82-92; N. Tiratsoo and J. Tomlinson, *State intervention and industrial efficiency: Labour, 1939-1951* Routledge (1993).
6. This assessment is constructed from C. Barnett, *The audit of war: the illusion and reality of Britain as a great nation* Macmillan (1986); G. Maynard, *The economy under Mrs.Thatcher* Basil Blackwell (1988) Oxford, pp25-8.
7. These points are covered more fully by Tomlinson's essay in this volume and Hinton, *Shop floor citizens* Edward Elgar (1994) Aldershot.
8. On wartime experience, see J. Hinton, 'Coventry communism: a study of factory politics in the second world war' *History Workshop Journal* 10 (1980), pp96-104.
9. *Report of proceedings at the 78th annual Trades Union Congress* TUC (1946), pp325-7.
10. AEU, *The Monthly Journal* November 1946.
11. 'The citizen on the shop floor: the idea of democracy in the British engineering industry, 1941-48', paper presented to a conference on Management, Production and Politics, held at Glasgow University in April 1992; *Shop floor citizens*.
12. 'The failure of the AACP', p82.
13. Middlemas, *Power, competition and the state*, pp66-7.
14. J. Tomlinson, 'A lost opportunity? Labour and the productivity problem' in G. Jones and M.W. Kirby (eds.), *Competitiveness and the state in twentieth century Britain* Manchester University Press (1991) Manchester.
15. *Economic survey for 1947* HMSO (1947) Cmd 7046; *Economic survey for 1948* HMSO (1948) Cmd. 7344, pp54-5.
16. L. Panitch, *Social democracy and industrial militancy* Cambridge University Press (1976) Cambridge, pp10-22; R. Jones, *Wages and employment policy, 1936-1985* Allen and Unwin (1987), pp35-7; A. Booth, *Economic policy, 1931-1949: was there a Keynesian revolution?* Harvester (1989) Brighton, pp158-63; A. Cairncross, *Years of recovery: British economic policy, 1945-51* Methuen (1985), pp47-57, 318-29.
17. Booth, *Economic policy*, pp158-9.
18. Public Record Office (PRO) CAB 124/785, National industrial conference, memo by E.M. N[icholson], 27 June 1946.
19. PRO LAB 10/1489, Proposals for closer consultation between the government and organised industry on all matters in which employers and workers have a common interest, NJC 1, no date.
20. A draft white paper on wages policy, 'Statement on the economic considerations affecting relations between employers and workers' was brought before the NJAC in late 1946 (PRO LAB 10/655, JCC 182, no date) but the unions found the message so uncompromising that they battled to change the text. The published version appeared under the same title in 1947 as Cmd. 7018, but with significant changes and additions (notably a new introduction calling for improvements in efficiency and productivity) drafted by the TUC. This was not enough for the Cabinet once the crises of 1947 began to break, and the government issued its second white paper, *Statement on personal incomes, costs and prices* HMSO (1948) Cmd. 7321, but this time without prior consultation with the TUC. For a fuller discussion, see Jones, *Wages and employment policy*, pp35-7.
21. TUC papers at the Modern Records Centre (MRC), Warwick University: MRC MSS 292/560.1/4, Economic Committee 7/4, 11 May 1947.
22. Middlemas, *Power, competition and the state*, pp148-9.
23. Cairncross, *Years of recovery*, p403.
24. Cripps told the 1948 TUC annual congress that labour efficiency was a necessary part of any programme of full employment: *Report of proceedings at the 80th annual Trades Union Congress*

TUC (1948), p216. The reference to the NJAC can be found in PRO LAB 10/652, NJAC 25th meeting, 27 October 1948.

25. Middlemas, *Power, competition and the state*, p257.
26. NPACI is the National Production Advisory Council for Industry which had been established during the war to bring about tripartite management of wartime production. The new terms of reference can be found in PRO BT 190/2, 33rd meeting of NPACI, 7 December 1951.
27. MRC MSS 292/560.1/8, Economic Committees 2 and 3 and special meeting 22 July 1952.
28. MRC MSS 292/560.1/8, Economic Committee 7/3, 'The need for higher productivity', 14 May 1952.
29. MRC MSS 292/560.1/8, Economic Committees 8 (11 June 1952) and 9 (9 July 1952). *Report of proceedings at the 84th annual Trades Union Congress* TUC (1952), p284.
30. A. Carew, *Labour under the Marshall Plan: the politics of productivity and the marketing of management science* Manchester University Press (1987) Manchester, pp202-3.
31. PRO BT 190/2, NPACI 42nd meeting, 28 May 1954.
32. Middlemas, *Power, competition and the state*, pp226-33.
33. Successive Presidential Addresses to the AEU National Committee during the 1950s drew attention to the need for higher productivity to make high wages possible and the pages of the *Monthly Journal* were frequently used to urge productivity growth. See, for example, W.J. Carron,., 'Automation' *Monthly Journal*, August 1955, which proposed that workers should welcome the more efficient methods which were necessary for the continued competitive strength of British industry and should be adequately paid for new work practices. The complex internal politics of the AEU at this period is the subject of continuing research by Joseph Melling and myself in a project funded by the University of Exeter.
34. Little is known about the content of pay bargaining during the late 1940s and early 1950s. It is possible that 'productivity bargaining' of the type which became fashionable in the 1960s was spreading much earlier. Carew has shown that publicity for such deals was spreading in 1949-50. See *Labour under the Marshall Plan*, pp147-57. See also M. Bufton, 'The Productivity Drive: an overview', University of Exeter (1995).
35. *Report of proceedings at the 86th annual Trades Union Congress*, TUC (1954), p298.
36. MRC MSS 292/560.1/10, Economic Committee 5/1, 10 February 1954.
37. Middlemas, *Power, competition and the state*, p235.
38. MRC MSS 292/560.1/10, Economic Committee, 8 May 1954.
39. *Report of proceedings at the 87th annual Trades Union Congress* TUC (1955), p249; *Report of proceedings at the 88th annual Trades Union Congress* TUC (1956), pp354-61, 512-25; MRC MSS 292/571.81/5, 'Meeting between the Production Committee and the CSEU, Notes for the Chairman.
40. PRO T230/309, Talk with the Trades Union Council, 28 February 1956.
41. The government issued a white paper, *The economic implications of full employment* HMSO (1956) Cmd. 9726. The decision not to discuss the text with the TUC can be found in PRO T230/310, Hall to Bridges, 'Trade Union Congress and wage restraint', 4 September 1956.
42. J.C.R. Dow, *The management of the British economy, 1945-60* Cambridge University Press (1970) Cambridge, pp90-106.
43. *Report of proceedings at the 90th annual Trades Union Congress* TUC (1958), pp255-6.
44. Carew, *Labour under the Marshall Plan*, p208.
45. *Report of proceedings at the 76th annual Trades Union Congress* TUC (1944), pp393-417.
46. See also Tiratsoo and Tomlinson, *Industrial efficiency and state intervention*, chap. 5.
47. J. Tomlinson, 'Attlee's inheritance and the financial system: whatever happened to the National Investment Board?' forthcoming.
48. *Report of the 1944 TUC*, pp418-22.
49. MRC MSS 292/560.1/4, Economic Committee 1, 11 December 1946.
50. PRO BT 190/2, NPACI 2nd meeting, 9 December 1946.
51. MRC MSS 292/557.1/1, NPACI (GC side), 7 December 1945; *Report of the 1946 TUC*, pp197-8.
52. PRO BT 190/2, NPACI 4th meeting, 5 April 1946.
53. Tiratsoo and Tomlinson, *Industrial efficiency and state intervention*, chap. 4.

54. PRO LAB 10/652, 17th, 18th and 19th meetings of NJAC, 5 June, 23 July and 6 August 1947. 54. PRO LAB 10/652, 17th and 18th meetings of NJAC.
55. PRO LAB 10/652, 17th and 18th meetings of NJAC.
56. The other main, regular task of the EPB was to scrutinise the annual *Economic Surveys*. The EPB was particularly useful in undertaking emergency work, such as when new principles of fuel rationing were required in the coal crisis. In general, the unions were marginalised on the EPB, though the General Council's representatives used the forum to fight investment cuts.
57. Middlemas, *Power, competition and the state*, p147.
58. Panitch, *Social democracy*, pp24-32.
59. PRO LAB 10/652, 17th meeting of NJAC. In engineering, employers believed that the introduction of piecework had brought a once-and-for-all increase of output by 30-50 per cent: F. Zweig, *Productivity and trade unions* Blackwell (1951) Oxford, p231.
60. Tomlinson, 'The failure of the AACP', pp83-4, 86-7.
61. P.D. Henderson, 'The Development Councils: an industrial experiment' in G.D.N. Worswick and P.H. Ady (eds.), *The British economy, 1945-50* Oxford University Press (1952) Oxford, p459.
62. 'The citizen on the shop floor', pp13-23.
63. *Power, competition and the state*, p157.
64. S. Blank, *Industry and government in Britain: the Federation of British Industries in politics, 1945-65* Saxon House (1973) Farnborough, pp88-104; K.O. Morgan, *Labour in power* Oxford University Press (1984) Oxford, pp285-329
65. See Tanner's Presidential Address in the *Monthly Journal*, August 1949. Significantly he repeated the sentiments after the Conservative government had been elected: *Monthly Journal*, June 1952.
66. *Productivity: report of the General Council to the special conference of trade union executives* TUC (1948); *Productivity: report of a conference of trade union executive committees* TUC (1948); MRC MSS 292/557.91/5, various papers.
67. *Productivity: report of a conference of TU executives*, pp4-5.
68. Jack Tanner told the 1947 AEU National Committee: 'The individual autonomy of affiliated unions is a fundamental strength of our movement and is the basis of its strength and stability. It must be maintained, but within these limits, the General Council of the TUC should be delegated more authority for rapid decision. Policy is decided at Congress, and accordingly, individual unions normally agree to General Council recommendations to implement that policy. But on urgent and new issues it is necessary to obtain their formal agreement before the General Council can speak on their behalf. In the urgency of present affairs this delay cannot be afforded. Power must be delegated, so that the General Council can act with the speed required, subject to the endorsement of affiliated unions, afterwards if necessary.' *Monthly Journal*, August 1947. Tanner's politics and contributions to the politics of the AEU is discussed in the essay by Alan McKinlay below.
69. MRC MSS 292/577.91/5, CSEU to PAC, 1 Apr. 1949; meeting with National Union of Pottery Workers, 16 June 1949; Richard Coppock (NFBTO) to Tewson, 27 September 1949.
70. PRO LAB 10/1489, NJC 46, 'Spread of industrial know-how in Great Britain: memorandum by the TUC', 10 January 1949.
71. *Productivity: report of a conference of TU executives*, p17.
72. Carew, *Labour under the Marshall Plan*, chap. 9; Tomlinson, 'The failure of the AACP'.
73. MRC MSS 292/557.91/5, Conference of CSEU, 7 January 1949.
74. *Productivity: report of the General Council*, p11.
75. MRC MSS 292/557.1/2, NPACI (GC side) 1/1, 28 September 1948; 4/2, 30 March. 1950.
76. Carew notes that only one US union employed such experts at the time: *Labour under the Marshall Plan*, pp147-53.
77. *Productivity: report of the General Council*, pp7-8.
78. *Years of recovery*, pp405-6.
79. Angus Calder has noted the wartime collapse of public trust in private industry and industrialists: *The people's war* Panther (1971), pp338-39. See the discussion by Joseph Melling in the Introductory essay to this collection, regarding the literature on the wartime conflicts and the new revisionist interpretations of the war and post-war years.
80. Hinton, 'The citizen on the shop floor', pp18-19.

81. Tiratsoo and Tomlinson, *Industrial efficiency and state intervention*, chaps. 4-8.
82. Carew, *Labour under the Marshall Plan*, p201.
83. Blank, *Industry and government*, pp86-110.
84. 'The failure of the AACP', pp90-91.
85. See the titles by Allen, Kilpatrick and Lawson and Phelps Brown cited in endnote 2 above. The whole literature is discussed in Booth, Dartmann and Melling, 'Institutions and economic growth: trade unions and the politics of productivity in West Germany, Sweden, and the U.K., 1945-1955', (forthcoming, 1996).

4. Labour-management relations, the Marshall Plan and the politics of productivity growth in Germany *

Christoph Dartmann

Introduction

The Federal Republic of Germany has a reputation for peaceful labour-management relations. Shop floor relations in particular have formed a cornerstone in what is often referred to as the 'Modell Deutschland'. A central feature of this socio-economic constitution, is the system of co-determination in the iron and steel and coal mining industries. This participation of organised labour in the control and management of private large industrial undertakings on an almost equal basis with the owners was, and remains, the high point of worker participation in Western capitalist economies. Neither post-war nationalisation in Britain, nor direct labour participation in management and profits in some sectors of the US economy, nor even the 'Swedish model' described by Ekdahl and Johansson in this collection, afforded an equivalent company level involvement. It is also noticeable that efforts to extend the German model to other, if not all EC countries since the 1960s, has not met with any real success despite the influence of Germany within the EU.[1]

The German system of co-determination is often perceived, in somewhat vague terms, as a continuation of the Weimar and Wilhelmine practices of 'organised capitalism', or perhaps corporatism.[2] The key reference points in such interpretations usually include the rights extended to works councils under the Weimar constitution and several subsequent laws, the *Zentralarbeitsgemeinschaft* instituting a corporatist set-up following an agreement between employers and trade unions in November 1918, and the demands by the socialist trade union umbrella organisation (the ADGB) for industrial democracy, culminating in Naphtali's detailed exposition of 1928.[3] If we conceive of industrial relations in rather narrow terms there may be some justification for this view, though any adequate explanation of the evolution of co-determination must be framed in terms also of its interrelationship with economic policy and development. It is arguable that the postwar industrial relations system of the Federal Republic contributed to the strong economic performance during at least the two decades following the reconstruction period. Since co-determination had a major impact on the conduct of the coal and steel industries, and perhaps more important indirect effects on the wider industrial relations framework, it provides an excellent test case for an assessment of the links between social, political and economic issues shaping industrial relations. This essay will argue, in common with some other contributions to this collection, that co-determination is correctly seen as a significant feature of post-war European reconstruction, and also that its success can be attributed more to its strategic function in forging a link between industrial relations and Germany's wider social and economic policies, than to the institutional practices of peaceful labour-capital relationships at the shop-floor and company level or as the result of trade union rights campaigns at these levels.

The introduction of co-determination

The German system of co-determination was introduced between 1946 and 1951. On 10 April 1951 the Diet of the young Federal Republic passed a bill giving the trade unions and workers equal representation with the employers on the supervisory boards of all major iron and steel producing and coal mining companies. The Act provided for a labour director on the managing board with equal status to the financial and commercial directors, and whose appointment required the support of the labour members on the supervisory board, giving those members and their organisations a virtual right of appointment for one management post. This strong form of workers' representation was extended to holding companies in the two industries in 1956, and in a weaker form to all companies above 2000 employees in 1976. In addition there was significant legislation in several areas of social policy and employment protection which consolidated the rights achieved under the co-determination laws in Germany.

The 1951 Act is, with some amendments, still in force today, though it covers fewer and fewer companies, following the decline of the two basic industries. The legislation actually institutionalised the form of participation already introduced in practice during the reconstruction of the iron and steel industry under British occupation from early 1947 onwards, as Abelshauser has also noted in this collection. During this process the big concerns of the Ruhr, which had been sequestrated by the British and put under a special authority, or *North German Iron and Steel Control*, were deconcentrated. Several new managing and production units, usually based on one major plant in an older firm, were established. These new companies were provided with supervisory boards of 11 persons. Of these, five represented labour: two - usually one white and one blue collar worker - came from the works council, and in practice they were invariably its chairman and his deputy. Two further members were nominated by the trade union umbrella organisation, the DGB, and by the *Industriegewerkschaft Metall* (IG Metall) respectively. A fifth member, without direct trade union ties, was chosen from public life; he had to be acceptable to the unions, hence the frequent choice of the Social Democrat mayor of the town where the plant was situated. The five members representing capital were chosen in arrangement with the erstwhile owners, three of whom represented the respective old combine, and one was chosen from amongst the managing boards of other newly established companies. A further member was selected without formal links to the employers' organisations, in line with the appointee from the labour side, whilst the German Trustee Administration (the *Treuhandverwaltung im Auftrag der North German Iron and Steel Control*), conducting the deconcentration measures under British control, nominated the final member, who served as an independent chairman of the supervisory board.

There is no doubt that the DGB, the Metal Workers' Union and especially the miners (IG Bergbau) found the introduction of co-determination problematic. Nonetheless, once it had been introduced in the decartelised steel companies, the *Wirtschaftswissenschaftliche Institut* of the DGB (WWI) under Erich Potthoff in particular developed clearer ideas about labour's participation in control and management.[4]   Between 1947 and the early 1950s, the demand for co-determination then became central in the DGB's platform, with nationalisation viewed as a secondary goal unless it was coupled with a genuine shift in power-sharing and direction. Once this position had been reached it remained central, although the German unions did not resist concomitant policies such as orienting economic and wages policy on the principle of following 'best-practices' companies and thereby threatening to drive bad performers out of business. The contemporary Swedish practices as depicted by Ekdahl and Johansson in their essay, were apparent to German unions. Most importantly perhaps, the German unions rejected the proposals of Viktor Agartz in the early 1950s for the pursuit of a very aggressive wages policy, familiar to unionists of the pre-Nazi era and similar to the productivity bargaining tactics of the United Automobile Workers in contemporary America during the 1950s. From the DGB's point of view, co-determination enabled the unions to resolve several difficulties of pursuing the different goals of wages, employment and the control over the production policies which the works councils had assumed on the shop floor. Since the Labour Director and the Advisory Board members had a right to influence employment matters, they could work with the works councils to avert large scale redundancies and protect job levels. The Labour Director could also influence wages and employment conditions, though here his position was less clear cut, and the DGB adopted an initial view that co-determination resolved the principle of wage setting. It is equally apparent that the DGB made a considerable political investment in co-determination, recognising its introduction as giving them an important position within the new German state.

Co-determination and productivity

With co-determination apparently meeting several of the unions' aims, the question of productivity and its relationship to wages and co-determination still remained unsolved. Whilst specific details may be disputed, there is no doubt that manufacturing labour productivity rose substantially in Germany during the 1950s and 1960s. There is also little doubt that organised labour played a significant part in this success story. The relationship between wages and productivity can be read as the most evident recognition of this contribution: during the 1950s and 1960s real wages rose in line with, or even less than, productivity growth trends. There is also agreement that this performance contrasts markedly with the pattern of growth since the 1970s as well as with the rates recorded in the Weimar period.[5] Before the early 1950s the axiom that past productivity growth should set the limit for wage increases had not been one which German unions accepted. Even in 1953-54 Viktor Agartz and others were fiercely challenging the assumption that wages should be set within the limits of output growth, thereby leaving room for price cuts and profits, with Agartz insisting that a labour strategy of 'expansive Lohnpolitik' should be pursued which would force firms to rationalise as wages were driven above past productivity levels. Agartz's powerful position as the economic theoretician of the labour movement before 1955 was abruptly ended when he was forced to resign from the WWI in a scandal over forged information, being also expelled from the SPD and his own union because of his pro-Communist sympathies. This is an important development for the German labour movement since Agartz's theories, derived from Hilferding's work on finance capitalism, included proposals for the nationalisation of basic industries, control of large sectors of private capital and a centralised management of the economy with union participation at all levels of economic life. Agartz's challenge to prevailing wages policy was based on the argument that union policies did not permit wage growth even to the limits of *labour productivity* growth, still less for appropriating any returns to capital. In the absence of aggressive wage policies, uniting the labour movement in a common programme of radical reforms, Agartz saw co-determination as having negative rather than positive consequences for the labour movement. The DGB made it clear as early as 1952 that they would not embark on the ambitious policy advocated by Agartz. His failure ensured that the German unions accepted the link between productivity and wages growth and during the 1960s there was some attempt to elaborate and formalise this connection with the onset of full Keynesian policies in Germany though with little tangible success.

Thus it can be seen that the main concern of the German unions in the early 1950s, and more particularly the DGB and IG Metall, was to use co-determination to secure influence over employment and wages questions, whilst also giving them an opportunity to strengthen their political presence and to manage industrial relations more effectively. The unions found the issue of productivity and the mentality of wage bargaining under the constraints of productivity growth, much more problematic. The pre-1945 experience of the unions in regard to productivity questions, or 'rationalisation', was at least ambiguous and frequently negative. In the early 1920s, the socialist umbrella organisation and several individual unions had initially welcomed the rationalisation movement. Fritz Tarnow, a representative of the woodworker union and one of the most influential union leaders, had taken up American ideas about the importance of high wages for rationalisation, for what later would be called productivity, and for purchasing power. In 1928, following a visit to the US, he actually wrote a widely circulated book entitled *Why be poor?*, strongly developing the point on purchasing power.[6] At the same time, the rights given to works councils at plant and company level under the Weimar Constitution and subsequent legislation, appeared to augur well for a successful union and worker participation in rationalising production by safeguarding jobs, wages, and the union's influence over employment conditions. These positive attitudes were soured during the 1924-25 'shake out' crisis, and even more so during the 1930s depression, when rationalisation was widely equated with unemployment. Such attitudes lingered after the war when Walter Freitag, chairman of the IG Metall, concluded that productivity meant rationalisation which was synonymous with unemployment. The reduction of wages during the Depression years of the 1930s across the developed World also had a formative influence on older union activists who survived the War to face new calls for rationalisation in production.

Two factors were to play a decisive role in organised labour's positive response to productivity drives in the post-war years. The first was the demand by German unions of co-determination rights in industry. The second was the American influence on productivity questions exerted via the Labor Division of the Economic Co-operation Administration (ECA), or the Marshall Plan. The combination of these two factors ensured both German labour's active participation in productivity questions *and* the introduction and survival of co-determination. Germany's unions, from peak organisations down, and from works councils up, embraced a productivity mentality during the early 1950s to which they were introduced via the Marshall Plan, and which they accepted along with guarantees of safeguards in the form of labour participation in control and management of the largest industrial undertakings. The vital link between productivity and co-determination was forged by the union members of the Labor Division of the Marshall Plan organisation. From early 1951 they recognised the potential that lay in the issue of co-determination for their promotion of a productivity mentality in German industry. This group of officials recommended to the German government, the American Occupation authorities, and to German employers and unions, that co-determination be implemented by law, enabling unions to utilise co-determination as an instrument for promoting productivity issues.

The figure within the ECA to directly advocate co-determination and its utilisation for American aims was Clint Golden. Golden, an official from the United Steelworkers of America and serving as the CIO representative in the post of Labor Advisor to the ECA, had also written 'Dynamics of Industrial Democracy' with H.J. Ruttenberg in 1942. This was a blueprint for the US unions' attempt to foster peaceful industrial relations through labour-management co-operation and consultation. After he had visited Germany between 20 and 22 January 1951, Golden reported to ECA Administrator, William Foster:

> Apart from the moral, ethical and other aspect of labor participation in management, this situation offers an unusual opportunity to explore the possibilities of developing an ECA technical assistance program directed towards improving the productivity of German heavy industry particularly and at the same time evolving means of insuring a better distribution of the fruits thereof.[7]

And a fortnight later:

> It seems to me if [the trade unions that have won co-determination] were given [...] the technical and other facilities which would help them to their share of the job of management, it might result in a quicker receptivity to new ideas about production than would be the case with management people of the old industrialist school.[8]

It was the 'quicker receptivity' by labour leaders and workers of American attitudes on productivity that the Labor Division would formulate into major policy goals of their own. Following Golden's intimations, they utilised co-determination as institutionalised in the German coal and steel industries. In the process the Division transformed the application of this political industrial relations institution into an economically viable new form of business organisation based on a broad acceptance of the mentality of productivity. The practical steps they undertook included asserting pressure via the State Department on the American High Commission in Germany and the French and British occupation authorities to remain at least neutral during the debate in the Bundestag on the co-determination and subsequent legislation. The same officials also exerted direct and indirect pressure on the American National Association of Manufacturers, who had been very active in Germany attempting to influence the legislation, to discontinue these negative efforts, whilst at the same time pressing German employers and the German Government to seriously consider the case for co-determination.[9]

These efforts to introduce the powerful elites at home and abroad were matched by the activities of the Labor Division in collaboration with American union officials employed by the US occupation authorities, as they undertook a crusade to persuade the DGB, German unions and their shop floor members that co-determination as a political strategy for redistributing power in society should be dropped, and that organised labour should exploit co-determination as a means to raise productivity and thereby improve wages and working conditions. In late spring 1951 the Division drafted an office memorandum on 'Criteria and Productivity Steps for Germany', where they argued that the American authorities must realise 'that German labor cannot be mobilised for any program whatsoever before the co-determination issue is out of the way'.[10]   Co-determination itself and the precise forms it would take, were of no interest to the Labor Division but they stressed that a *'change of attitude* has to be achieved quickly on a much wider basis'. Although German unions had registered their support for increased productivity, a full conversion to the goals of productivity and stability was only to be expected after the settlement of the political-economic programme of the DGB. Then,

> if some kind of co-determination settlement has been reached in Germany, it should not be too difficult to convince the German trade union movement that it needs a broader adjunct to its co-determination philosophy which would bring not only some immediate benefits to labor but to the German people as a whole. The German trade unions should be persuaded to pursue a policy of expanding economy which would bring the benefits of industrial peace, established under co-determination, to labor as well as to all consumers and to business. German labor would get with this an argument which could be presented to the German people and which would demonstrate that co-determination can mean more than simply the participation of labor in the administration of German industry.

During 1951 and 1952, the German unions succumbed to this strategy, joining the *Rationalisierungskuratorium der Deutschen Wirtschaft* which (on the lines of the Anglo-American Productivity Council discussed by Tomlinson in his essay), served as Marshall Plan Productivity Centre, and facilitated the utilisation of co-determination bodies for productivity measures. The construction of this link between productivity and co-determination by the Marshall Planners, coupled with the pressures from Adenauer and his economics minister Ludwig Erhard - and the Ruhr industrialists depicted in Abelshauser's essay - served to strengthen the case for the unions' acceptance of the productivity principle. Although the DGB had not made the introduction of co-determination a condition of their co-operation in the productivity drive, once the link between co-determination and wages and employment levels as well as productivity was accepted, the unions pushed hard for productivity growth measures.

After the introduction of co-determination, it was the labour directors who were the earliest and most active promoters of the idea of 'productivity' and its relation, *inter alia*, to wages. Adolf Jungbluth, one of the first labour directors, made all aspects of 'productivity', and especially the human aspects or what he called 'psychological rationalisation', a personal crusade.[11]   Abelshauser has shown how labour directorships were introduced in the case of the Ruhr region.

More generally, the labour directors in the iron and steel industry took it upon themselves to improve productivity, and as a first step produced statistics on output per man-hour in order to ascertain equitable wages.[12] In the early 1950s they calculated that output per man-hour in the iron and steel industry had risen substantially initially due to the reduction of absenteeism and later in the decade improvements were attributed to the successful introduction of new technology and machinery. In both of these issues the labour directors were very active, in the first instance by reducing absenteeism, and in the second case by promoting workers' co-operation in the introduction of new technology. For the coal industry, the *Deutsche Kohlenbergbauleitung* played down the importance of productivity statistics, as problems of technical development and the lack of investment influenced output so greatly as to make comparisons with pre-war levels meaningless.[13] But there are indications that the introduction of full mechanisation in the coal mines went substantially faster and smoother in Germany than in the UK, as the essays by the Wintertons and Melling would suggest. As a general rule it appears that labour directors under co-determination became heavily involved in productivity questions, featuring prominently in the general meetings of all labour directors which were organised by the DGB together with the WWI. These organisations hoped that such meetings would develop into a quasi-official central policy making body for Germany's heavy industry.[14] On the supervisory boards, union members also played a significant part in the promotion of productivity by agreeing to, or even pressing for, major investment schemes.

Conclusions

This brief essay has argued that the introduction of German co-determination was substantially influenced by American unionists working with the Marshall Plan in Europe and that the result was the first moves to what is sometimes referred to as a productivity coalition. This cannot be read simply as a manipulation of German labour politics and its union movement by transnational actors who secured productivity growth as a consequence of skilful institution-building. The productivity effects were as much an indirect consequence of rising wage and social costs as they were an outcome of a stable regime where wage claims were constrained within the region of (or below) past productivity growth, thereby encouraging labour saving investment without unemployment. At the same time, the dualism between unions and works councils was resolved, though for many trade unionists in an unsatisfactory fashion. There arose a clear division of responsibilities as unions assumed the task of bargaining over wages in the light of industrial and national productivity rates, whilst works councils were engaged in the introduction of new technologies and working methods on the shop floor of industry. Such an arrangement appears to have functioned in favour of productivity growth as technology and the control of work were effectively removed from the bargaining arena, in contrast to the contemporary situation in the UK.

It may be argued that the durability of the co-determination arrangements in modern Germany should be seen as a monument to their function in enhancing productivity growth rather than their scope for transforming labour-management relations at company level. Peaceful industrial relations have been secured in a system which has given organised labour a substantial influence in the running of private capitalist undertakings, whilst improving the flexibility of the workforce when faced with productivity reforms. Decisions on investment, the introduction of labour saving machinery, or product choice, amongst others, were usually the subject of unanimous support on the supervisory boards of companies subject to co-determination.[15] This collaborative and co-operative quality of the co-determination system can be better understood in relation to the evolving economic politics and policy-making process in Germany than by reference to the traditional character of German industrial relations. In turn, the combination of co-determination with productivity questions, or the 'Americanisation'[16] of German industrial relations, allowed not only co-determination to be instituted and to remain successful, but also ensured largely peaceful industrial relations which seem so familiar to the 20th century historian of German economic and social history.

Notes

* This essay arises out of my doctoral research. I am particularly grateful to Joseph Melling for his suggestions on the presentation of these ideas.

1. The UK undertook experiments in the steel industry and the Post Office, both of which were allowed to lapse, and the debates over the implementation of the Social Chapter of the Maastricht Treaty continues. Efforts, futile thus far, to extend industrial demoracy can be seen in the fate of the UK 'Bullock Report' and the European 'Fifth Directive'. US firms display renewed interest in labour's contribution to management, production control and profits, but recent experience of American airlines industry shows this can entail employee ownership for bankrupt companies!

2. See for example, A.D. Chandler, *Scale and Scope. The Dynamics of Industrial Capitalism* Belknap (1990) Cambridge, Mass.; R. Hilferding, *Finance Capital. A Study of the Latest Phase of Capitalist Development* Routledge (1981, originally Vienna, 1910); H.-A. Winkler (ed.), *Organisierter Kapitalismus. Voraussetzungen und Anfänge* Vandenhoeck and Ruprecht (1974) Göttingen; S. Berger (ed.), *Organizing Interests in Western Europe. Pluralism, Corporatism, and the Transformation of Politic* Cambridge University Press (1981) Cambridge.

3. F. Naphtali, *Wirtschaftsdemokratie. Ihr Wesen, Weg und Ziel* Verlagsanstalt des ADGB (1928) Berlin.

4. Wirtschaftswissenschaftliches Institut des DGB (WWI), E. Potthoff, *Die Aufgaben des Arbeitsdirektors. Dienststellengliederung des Fachbereichs Arbeitskraft* (1947) Cologne.

5. See figures from E.H. Phelps Brown and M. Browne, *A Century of Pay. The Course of Pay and Production in France, Germany, Sweden, the United States of America, 1860-1960* Macmillan (1968) , p312, table 30, which shows an annual growth of 4.86% for industrial productivity for 1950-59, and an annual increase of 4.66% for real wages; see. also wages and productivity data in J. Bergmann and O. Jacobi, *Gewerkschaften in der Bundesrepublik. Bd.1: Gewerkschaftliche Lohnpolitik zwischen Mitgliederinteressen und ökonomischen Systemzwängen* Europaische

Verlagsanstaldt (1976) Frankfurt pp450, 455; P. Gourevitch et. al., *Unions and Economic Crisis: Britain, West-Germany and Sweden* Allen and Unwin (1984), p176.

6. F. Tarnow, *Warum arm sein?* Verlagsanstaldt des ADGB (1928) Berlin; for rationalisation and labour's reaction G. Stollberg, *Die Rationalisierungsdebatte 1908-1933. Freie Gewerkschaften zwischen Mitwirkung und Gegenwehr* Campus (1981) Frankfurt and New York.

7. Report Clint Golden to William C. Foster on European Trip Jan. 3 to Feb. 5, 1951: Historical Collections and Labor Archives, Pennsylvania State University, Collection Meyer Bernstein [2], September to November 1951.

8. Letter Golden to Bernstein, 17.2.1951: Historical Collections and Labor Archives, Pennsylvania State University, Clinton S. Golden Papers 2-24.

9. For a more detailed account see C. Dartmann, *Re-Distribution of Power, Joint Consultation or Productivity Coalitions? Labour and Postwar Reconstruction in Germany and Britain, 1945-1953* Brockmeyer (1996, forthcoming) Bochum.

10. National Archives RG 469 Office of Labor Affairs, box 2, folder Germany 1951, and the following quotations, emphasis in the original.

11. Almost all of Jungbluth's publications dealt with this aspect; see minutes 1. Sitzung des Rationalisierungsausschusses der ZTK, 29.11.1948, and his Referat, 'Rationalisierung und Gewerkschaft', 22./23.1.1949: DGB Arciv, Zonale Techniker Konferenz 1947/48.

12. 'Voraussetzungen zur Produktionssteigerung in der eisenschaffenden Industrie', Bericht des Ausschusses der Arbeitsdirektoren zur Produktionssteigerung, Mai 1948: Budescarchive (BA) B 109/5131; Rundschreiben STV 5/52, 7.2.1952, 'Die Entwickllung der Belegschaft': Bundesarchiv B109/669.

13. Bericht DKBL March 1948: DGB Kohle 1945-1955; cf. Kost, Heinrich, 'Die Tätigkeit der Deutschen Kohlenbergbauleitung. Schlußbericht', *Glückauf* 90 (1954), 93-94.

14. Minutes Arbeitsdirektoren-Tagungen: IGM Zweigstelle Düsseldorf.

15. For the early period see W.M. Blumenthal, *Co-determination in the German Steel Industry. A Report of Experience* Princeton University Press (1956) Princeton, New Jersey.

16. C.f. V.R. Berghahn, *The Americanisation of West German Industry 1945-1973* Berg (1986) Leamington Spa.

5. The end of a historical compromise? The Labour movement and the changing balance of power in Swedish industry, 1930-1990 *

Lars Ekdahl and Alf O. Johansson

In *The working class in welfare capitalism* Walter Korpi claimed that Swedish Social Democrats (SAP) in the 1970s were facing 'the major task of implementing economic democracy'.[1] Korpi argued that since the 1930s the labour movement's 'power resources' had increased consistently and these advances created the opportunity to realise the central goals of the SAP programme, which were summarised as the complete reconstruction of Swedish society in ways which would place the control over the means of production and distribution in the hands of the people. In the Social Democratic vision, Sweden's citizens were to be 'freed from any kind of power groups outside their control, and the class-based social order [was] to be replaced by a community of individuals co-operation on the basis of liberty and equality'.[2] For Korpi the moment had arrived for a decisive step beyond even economic democracy and towards democratic socialism.[3] Such an assessment was based on Korpi's view of stable progress towards the Social Democratic goals of a welfare society based on rapid industrial development, full employment, and a continuous expansion of the welfare state. These goals had been pursued in close correspondence with the Swedish union movement and writers such as Korpi assumed that this relationship would sustain the Social Democrats as they moved to extend employees' influence within capitalist enterprises and to create the wage earners' funds which would enable workers to share ownership of the companies themselves.[4]

In the event, the development of Social Democracy from the 1970s was to take a very different course from that envisaged by Korpi and many of his contemporaries. In 1976 the Party's long reign was ended and after returning to power in the 1980s, Social Democrats were again turned out of office in 1991. The tender plants of industrial and economic democracy which were introduced by legislation in the 1970s and 1980s withered even if they were not completely uprooted during the conservative administration of 1991-94. The SAP itself has been increasingly influenced by neo-liberal ideas in the past decade and frequently in conflict with the demands of the Swedish union movement (LO). In common with social democratic parties throughout Europe and the capitalist world, the Party has given priority to squeezing inflation at the expense of full employment and has contemplated cuts in the welfare state which it had created in earlier decades.[5] Such policies have weakened the union movement as it sought to retain the older principles of Social Democracy. In particular, the fundamental goal of realising common ownership and control seems to have slipped from the agenda of the SAP if not from that of the union movement. It is possible to cite these developments in dismissing Korpi's optimistic assessment of economic and political reform during the 1970s.

We would argue that Korpi's theoretical approach *does* suffer from normative and idealistic assumptions about the natural advance of social democracy, though this was not primarily due (in our view) to his close involvement in the complex political and ideological process which he was appraising. These normative and idealistic assumptions are reflected in his both vague and ahistoric understanding of the 'power resources' of the main contenders of the Swedish labour market. While leaving the state largely outside the analysis, the influences of capital and labour on the character of the Swedish economic and social system in rather mechanical terms are seen as outflows of the 'control of means of production' of employers and of the degree of organisation of workers in the labour movement.[6]

In the following section we offer a critique in more depth of the view of 'power resources' and conceptual issues raised in Korpi's work and suggest an alternative model for explaining shifts in the strategy and orientation of the Swedish labour movement during the six decades before 1990. We provide an empirical exposition of this model in a later section of the essay where we chart the origins and growth of the 'historical compromise' between capital and labour in Sweden from the 1930s to the 1980s. Throughout the chapter we argue for a shift in analysis of the origins and growth of that compromise from the programmes of central institutions, to an exploration of the continuing dialogue between central and local actors as a context for the initiatives which were adopted by the protagonists.

The Swedish labour movement at the crossroads

A key theme in Korpi's analysis of Swedish Social Democracy is that its success can be traced to a series of political compromises reached between employers and the labour movement in the 1930s. This process implied a wider, if tacit, agreement on the division of power and influence in Swedish society. This concordat was based on the industrialists' realisation that the influence of the Swedish labour movement was likely to remain for the foreseeable future and that the movement would use the state to create a comprehensive welfare system. The reciprocal concession from the unions was their agreement not to question the prerogatives of the owners of capital and that decisions on production, investment, employment and the disciplining of labour would remain in the hands of the employers. The trade-off was therefore based on the assumption that labour organisations would not exploit their political influence to undermine the employers' power to manage, whilst the business community recognised the unions' right to bargain on wages and conditions of employment as well as its wider social programme. Korpi attached great importance to these (often unwritten) assumptions and the formal understanding which was established between capital and labour in the 1930s, which led him to coin the celebrated phrase Sweden's 'historical compromise'.[7] In fact, Korpi appears to have adopted much of the ideology which contemporary Social Democrats used in presenting themselves in the political arena during this crucial phase of activity. Korpi refers specifically to a speech by Ernst Wigforss, delivered as the Minister of Finance, to a group of industrialists on the eve of the Second World War. Wigforss advised his audience, that it was essential that

> those who have influence in large or small sectors of private business do not found their actions on the presumption that the present tendencies of the state are of a temporary nature, that a political realignment will take place in such a near future that a discussion based on the potential for concessions, accommodations, and compromises, becomes superfluous.

For their part, Wigforss promised, the political representatives would respect the need for the state to maintain favourable conditions for private enterprise.[8] Korpi not only privileges this speech as an expression of the spirit of what became the 'historical compromise' but he also absorbs the SAP's evolutionary perspective, implying that the strength of the labour movement would expand with the maturation of capitalism and amass such power resources as to be able to challenge for control of industrial capital itself.[9] In this way, the historical compromise would give way naturally to a programme of economic democracy.[10]

Korpi interpreted the widespread industrial unrest which erupted from the late 1960s as an indication that employees and their unions, strengthened by their accumulating power resources, were now dissatisfied with their influence within capitalism and ready to embrace economic democracy.[11] It is not surprising that Korpi found the electoral collapse of the Social Democrats in 1976 somewhat perplexing. He attributes this setback to the growth of discontent with the effects of the SAP's strategies for economic growth within the terms of the historical compromise.[12] To resolve the classic contradictions of social reformism, Korpi urged that the economic and political wings of the Swedish labour movement should cooperate in implementing economic democracy. Continued compromises with capital would merely deepen the contradictions within the Party's programme and policies.[13] When faced with the logical question as to why a labour movement which had steadily amassed greater power resources in previous decades should actually face such dilemmas and political defeats, Korpi merely asserts that the Social Democrats had chosen misplaced policies which had eroded their own hegemony.[14]

Whilst Korpi's analysis of a new distribution of power in the 1930s, based on a tacit accommodation or 'historical compromise' has much to commend it, we would argue that such a model lacks a critical assessment of the *terms* on which each organisation was able to mobilise its membership in support of a particular set of goals which were highly specific to the historical conditions of Swedish capitalism and society in the middle decades of the twentieth century.[15] Such a mobilisation of what we might term 'power resources' was not purely an ideological or political exercise but depended on the identification of material and other interests within the ranks of the membership and the changing perceptions (and articulation) of these interests over the decades which followed.

The bulk of the literature on the historical compromise presents a somewhat monolithic view of the Social Democratic and labour movement in Sweden, where the conflicts between unions and Party, nor even the strategic calculations in favour of compromise with employers at different moments, are accorded particular prominence.[16] This homogenous portrait of popular politics and the labour movement is due in part to the conscious and consistent representation of Swedish progress by such prominent ideologues as Rudolf Meidner, joint architect of the celebrated Rehn-Meidner model (see below). Such advocates of Social Democracy have attributed the dominance of collaborative institutions to the growth in the numerical strength of Swedish unions and their systematic pursuit of democratic and welfare solutions to economic and social problems. The fusion of ideology and strategy in the *praxis* of Social Democracy is reflected in Meidner's assessment of the labour movement's programme as the 'values and commitment of a political movement, that was destined to play ... a dominant role during a long period of Sweden's development into a modern welfare state'.[17]

This ideological construction of the movement's goals from the interwar period onwards, was greatly facilitated by the network of local unions and political clubs which sought to integrate the Social Democratic vision of the needs of the individual and local community with strategies for national economic and social growth.[18]

Whilst other, more critical, perspectives on the origins and evolution of the Swedish Model have been provided by scholars since the 1970s, it is only in recent years that research has exposed the complexity and frictions within the Swedish labour movement. Similarly, the relative unity and coherence of the business community within Sweden when compared with the fragmentation and diversity of capitalist organisations abroad, has deflected attention away from the divisions which *did* exist within the ranks of Swedish capital.[19] Scholarship has recently sought to deconstruct the monolithic blocks of capital and labour in Sweden, exposing the fault lines which remained largely hidden in the years of growth and stability but which were increasingly visible as conflicts emerged in industry and society during the 1970s.[20] In his analysis of the Swedish Model, Anders Johansson has developed a very different interpretation of the historical compromise from that advanced by Korpi. Johansson argues that the collective agreements of the interwar period did not constitute a political class compromise but was rather the expression of a 'convergence of material interests regarding industrial peace, rationalisations and growth' amongst the representatives of capital, labour and the state. Although Johansson's reassessment of the rationale behind the agreements of the 1930s provides a plausible alternative to Korpi's somewhat naive assumptions about the coherence of the distinctive interests, Johansson's revisionist view also reduces the scope of politics to merely a register converging interests which were inevitably drawing together. As with Korpi's interpretation, there remains the unanswered question as to why the Swedish model should have risen and then declined, since it is suggested that the leading actors continued to pursue homogenous and non-contradictory (as well as converging) interest goals and to favour economic progress as a means to satisfying their constituents.[21]

Other writers have taken issue with Korpi but presented a more persuasive account of the continuing complexity and fragility of the coalitions which assembled within the Swedish labour movement and amongst the employers. Olsen, Pontusson and Swenson all emphasise the antagonisms which persisted in the ranks of both capital and labour during and after the period when the historical compromise was reached. Olsen and Pontusson have stressed the shifts in the strategies which were developed by Sweden's leading companies and business organisations over the decades. Opinion varied within the employers' associations over the utility of central negotiations and also the influence of distinctive clusters of firms who faced different market conditions. The impression of consistent and active support for the historical settlement has to be modified in the light of such research.[22] On the other hand, Swenson's study of business politics in the 1930s demonstrates the extent to which Swedish employers *promoted* the policies of compromise and the degree to which the Social Democrats depended on such activities as a tacit endorsement of their own policy preferences. The Social Democrats were galvanised into an active pursuit of such a settlement in the labour market by the industrialists' threat of a general lockout. It is this market power which, Swenson argues, needs to be understood in any evaluation of the origins of the political settlement reached in the period, rather than mechanically assuming that numerical strength or electoral position explains the balance of power within Swedish society.[23]

The insight to be derived from such recent research is that we cannot retain an unproblematic understanding of collective interests, or assume that those demands which are visible at macro level express the homogenous aspirations of the constituencies which the organisations which articulate them actually represent. In particular, groups of capitalists and labourers operate at different levels in the power and interest hierarchies of these organisations and almost certainly will vary their perceptions and demands over time. Research on the workplace, social campaigns and political mobilisation at local and micro levels appears to suggest that a crucial prerequisite for the historical compromise reached nationally in the late 1930s was actually the negotiation of similar (if necessarily distinctive) settlements at local level in previous decades. At the same time, national parties and labour unions were working to cultivate support for their own agendas and to promote their version of the 'rules of the game' in bargaining and political representation. The impact of such national bodies on local labour relations and Party activities is much better understood and emphasised than the ways in which workplace reforms in production and local campaigning has generated demands and aspirations to which the central representatives have responded in formulating their programmes.[24] In the remainder of this paper we seek to make some references to such adjustments whilst emphasising throughout that the creation and preservation of the historical compromise has depended on the continuing adjustment to converging and diverging interests which were pressing on it. Even in its heyday, we suggest, the historical compromise was potentially unstable and continued to function as far as it could respond not merely to the large blocs of supposedly coherent interests represented at central level, but also to the variety of industrial and community struggles among constituents on whom these blocs themselves rested for support.

From confrontation to industrial peace

The 1920s were a decade of transition for Swedish labour. Initial and severe depression was followed by continued high unemployment (10-12 per cent) and bitter conflicts in the labour market. These struggles compelled both unions and their employers to reappraise their strategies. We can trace the slow emergence of alternatives to confrontation as both local firms and their workers came to appreciate the costs of conflict in terms of continuing unemployment and a deterioration in the competitiveness of Swedish industry.[25] In addition to these market constraints, there was a new political context to these struggles since the universal franchise was introduced in 1920 and workers increased their participation in political institutions at local level in campaigns which focused on finding ways of alleviating unemployment and the introduction of assistance schemes for those most severely affected. For the first time, local workers' organisations discovered an opportunity for negotiating with the bourgeois parties and particularly with those business representatives who were prominent in local politics.[26] This combination of economic crisis and political mobilisation appeared in numerous localities across Sweden and helped to create the conditions in which the national parties shifted from strategies of confrontation to learning the skills of coexistence and, to some degree, of co-operation.

The process was not a simple one and clearly did not involve a coherent *praxis* being devised at local level for grafting on to the national scene, if only because the national leaderships were pursuing their own agenda for peace in industry. Rather it was the multitude of local disputes following the First World War and in the early 1920s which pushed both the political parties and the bargaining organisations into an almost permanent state of central negotiations around compensation questions. These pressures served to convince prominent sections of LO and the Swedish employers (SAF) to formulate arrangements for a more peaceful order, in close consultation with the Swedish state. At the end of the decade the conservative Government initiated an industrial peace conference which resulted in the creation of joint consultative bodies between capital, labour and the state and the formation of a certain consensus on the desirability of peace relations as well as the need for achieving rapid industrial growth by means of rationalisation and the adoption of efficiency measures in production.[27] The economic crisis of the early 1930s interrupted these moves to conciliation, particularly as the unions identified rationalisation and labour-saving reforms as a source of further unemployment.[28] Whilst local unionists and political activists had acknowledged the need for co-operation at the end of the 1920s, the return of economic crisis led to a resurgence of anti-capitalist attitudes amongst Swedish workers.

The conversion of the union membership to a fresh outlook on industrial innovation can be traced to the triumphant election campaign of the Social Democrats in 1932. The new Government launched a Keynesian economic programme to fight unemployment whilst also initiating a new round of negotiations with LO and SAF on rules and procedures in collective bargaining. SAF proposed that the industrial organisations should reach a resolution without state intervention, which resulted ultimately in the famous Basic Agreement at Saltsjöbaden in 1938. This was essentially a declaration of intent containing the principles for future central bargaining with a joint standing committee to settle conflicts over rationalisation and the consequent redundancy of labour.[29]

Although the state was not directly involved in the drafting of the Agreement, the Social Democratic Government provided a vital context for the concordat by implementing unemployment policies which eased relations in the labour market and also by threatening to intervene more directly to codify labour agreements. This threat convinced SAF of the urgent need to reach agreement with LO on the institutionalisation of collective bargaining. The result was a division of responsibility between labour market negotiators and the state which became a defining feature of the historical compromise. Whilst the state accepted responsibility for safeguarding employment, it was the responsibility of the bargaining organisations to maintain industrial peace, set wage rates and promote technical efficiency.[30]

The 1938 Agreement with organised labour was not achieved without friction and controversy inside the Swedish business community. Divisions were most apparent between those firms oriented to the domestic market and those who were geared to export sales.[31] Industrialists producing for Swedish consumers were able to weather the crisis of the 1930s reasonably well and offset increased production costs by increasing prices. They were understandably more sympathetic to economic policies which fuelled domestic demand and full employment. Exporting firms were much more critical of active unemployment programmes and social reforms which increased their unit costs and impaired their competitiveness abroad. The domestic producers had secured a dominant position with SAF at a time when intensified competition in overseas markets weakened the position of leading exporters. In response, the exporting firms formed the 'Executives Club' as a forum and lobbying association which worked to politicise SAF in opposition to the unemployment and welfare policies of the Social Democrats.[32] Viewed from this perspective, the historical compromise of the 1930s appears less as a permanent institutional formation than as a temporary and pragmatic solution to immediate pressures on the different actors. The term 'compromise' is particularly appropriate when we recall that amongst those conceding ground were the Social Democrats, who were forced to abandon their plans for nationalisation and economic planning of industry in return for the business community's acceptance of the Keynesian economic policies and welfare legislation pursued by the Government. A parallel process of political compromise was undertaken between the Social Democrats and the agricultural interests, with the farmers winning subsidies for small and medium-sized producers in return for their approval of unemployment programmes. These compromises did not merely protect the status quo, however, but represented a decisive advance in Swedish politics and the formation of a new governing coalition. Those parties historically identified with the industrialists, the conservatives and Liberals, were marginalised by the new settlement and appeared as negative critics of the whole spirit of historical compromise.[33]

The implications of the historical compromise for the union movement were also profound. A series of statutes adopted by the LO at its 1941 Congress confirmed the trend towards centralisation of power and decision-making which the Basic Agreement had foreshadowed. These new procedural rules prescribed that permission was needed from the LO Secretariat before a strike could be called affecting more than three per cent of a member union's members. Financial support depended on this rule being respected. New statutes also provided that the national leadership of the unions should be the final arbiters in cases of dismissal and to approve or reject agreements. In this way, the final decisions about collective bargaining came to be taken in joint co-operation between LO's Secretariat and the boards of the national unions.[34] At the same time the grassroots movements to extend the influence of labour in the workplace and company decision-making, as well as their claim to be consulted over the rationalisation of production, was virtually abandoned. There was a clear, if tacit, agreement between the central organisations that the strategy for economic growth would be formulated and implemented by the business leaders.[35] It would be wrong to interpret these shifts in the strategic thinking of the union movement as merely the logical outcome of political bargaining. There were also tensions within the Swedish unions which created difficulties for both leaders and members. During the 1930s unions were divided by the distinctive bargaining conditions which existed in different sectors of industry. Unions based in trades producing for domestic markets, including those organised on older craft lines such as building and printing, achieved wage rises which outstripped those conceded to workers in the export-oriented manufacturing occupations, whilst more weakly organised textiles and agricultural employees also lagged behind. The important construction strike of 1933 indicated how lower-paid workers often found themselves drawn into struggles amongst higher-wage groups as the employers used the lockout as a powerful weapon against the unions. It was out of this bitter experience that the Metal Workers' Union (Metall) adopted the principle of 'solidaristic' wages, with the aim of reducing wage differentials amongst LO unions, thereby initiating the LO campaign for central negotiations to secure solidaristic wage regulation.[36]

Central direction was seen as an instrument for securing greater equality of treatment in the labour market. Those forces within the LO pressing for a solidaristic wages policy were helped both by the state's unemployment policy and the employers who now found that growing scarcity of labour increased the cost of searching for and hiring workers. Firms producing for the domestic market could pass on wage costs more easily in prices rises than the exporters and it was the latter who were pressing for central negotiations as a means of disciplining wage rises. The ruling Social Democrats were also anxious to secure industrial peace and contain wage inflation by means of central bargaining as a platform for their economic policies and saw in 'solidaristic' wages an instrument for containing a leap-frogging of wage demands from unions.[37]

Such an interpretation of the context for the historical compromise of the 1930s is quite different from that offered by Korpi. We can see the Basic Agreement as the culmination of a series of initiatives which involved compromises on various fronts and between distinct interests in Swedish economy and politics. Actors were forced to devise strategies in the midst of the intended and unintended consequences of the economic environment and the proposals of other groups. The pursuit of interests involved a complex game of rational choice where success depended on understanding the opportunities created by the new conditions of compromise. This is clearly visible in the case of the export industries. The exporters yielded on such issues as the Social Democrats' unemployment policy. At the same time, they seized on the opportunity to support policies which would restrict competition for labour in a period of growing scarcity. Similarly, the low-wage unions within the LO found some occupations benefited from the wage movements in the domestic industries as Keynesian economic policies took effect, whilst they could endorse the moves to central bargaining and solidaristic wages proposed by the LO and supported by the state and business. It is evident that in the longer term the historical compromise marked an important step towards a tighter and more centralised organisation of both workers and employers in Sweden, though this was achieved not simply as a result of the logic of organisational growth or the natural evolution of the 'historical compromise'. It was the outcome of specific calculations and initiatives framed by actors pursuing their conception of the optimum advantage to be gained from changing conditions. What is undeniable is the shift in the perspective of the labour movement from a concern with local consultation over the path of industrial change and the impact of unemployment, to an outlook in the 1940s where management prerogatives were virtually accepted. The unions, led by the low-wage occupations, were much less concerned with the threat to jobs from rationalisation and piece rates and now embraced the spirit of compromise expressed at Saltsjobaden. This marked a defeat for those unions which had opposed the paragraph of the Agreement which explicitly recognised the employer's power to manage, and the advocates of industrial democracy were disregarded as the Swedish labour movement came to focus on issues of distribution.[38] Tensions between radicals who continued to emphasise the principle of participation and the leadership of organisations who were increasingly concerned with the management of procedures were to break the surface during the debate on the 'Works Council Agreement' of 1946.

Compromise on a contested terrain: Swedish labour's post-war offensive

The war and the immediate post-war years placed great strain on the settlement constructed in the 1930s. To defend Swedish neutrality and to promote unity in the face of acute economic dislocation, the Social Democrats formed a coalition government with all the opposition parties. State control and the extension of state planning was often implemented by prominent representatives of industrial capital rather than bureaucrats or socialists. The presence of such business leaders in government did not calm the fears of the large export companies, gathered in the 'Executives' Club' that the labour movement was preparing the ground for a permanent post-war regime of state controls.[39] There were some grounds for these anxieties as the war drew to a close, as significant elements within the labour movement openly advocated the continuation of economic planning as the means for securing the restructuring, development and rapid growth of the Swedish economy.[40] Their ideas were embodied in the *Post-war Programme* presented by the Social Democrats in 1944, prepared in consultation with LO and receiving the approval of the Communist Party. The avowed purpose of the *Programme* was to avert economic crisis and mass unemployment on the return to peace, yet the document also argued that industrial production should be organised for the social good and on lines which society itself approved. A logical development of this strategy was the introduction of industrial democracy, since it was assumed that an improvement in industrial efficiency could not be achieved without 'a larger measure of economic democracy within the economic organisation'. The means proposed for such an enlargement of economic decision-making was not, however, state legislation but rather agreements between those engaged in collective bargaining.[41]

These proposals had the affect of uniting industrialists and the political bourgeois parties much more coherently, with the 'Executives' Club' leading a propaganda campaign against the moves to national economic planning.[42] The counter-offensive from industrial capital and the bourgeois parties resulted in significant electoral losses by both the Social Democrats and the Communists in the 1948 elections. The major beneficiaries were the Liberals, closely allied to the big employers and able to consolidate their position at the end of the 1940s. Within the ranks of the Social Democrats, moderate sections increased their influence as they argued for a return to the co-operative relationship established with business in the pre-war years. As the Party retreated from far-reaching demands for nationalisation of key industries and direct state control of industry, so the road was opened for more conciliatory politics and a fresh coalition with the Agrarians.[43] The capacity of the SAP to carry forward a radical programme was also inhibited in the immediate post-war period by internal conflicts within the trade union movement. war production had brought a fall in unemployment but also a significant decline in real wages. Each union was concerned with the restoration of pre-war income levels, though once again the capacity of the labour organisations to achieve substantial increases varied across the LO membership. As unions pushed for wage rises there was a real danger that wage differentials would widen considerably between the different occupations. In this context the demand for central negotiations and a solidaristic wage policy was heard once again in the union movement.[44]

This debate was intensified and complicated by the intense political divisions within the Swedish labour movement demonstrated in the six-month strike which swept the mechanical engineering industry during 1945. During the interwar years the Social Democrats and LO leadership had effectively contained the influence of Communist activists within the trade unions, though support for Communists had increased in some unions during the war years as falling real wages fuelled discontent on the shop floor. The great strike of 1945 reflected both this grassroots discontent and the organising abilities of the Communists within the Metall Union. Communist activists had espoused the cause of local union initiatives and resisted the claims of 'capitalist rationalisation' during the 1930s and the triumph of the historical compromise, as well as its recreation in the 1950s, involved the suppression of Communist opposition within the unions as LO and SAF reached an understanding on industrial peace.[45] When dissatisfaction in the local union branches was at its height, in the closing years of war and immediate post-war years, the leadership of LO and SAF sought to uproot the causes of discontent by extending the Basic Agreement of 1938 and the supplementary agreements on workers' health and safety, and on apprenticeship, passed during the war, with a scheme for enlarging employees' influence within the enterprise. This resulted in the Works Council Agreement of 1946 and the Agreement on Rationalisation and Time and Motion Studies approved in 1948.[46]

Although these measures raised expectations of industrial democracy, their limitations quickly became apparent. These limits were evident in the different aspirations which the architects of the agreements brought to the drawing board. Both SAF and LO were anxious to meet too widespread demands for increased employee influence, though the employers wanted the new works councils to be instruments for raising productivity and reducing conflict in industry. The industrialists sought to open up an alternative channel of information to their workers, on such questions as rationalisation and investment, to that provided by the unions. For their part, the LO leadership felt deeply ambivalent about the opportunities created by the works councils, since a successful role for the new bodies was bound to call into question the lines of authority and prerogative drawn at the time of the historical compromise. There was also the prospect that local unions would face confusing demands as the councils promoted the interests of individual firms as well as their workers, possibly undermining the authority of the unions themselves. Given these concerns, it is not surprising that works councils were given a largely advisory role and were staffed by management and union (both not employee) representatives. The councils were stripped of the ability to negotiate company policies and the management was instead placed under an obligation to report on the firm's financial circumstances and to announce, in advance, proposals for extensive reforms in production, investment and the organisation of work. Local unions could exploit such information in the normal process of bargaining.[47] Although research on works councils is limited, it seems clear that the trade unions quickly lost interest in them. Their disenchantment is partly explained by the refusal of managements to cooperate fully with the agreement and place relevant issues on the agenda, whilst in other cases firms sought to direct key problems to the councils rather than the established negotiating machinery. This tendency of works councils to complicate the unions' role and their relations with management accounts for the demise of the works councils, though the underlying causes of discontent and demands for participation often remained and were to surface again in later years.[48]

A similar pattern can be traced in the workings of the agreement on time and motion studies reached in 1948. After extensive discussions, both LO and SAF agreed that rationalisation was essential for continued economic growth and that time and motion studies, correctly conducted, constituted an effective instrument for raising productivity. LO demanded that time and motion study councils be set up at company and branch levels, with complaints and disputes to be referred to the latter. The employers resisted and further debate resulted in the creation of a national council for time and motion studies, briefed to promote higher efficiency in industry. Negotiations on piece rates and time and motion studies were to remain matters for local bargaining. There remained also an important contrast between the widespread complaints and bitterness over the unfair working of piece rates and charges of sweating, and the modest fruits of the LO campaign for an increase in employee influence over the enterprise.[49] It can be concluded, therefore, that the terms of the historical compromise of the 1930s actually constrained radical departures in the areas of works councils and time and motion studies. Rather than a shift in the balance of power during the post-war years to the union membership, the actual operation of the new agreements served to confirm the tripartite relationship between the LO, SAF and the Swedish state. There was something like a productivity coalition built in the 1940s, based on the spirit of compromise. In comparative terms the Swedish model appears to have been successful in delivering economic growth, though it could be argued that the effectiveness of this coalition in raising productivity may have been greater if the influence of workers over production questions had been extended.[50] It is certainly true that the upsurge of unrest which appeared in the late 1960s seems to have deep roots in the discontents of the post-war years.

The golden age of historical compromise and the origins of crisis

The 1950s and 1960s were the years when the historical compromise enjoyed widespread support and appeared to deliver a golden age of stability and high growth. Sweden's gross national product increased by more than three per cent per annum, only surpassed by the USA during the 1960s. Industrial productivity (per hour) grew in the four quinquennial periods 1950-70 at an average annual rate of 4.4, 5.9, 7.4 and 6.9 per cent respectively. These were also years of successful labour market management and virtual full employment, with unemployment standing at less than two per cent by the late 1960s.[51] We would argue that reforms in the labour market provided some of the pre-conditions for this golden age of Swedish capitalism, not least in the creation of centralised collective bargaining between LO and SAF. Sweden's employers were the driving force behind this movement in the mid-1950s as SAF and those unions which had fallen behind in wage rises combined to push for central negotiations and a solidaristic wage policy as a means for realising their separate goals. Supported by the individual unions, SAF and LO could legitimately claim to offer themselves as the guarantors of industrial peace and the defenders of the legacy of Saltsjöbaden.[52] It is clear that, once again, the economic conditions of post-war growth do not in themselves provide a full explanation of the reforms introduced at this period. The political conjuncture was a vital context for the consolidation of the post-war settlement. The red-green coalition formed with the Agrarians in government (1951-57), compelled the Social Democrats to retreat from several of the commitments of the post-war *Programme*, whilst the dilution of the Party's strategy for economic planning was an important element in the building of a closer relationship with the employers.[53] During the 1950s these relations were confirmed in the establishment of a number of corporatist institutions which bound the state, LO and the industrialists closer together.[54] Significantly, the militantly anti-corporatist 'Executives' Club' ceased activity in 1953.[55]

The principles of central bargaining and solidaristic wages were not merely pragmatic responses to the specific needs of employers and particular unions. They also provided the basis for an imaginative intellectual formula which would guide the thinking of the labour movement for much of the post-war period. This was the so-called Rehn-Meidner model, outlined in the early 1950s by two LO economists Gösta Rehn and Rudolf Meidner and designed to resolve the dilemma of how to combine full employment with price stability. The authors assumed that it was the responsibility of the state to pursue both an active labour market policy to secure full employment and a rigorous fiscal programme in order to restrain both excess demand from consumers and the 'excess profits' of private firms. A key premise of the model was that bargainers would adhere to solidaristic wage policies, based on the classification of work for wage purposes. The main purpose of this formula was to fix wages at a level which enabled the more efficient and profitable companies to generate more investment funds whilst the less productive firms would be forced to rationalise their operations or squeezed out of business by competitive pressures.[56] Whilst opinions vary on the actual contribution which the Rehn-Meidner model made to the rapid restructuring of industrial production and productivity growth in the 1950s and 1960s, it seems clear that the model *did* lead to a compression of wage differentials as well as a concentration of the industrial base and increased capital exports at this period.[57] By the end of the 1960s the affects of the model were also generating a set of demands for political measures to correct its impact.[58]

The surge of economic growth in these decades also had important consequences for local bargaining and union activity at local level. Full employment and state labour market policies served to strengthen the influence of unions within the company, whilst centralised bargaining provided a backbone for local wage bargaining. Social welfare reforms also gave unions a network of support structures in areas such as training and education, pensions and compensation.[59] But these achievements also had adverse affects on the scope of local union activity compared with the pre-war decades. The growth of state welfare placed benefit issues on the welfare agenda and removed it from the concerns of local unions, whilst the expansion of labour market programmes created a large assembly of institutions and experts which assumed control over matters that previously had devolved on to local unions and their employers. Official LO support of rationalisation and technical innovation introduced by the firm also restricted the capacity of local unionists to intervene in questions of work design and the local bargainers turned their attention increasingly to the piece rate systems and the time and motion studies on which they were based. Unions in general welcomed the spread of systematic piece work in Swedish industry, including Method Time Measurement (MTM), since these were perceived as removing the arbitrary power of the supervisor to decide job prices. Whilst the rapid spread of measured piece rates opened up the possibility of union influence over work organisation and manning levels, the bargaining over rates became more technical and were left in the hands of trained union officials or experienced representatives which reduced the capacity for interventions from the ordinary members.[60] The logic of centralised bargaining also restricted the scope for local initiatives, placing upper limits on any increases negotiated by union representatives. This trend intensified with the major reorganisation of the LO in 1962 which resulted in a merging of former sections into fewer and larger units. Even though the number of local clubs also rose, such developments appear to have tilted the balance of influence away from members and towards officials. The influence of professionals was also felt in another direction: signs of discontent were now met by the intervention of psychologists, work sociologists and other functionaries who organised, for example, the controversial 'Mental Health Campaign', seeking to identify the sources of friction in the personalities of the workers rather than their environment and attempting to fit the employee to the work process designed for efficient output.[61]

There is evidence, therefore, that the fruits of the historical compromise in terms of higher growth rates and improved living standards were gathered at the cost of diminished local influence and democratic accountability at work. Unions were themselves governed by a small number of full-time officials and re-elected members who controlled affairs whilst apathy spread amongst the wider membership.[62] This was the result not merely of the growth of corporatist arrangements but also reflected the determination of the Social Democrats to limit the influence of the Communists who often fought centralisation in these years. Critics of the prevailing bargaining system were often branded as Communists in order to marginalise and harass them, which removed the basis for active debate on the prevailing model until the late 1960s.[63] When the critique did emerge, it came in the form of a sudden explosion in December 1969. A two month strike erupted at the Norbotten mines of the state-owned LKAB as workers campaigned against the rising work pace which resulted from the piece rates system and also against the increasing bureaucratisation of the enterprise. The miners demanded monthly salaries and more influence over work organisation, though they also attacked the solidaristic wage policy which had led to a decline in the relative standing of mineworkers. In its outlook and practical organisation the strike movement opposed centralisation and was led by an elected strike committee rather than the local union officials. The strike committee was dominated by Communists who were battle-hardened against further attempts by the Social Democrats to marginalise local activists.[64] The conflict at LKAB provided the spark for a conflagration of strike activity that was unparalleled since the 1920s. Widespread demands emerged for monthly wages, an end to sweating, centralisation of decision-making, and a narrow concern with distribution questions. The unrest peaked in the dock workers' disaffection from the Transport Workers' Union as they formed their own breakaway organisation outside LO.[65] The pressures on the labour movement to engage in a strategic reorientation were intensified when the Central Organisation of Salaried Employees (TCO), as well as opposition parties linked to the civil servants, argued for greater democratisation of the working life. These demands prompted the Social Democrats to formulate solutions which were to be implemented in the labour legislation of the 1970s.[66]

The turmoil in the spheres of labour relations and politics had deep repercussions for Swedish industry. Some of these difficulties had themselves contributed to the wave of unrest that was sweeping the production system. Taylorism had been pursued *in absurdum,* leading to a visible decline in motivation, co-operation, and quality of work. The wage system did not provide incentives which both firms and their employees wanted. Companies found recruitment more difficult and labour turnover increased. The employers were forced to seek new strategies for management and organisation. SAF as well as individual companies had initiated the concept of 'new factories' with a work organisation based on 'semi-autonomous groups' and a wage structure which favoured increased flexibility. Paradoxically, it was the large export companies that led this movement. One of the consequences was that the central bargaining system and the solidaristic wage policy were called into question.[67] The prominence of the exporting firms can be explained in the light of their rapid growth during the late 1960s, based on rapid technological change and increased international competition which pointed to the need for more flexible wage structures to attract specialist staff and reward increased effort. Whereas such firms had been concerned in the 1930s to retain uniform wages and contain wage costs (which formed a large proportion of production costs) by central negotiation, by 1970 the proportion of trained technical employees was much larger and these grades were now organised in their own unions. Individual contracts had given way to collective agreements. As their contribution became more valuable to the enterprise and wage costs were a less significant element in total production costs, so powerful sections of the export industry demanded a return to a free labour market with salaries set at company level and questioned the utility of the central bargaining system and solidaristic wage policies.[68] The ferment in labour relations was only one of several forces which appeared to be transforming Swedish society and challenging the hegemony of the Social Democrats at this time. Two major surveys conducted in the 1960s on Swedish living standards revealed the surprising extent of relative poverty in the country.[69]

There was rising discontent with the affects of the regional concentration of industry and the active labour market policies which resulted in extensive geographical mobility within Sweden.[70] Concerns were expressed about the concentration of wealth in society and of capital ownership in industry.[71] Yet it was the threat of rising unemployment which provided the most acute dilemma for the Social Democrats, aggravated by growing exports of capital abroad.[72] Despite the evidence of dissatisfaction with the expanding bureaucracy in national and local politics and the pressures for greater freedom in business strategy from the leading companies, there was a strong countervailing demand within the SAP and amongst radicals for *increased* state control of capital formation and for a more active industrial and labour market policy.[73] The emerging economic crisis contributed to a deep political crisis within the Swedish order, where the consensus of the historical compromise gave way to the controversies of open opposition.

The end of compromise: from convergent to divergent interests

At the beginning of the 1970s it was increasingly apparent that the growth strategy of the earlier decades had generated a number of unresolved problems. Less obvious was the important shift which had occurred in the power relations and alignments of the major partners to the original compromise and their perception of their material interests in the changed conditions of the 1960s. These groups now calculated their opportunities and interests in quite different ways than they had done in the era of convergence and compromise. The conditions which eroded the compromise were both economic and political. The evidence of disintegration was visible when the Social Democrats were forced to surrender power to an alternative bourgeois coalition in 1976, after more than four decades of power. Rather than break with the past, the new coalition adopted a familiar mix of policies to fight stagflation whilst seeking to rescue the staple iron and shipbuilding industries by crisis management. A more distinctive conservative programme was only formulated in the late 1970s as political realignments marked the gradual decay of Swedish social democratic ideals, as electors turned away from their historic allegiance to the Social Democrats and the ethics of the historical compromise.[74]

Once again the position of the employers as well as the unions was to be critical in determining the fate of the Swedish settlement. By the 1970s it was clear that the export industries were in the ascendant and were dominated by multinational companies which expanded their activities overseas and came to control the leadership of SAF. This group now recognised that an opportunity existed to achieve what the 'Executives' Club' had been forced to bargain away in the 1930s: namely, the reduction of welfare programmes which imposed high costs on Sweden's competitive industries, whilst also breaking up the system of central bargaining and solidaristic wages that no longer served the needs of the exporters. Firms were already having to pay a premium to attract scarce skilled labour and with rising unemployment the wages of the less skilled could be contained without central agreement. Issues of work organisation could also be stifled by the application of a flexible wages policy.[75] The erosion of the central bargaining system was also assisted by the frictions which re-emerged in the ranks of the unions at this time of debate on solidaristic wages. Here the Metall Union played a key role as it drew the bulk of its members from employees in the export trades. The Metall Union also sought to break away from the central machinery and solidaristic wages policy in response to changes in both technological and market conditions within the metalworking sectors, corresponding to the demands made by their employers.[76]

This convergence of criticism does not imply that the demands of such unions as Metall for increased influence over work content and wage determination were welcomed by their employers. Such calls led to sharp conflicts both with industrialists and with established union officials. Whilst many firms sought to break up the existing bargaining structures, they were clearly opposed to replacing them by institutions which gave their employees real influence over management decisions. The growing pressures on the unions and the LO to develop a fresh strategy, permitting local unions to have greater scope for action and to address production questions, presented the official leadership with a dilemma. Responding positively to such calls would imply a departure from the famous Paragraph 23 (later 32) of the Compromise which had its origins in the original 1906 agreement between SAF and LO protecting the absolute prerogatives of management. At the same time there were unmistakable signs that the structure of Swedish capitalism and the balance of power within economy and society were shifting in ways that the unions needed to address. The process of internationalisation led to the rapid growth in size, profitability and investment resources of some leading companies, which strengthened the dominance of these enterprises at a time when Sweden's industrial base was shrinking. Together with a host of smaller, rapidly growing firms based in the new technologies, such firms took advantage of prevailing economic policy to make 'excess profits' without increasing domestic employment. This trend was strengthened by the impact of the 1970s oil crisis as well as the economic recession which brought a fall in industrial investment, slower productivity growth and rising unemployment.[77] The larger transnational companies were increasingly dominant in both export markets and domestic markets and whilst many medium and smaller enterprises flourished, they were often tied as sub-contractors to the larger firms which controlled much of the Swedish economy. The affect of these shifts was to give both the large firms and the advanced firms of various sizes in new sectors a sharper orientation to international markets and their collective strategies were framed in this context.[78]

These important changes in the economic and political landscape of Sweden were accompanied by an ideological reassessment of the bonds of loyalty within Swedish society. Alterations in the occupational structure and the growth of urbanisation during the 1960s had broken up many of the labour movement's former strongholds. The ideal of loyalty towards the wider movement was not as prevalent amongst the new generation of workers as it had been in earlier decades, partly because of the growth of non-LO unions in both the private and public sectors.[79] The allegiance of the public sector workers was still uncertain during the 1970s, whilst confidence in the resilience of the historical compromise and its capacity to deliver sustained economic growth was clearly waning amongst the leadership of the wider labour movement.[80]   Whilst viable alternatives were still lacking in public life, doubts about the historical compromise were now surfacing in different quarters and creating an ideological vacuum into which radical new ideas could rush.

Industrial democracy on the agenda

It is against this background - the structural change in the economy, the protests at the work places and the growing political uncertainty - that we should consider the strategy launched by the Social Democrats during the first half of the 1970s. The official rhetoric of the Party presented the coming of economic democracy as a natural third step after the achievement of political democracy with universal suffrage and social democracy with the arrival of the welfare state. In reality, the Social Democrats sought to promote industrial democracy via labour legislation designed to strengthen employee influence at the workplace, whilst the LO initiated the question of economic democracy.[81] Rudolf Meidner had chaired an LO commission in the early 1970s to investigate the scope for breaking capitalist concentration of ownership and control by regulating 'excess profits' and securing a collective formation of capital. The result was the celebrated proposal for wage-earner funds which could fundamentally transform the ownership structure of Swedish industry within a relatively short period.[82] It was the LO, therefore, which had set the pace in the discussion of democratic ownership and control of industrial capital.

On the labour legislation front, co-determination was pursued through a package of new laws.   Membership of company boards for employee representatives was enacted in 1976, following the 1974 legislation on security of employment. This measure restricted the employer's right to hire and fire workers, restricting the famous Paragraph 32 (23), by specifying the terms on which employees could be dismissed. Union representation within the firm was strengthened by a measure also passed in 1974, whilst in 1976 came the law on co-determination at work (MBL), which annulled that section of Paragraph 32 which gave employers the exclusive right to manage and allocate work. Henceforth, management was obliged to negotiate with local unions all major questions concerning the terms of employment including personnel reallocation, notice to leave, recruitment, managerial appointments, new working methods, new products, the preparation of budgets, and organisational changes.   The union's right to negotiate did not, however, invalidate management's right to decide. If consensus was not reached between the parties, management was responsible for making the ultimate decisions single-handed. Eventually, in 1977, the work environment law which had been enacted four years before was amended, including the right of unions to veto hazardous technology.[83] It is clear that even though the objects of this legislation were limited, they violated the principles embodied in the historical compromise. Political power and legislation was now being used to regulate labour relations and the rights of management, and workers should now be involved in areas of decision-making previously reserved for the employer alone. The most controversial measure - that on co-determination at work - remained an optional statute which could be invoked once central and local agreements were reached, thereby indicating the concern of the legislators to retain the framework of local negotiation and consent.

Changed political conditions at the end of the 1970s enabled SAF to delay entering into the proposed agreements. Not until 1982 were LO and SAF ready to sign the 'Development Agreement', which transferred the law on co-determination at work to collective agreement paragraphs in the LO-SAF domain. Further obstacles remained at local level and the Agreement has been fairly described as a successful outcome of SAF's determination to restrict the application of co-determination at work. There are also parallels with the works councils agreement of 1946, since in each case employee influence was circumscribed by the readiness of the employer to provide relevant information and participate in negotiations on such matters prior to deciding on policy.[84] The scepticism of LO regarding the vague character of the original reform legislation was confirmed in the early 1980s when it became apparent that the Social Democrats had no intention of fulfilling their promise and take concrete legislative proposals on industrial democracy to the Swedish Parliament. Rather than pursuing a radical programme of reform, the Social Democrats were again seeking to reach a new form of compromise with the powerful employers, thereby provoking further frictions within the labour movement.[85]

Meanwhile, the agenda of economic democracy proposed initially by Meidner in his wage-earn fund scheme of the 1970s, generated intense controversy within Sweden. The wage fund solution can be seen not merely as a response to the problems of the Swedish economy in recession but also as a continuation of the labour movement's strategy for achieving the goals which were identified when the Rehn-Meidner model, central bargaining and solidaristic wages were approved by the unions. On the other hand, the *political* challenge represented by the new Meidner plan was a more profound breach with Sweden's established order than the contemporary labour legislation, since the proposals openly questioned the distribution of ownership in a capitalist society and Meidner himself declared:

[W]e want to deprive the capitalists of the power that they exercise by virtue of ownership. All experiences show that it is not enough to have influence and control. I refer to Marx and Wigforss: we cannot fundamentally change society without changing its ownership structure.[86]

There was substance as well as rhetoric in Meidner's scheme since it was calculated that majority ownership of the larger and more profitable companies would have passed to the employees within two decades.[87] The reform had three main objects: firstly, to appropriate the 'excess profits' returning to private firms from the working of solidaristic wage policy; secondly, to increase collective capital formation to avoid the continued concentration of private ownership and thereby to assist the investment demands of domestic industries and limit capital exports; and thirdly, to complement labour legislation by enhancing employee influence in the firm and providing the local unions with the right as shareholders to appoint directors to the board.[88]

The principles of the Meidner proposal were initially welcomed by the LO, though the Social Democrats expressed significant reservations.[89] Successive government commissions were appointed on which business representatives also sat, to consider the implications of the scheme and SAF mobilised a strong campaign of opposition to the wage funds idea.[90] Supported by the opposition parties, SAF's campaign developed into a general attack on the whole fabric of welfare capitalism in Sweden, including social benefits, labour market policies and the Rehn-Meidner model itself.[91] By the time a diluted version of Meidner's scheme was legislated on the Social Democrats' return to power in 1982, the provisions simply guaranteed access to investment capital without any trace of employee influence retained.[92] Even so, the opposition of the business community continued and with the return of a new bourgeois government to power in 1991 the funds were abolished.[93] These confrontations over the wage-earner funds marked a turning point both in Swedish politics and in its labour relations. Antagonisms between the organisations of capital and labour were harsher even than those of the post-war years as the basic consensus on the questions of economic growth and welfare distribution evaporated. Underlying the attack on the funds by SAF and the conservative parties lay a determination to settle accounts with the historical compromise and to roll back the gains of central bargaining, solidaristic wages, the Rehn-Meidner model and particularly the welfare state. The importance of the opposition campaign, therefore, was as an exercise in ideological reconstruction, whereby SAF opposed even the policies of the conservative-liberal coalition as it sought to retain Keynesian measures in its fight against unemployment. In contrast to Britain where Thatcherism provided the ideological leadership for the business community, Sweden's neo-liberal economic philosophy and its calls for cuts in public expenditure and privatisation, was heard most audibly in the corridors of SAF before it gained widespread political currency.[94]

Whilst the wage-earner funds proposal served to promote a fresh ideological and political coherence on the right, the issue confused and divided the Swedish labour movement. The SAP criticised the radical content of the reform whilst the Communists questioned its veracity and effectiveness.[95]   After their initial endorsement of the principles of Meidner's scheme, the LO leadership retreated under the fire of criticism to concede important elements of the plan.   No prominent union stepped forward to defend the proposal whilst the white collar unions vacillated in the face of internal divisions and the impetus behind the proposal was lost.[96] These setbacks did not alter the underlying conditions which the Meidner solution was intended to address: structural change, excess profits, widening wage differentials and workforce discontents continued unabated. Sectional strategies began to emerge as some groups of workers entered into 'co-workers agreements' with the company employing them and differences in employment and working conditions sharpened further.[97]   When the Social Democrats returned to government in 1982 it was apparent that the movement for employee influence within the enterprise had been largely dissipated and the Party failed to extend earlier labour legislation and declared the continuation of wage-earners funds to be out of the question.[98]

Not only did the Social Democrats abandon the cause of increasing workers' power but they also reoriented their strategy for growth away from the principles of the historical compromise.   The policy christened 'the third way' was essentially incompatible with the aims of the Rehn-Meidner model. To halt the decline in the competitiveness of Swedish industry a radical devaluation of the currency was undertaken, paving the way for increased profits and private investment.   The responsibility for industrial restructuring and improving productivity growth was placed clearly in the hands of the employers. There was also a deregulation of the credit market and of foreign exchange transactions at the end of the 1980s.   The result was not an investment boom in domestic industry but a tidal wave of capital exports and speculation followed by a collapse of the credit market in the early 1990s. As wage earners pressed for increases to compensate for falling purchasing power in the late 1980s, much of the competitive advantage resulting from devaluation was lost. Firms did not engage in the painful process of restructuring Swedish industry until the late 1980s when the declining competitiveness of traded products contributed to the wider problem of budget deficits as welfare expenditure continued to grow.   In the face of permanent deficits, pressures mounted to cut public expenditure and the Social Democrats inexorably moved from prioritising full employment to a commitment to reduce inflation.[99] This shift has placed further strains on the fragile unity of the Swedish labour movement in a period of economic crisis, as the state was drawn into protecting the interests of the export industries as a platform for future economic success. Unions faced rising unemployment and an erosion of the state benefits which had underpinned their bargaining position and political legitimacy.

The demise of central bargaining and solidaristic wage policies

Against this background of rapid changes in Swedish industry during the 1980s, new forms of bargaining began to emerge which were at clear variance with the assumptions of the historical compromise. As in earlier periods of transition, there have been both economic and political shifts in Sweden that have enabled strategic groups to alter the power balance within society and to decisively break with the institutions of corporatism. The result has been a fragmentation of interests which were previously considered organic and a reorientation in the agenda not merely of the leading economic groups but also of the Swedish state itself as transnational companies extended their power base beyond the national frontiers. Once again a key role was played by Swedish industrialists and in particular the large transnational firms which dominated the Swedish Metal Trades Employers' Association and through it the SAF itself. The big firms used this position to alter SAF statutes, enabling trade associations to reach agreements with individual unions and even impose a lockout without the approval of SAF.[100] This policy removed the cornerstone of central control and industrial conciliation which had secured the historical compromise of the 1930s and as a confirmation of this break with tradition the metal employers formed their own dispute fund. Their Association attempted to introduce the decentralised wage bargaining which the larger companies had been considering for a decade.[101]

The metal firms were assisted in their strategy during the wage round of 1982-83 by the changing policy of the union which had been instrumental in the formation of the historical compromise and solidaristic wages. The membership of Metall Union recognised the opportunities offered by new technologies to upgrade their work tasks and redesignating their work as white collar tasks. Faced with the prospect that such skilled labour could defect to the white-collar unions, Metall itself accepted the case for more flexible, differentiated wage rates, thereby breaking the collective front of LO.[102] Metall did not decisively abandon central negotiations but its readiness to cooperate in separate bargaining enabled the SAF to openly advocate an end to central bargaining, whilst at the same time it withdrew its representatives from a wide range of corporatist bodies which had cemented its relationship with LO and the state since the 1950s.[103]

At the same time that LO was confronted with the erosion of the central bargaining structures in which it had invested many years of effort, it was also challenged by a resurgence in local union activity which followed on the passing of co-determination legislation by parliament. Although this measure did not alter the distribution of power within Swedish companies, it did encourage workers and unions to participate in discussions on new technology, work layout and future planning. The rapid spread of new technologies and the affects of the legislation combined to increase the levels of worker engagement and local union activity at enterprise level during the 1980s. In response to such developments the Congresses of the Metall Union and later of the LO, produced reports in 1985-91 which focus on the need for a strong local union presence capable of responding to these new conditions.[104]   Therefore the new conditions of production and of bargaining are far removed from the aspirations of those who promoted works councils and labour legislation in the 1970s, but these changes have offered Swedish unions fresh opportunities to influence company policies at local level. The capacity of the unions to exercise this influence is dependent on the wider bargaining environment, however, and it is clear that rising unemployment, widening differentials and the erosion of welfare benefits have reduced the leverage which unions can bring to bear on private employers.

The crucial step towards this new environment was arguably taken by the Social Democrats when they abandoned the commitment to economic growth via the historical compromise without formulating a viable alternative. Consequently the two branches of the Swedish labour movement lack a coherent strategy for growth, whilst the unions face the added difficulty of growing localised struggles and initiatives on production without a framework for industrial development and wage movement which would bind the movement together. The divergence in strategic thinking between the two sections of the labour movement was vividly expressed during 1990 when the Social Democrats applied for membership of the European Union, which lacked the enthusiastic support of the unions.   One interpretation is that the Social Democrats no longer expect a new historical compromise within national boundaries with the employers and that membership of the EU can provide the political counterweight to the transnational companies and to recreate the conditions of equipoise between state and economy which was reached in the 1930s. Simple figures describing the growing weight of the transnational firms can support such a view. These firms have been few compared to those of the USA, Japan and other leading nations, but their relative weight upon the economy of the mother country has been larger. From 1960 to 1990 the share of employment (of total domestic industrial employment) of the 20 largest multinationals had grown from around 30 to around 50 percent. During the same period their expansion abroad was still more impressive. In the 1980s they invested eight times more abroad than in Sweden and the larger part of their growing employment took place in their factories abroad.[105] The campaign to join Europe has also divided the labour movement between unions recruiting in the export trades who have accepted the case for membership and those based in domestic industries and the public sector who have been more sceptical of the benefits.[106] The historic fault lines between domestic and export employment sectors have again been exposed, though this time dividing the workforce rather than their employers.   It is certainly difficult to envisage conditions within the European context for the Social Democrats to play the influential role in managing society that has been such a feature of Swedish development.

Conclusions

There have been many interpretations of the development of the historical compromise in Sweden, though that provided by Walter Korpi has been one of the most influential and continues to shape our understanding of Swedish Social Democracy. Korpi sees the labour movement as the main agent of social transformation and the political vision of labour as the driving force behind this great transformation. Compromises with other classes are made on strategic grounds and for temporary purposes since in the longer term the working class is able to create sufficient power resources to disarm the opposition of capitalists and conservatives. In Korpi's view the historical compromise of the 1930s, made with the Agrarians on the political level and with the owners of industrial capital, constituted a necessary but temporary solution to immediate problems in the forward march of Swedish labour. Although the economic power of the labour movement was restricted, the compromise enabled the movement to build on its policies for economic growth and a welfare state which laid the foundations for a transition from agrarian to industrial production and the bargaining rights of wage labour. The readiness of the reformist Social Democrats to legislate to increase employee influence in capitalist firms and to frame measures for wage-earner funds, the final stage in the socialist transformation of society appeared to have dawned in the 1970s. Industrial and economic democracy would supersede the historical compromise of the transition period. Korpi acknowledged the existence of political choices for the Social Democrats, between the continuation of compromises with bourgeois interests or to launch into economic democracy, though he argued that membership pressures would continue to build on the unions until they assumed their historic role to exercise power in the transformation of society.

The flaws in this analysis are not difficult to detect. Korpi assumed that Swedish capitalists would continue to support the policies of state regulation, labour market intervention and centralised bargaining whilst also concurring in a radical diminution in their own control over production. The complex calculations which guided both capitalist strategy and union demands in reality were hardly considered. The power resource model turns on a rather simple equation of power distribution and assumes the coherence of interests within the labour movement which has been seriously questioned by divisions at various levels. Our essay suggests an alternative interpretation to that provided by Korpi's power resource theory of Swedish labour. We do not argue that the membership, organisation, planning and strategic action is unimportant in an understanding of the power of organised labour. These power resources are only realised in action, when people are motivated to engage in collective support. Their willingness to do so depends on their comprehension of a complex array of information on the best way to fulfil their own needs and interests. Converging and diverging interests will coexist at any one moment. The second point we are seeking to make is that these calculations and the environment in which they are made are *historically dynamic* and that we need an historical analysis of the competing opportunities which existed for action in order to understand the strategies which were developed. Korpi's perspective is implicitly teleological and presents history as a background to the march of modernising social democracy.

Viewed in a dynamic perspective, the historical compromise of the 1930s can be seen as an expression both of the existing power relations and the preferred solution to the economic and social problems perceived by the prevailing interests in Swedish society. It is often claimed that the Social Democrats were the real architects in this process, though our analysis shows the extent to which their strategy was the product of negotiations with and between a variety of interested parties. The historical compromise emerges as the work of several actors - even if the Social Democrats constituted the axis around which the drama revolved. We can see that the positions adopted by the respective parties shifted over time in response to changing (especially foreign) markets and as a consequence of the growth generated by the compromise itself. During the 1950s the leading employers were as enthusiastic as LO about central agreements to regulate labour at a period of full employment. By the end of the 1960s the constellation of power and interests which had sustained the historical compromise had clearly changed. Firstly, the adverse affects of the growth strategy was increasingly directed in political criticism of the Social Democrats. This undermined the hegemony of the SAP and gave opposition parties scope for a serious challenge. Secondly, and more importantly, growth brought structural changes in the Swedish economy including the rising influence of transnational exporting companies and a long tail of smaller enterprises which were interested in export markets. These changes weakened the bonds between industrial capital and the Social Democratic strategy of national economic development.

This breach between the SAP and the industrialists was dramatically exposed by the SAF's aggressive political strategy following the disorders of the 1970s. The strategy can be seen as a re-enactment of the Executives' Club opposition in the 1930s. In both periods the large metalworking firms sought to politicise SAF in a bid to settle the agenda of economic policy-making and oppose the labour market and welfare reforms provided by Social Democracy. During the 1930s and again in the 1950s this section of industrial capital saw the benefits of supporting arrangements which would deliver low, stable wage levels without industrial confrontation. The employers could establish a community of interests with the Metall Union and other unions seeking to promote solidaristic wages. Changing economic conditions and the ascendancy of the larger Swedish metal manufacturers persuaded such firms to pursue a fresh political and industrial strategy in recent years. These employers face a different cost structure, demanding more flexible and skilled workers and are much less sympathetic to the claims of the historical compromise and its rationale for growth. The metal employers have forged a new and different community of interests with Metall whilst dealing a heavy blow to central bargaining and solidaristic wages.

Sweden's industrial employers emerge from our analysis as key actors in the period when the historical compromise was designed, elaborated and undermined. In contrast to the view provided by Korpi, their resources have continued to be formidable even in periods when they were compelled to compromise with organised labour. The changing circumstances of the 1970s released the business community from their obligation to co-operate with Social Democracy and the unions once it was clear that the option of economic democracy had withered away. Labour was left without an alternative strategy. The poverty of the Social Democrats' position is reflected in the pursuit of a new national settlement within the fold of the European Union. We suspect that this bid may conceal a Utopian vision as flawed as that offered by Korpi in the 1970s. For in retrospect it appears that the historical compromise, so long regarded as a monument to rational Social Democratic planning, was the product of an historical conjuncture grounded on specific conditions and constellations of interests rather than as the first step towards a socialist transformation of Swedish society. This remains the main conclusion of our analysis. We do not deny the importance of the role which the Social Democrats have played in the formation and reformation of the coalitions of interests that held the historical compromise in place, though we argue that their role, like that of other leading actors, be subjected to an historical analysis in which neither interests nor power resources are pre-ordained.

Notes

* We wish to offer particular thanks to Joseph Melling for his invaluable, extensive editorial work. We are grateful also to Alan McKinlay and the other participants in the conference 'Management, Production and Politics' held at Glasgow University in 1992 for constructive criticisms of an early version of this paper. Aina Godenius-Berntsson made a dedicated effort to translate our text into persuasive English.

1. W. Korpi, *Arbetarklassen i välfärdskapitalismen. Arbete, fackförening och politik i Sverige* Prisma (1978) Stockholm, p367. See also W. Korpi, *Den demokratiska klasskampen. Svensk politik i jämförande perspektiv* Rabén and Sjögren (1981) Stockholm.
2. Quoted in Korpi, *Arbetarklassen*, p367.
3. Korpi, *Arbetarklassen*, pp358-61; Korpi, *Den demokratiska*, p 251.
4. Korpi, *Arbetarklassen*, pp97-103, 349-54.
5. On the disassembling of the welfare state, see K-O. Feldt, *Rädda välfärdsstaten* Norstedts (1994) Stockholm; A. Isaksson, *När pengarna är slut. Välfärden efter välfärdsstaten.* Brombergs (1992) Stockholm; P-M. Meyerson, *Den svenska modellens uppgång och fall.* SNS (1991) Stockholm.
6. Korpi, *Arbetarklassen*, pp32-40.
7. Korpi, *Arbetarklassen*, pp97-103, 349-54.
8. Quotations from Korpi, *Den demokratiska*, p 26.
9. Korpi, *Den demokratiska*, pp26-27; Korpi, *Arbetarklassen*, p100.
10. Korpi, *Arbetarklassen*, pp339-68.
11. Korpi, *Arbetarklassen*, pp107-8, 354-58; Korpi, *Den demokratiska*, pp222-23.

12. Korpi, *Arbetarklassen*, p361-63.
13. Korpi, *Arbetarklassen*, p363-68.
14. J. Pontusson, 'Socialdemokratin inför socialismen?' in *Häften för Kritiska Studier* 2 (1982), p43; Korpi, *Arbetarklassen*, p366.
15. For the mobilisation of power of groups of people in different situations, see J.A. Seip, 'Studiet av makt' in J.A. Seip, *Problemer og metode i historieforskningen. Artikler, inlegg, foredrag 1940-1977* Gyldendal (1993) Oslo, pp228-62; A.O. Johansson, 'En energi hade vi innerst inne. Om verkstadsarbetarnas makt i produktionen' in A.O. Johansson, S. Lundin and L. Olsson (eds.), *Dagsverken. Tretton essäer i arbetets historia.* Historiska Media (1994) Lund, pp136-63.
16. J. Pontusson, *The Limits of Social Democracy. Investment Politics in Sweden.* Cornell University Press (1992) Ithaca, p5.
17. R.Meidner, 'The Rise and Fall of the Swedish Model' in W. Clement and R. Mahon (eds.), *Swedish Social Democracy. A Model in Transition* Canadian Scholars' Press (1994) Toronto, pp338-39. See also Korpi, *Arbetarklassen*, pp84-90, 97-103.
18. A forceful plea for such an interpretation is given in A. Hedborg and R. Meidner, *Folkhemsmodellen.* Rabén and Sjögren (1984) Stockholm, pp11-22.
19. G. Ingham, *Strikes and industrial conflict. Britain and Scandinavia.* Macmillan (1974) London, pp38-42. For critique, see P. Jackson and K. Sisson, 'Employers' federations in Sweden and the UK and the significance of industrial infrastructure' *British Journal of Industrial Relations* XIV, 3, pp306-323; For a theoretical comment and an alternative analysis, see A. Johansson and J. Melling, 'The roots of consensus: bargaining attitudes and political commitment amongst Swedish and British industrial workers, c.1920-1950' *Economic and Industrial Democracy* 16 (1995), pp353-97.
20. Pontusson, 'Socialdemokratin', pp30-58; Korpi, 'Replik' in *Häften för Kritiska Studier* 6 (1982), pp59-64; J. Pontusson, 'Socialdemokratin och tredje vägen' in *Häften för Kritiska Studier* 5-6 (1983), pp64-73; G. Olsen, *The Struggle for Economic Democracy in Sweden*, Avebury (1992) Aldershot, p2; Pontusson, *Limits*, pp17-18.
21. A.L. Johansson, *Tillväxt och klassamarbete - en studie av den svenska modellens uppkomst.* Tiden (1989) Stockholm, chaps. 5-6; summarised in Johansson, *Den svenska modellen. En analys.* Brevskolan (1994) Stockholm.
22. Olsen, *Struggle*, pp15-17; Pontusson, *Limits*, pp10-34.
23. P. Swenson, 'Bringing capital back in, or Social Democracy reconsidered: Employer power, cross-class alliances and centralisation of industrial relations in Denmark and Sweden', in *World Politics* 43, 4 (1991), pp513-44. Also P. Swenson, *Fair Shares. Unions, Pay, and Politics in Sweden and West Germany.* Cornell University Press (1989) Ithaca.
24. The argument that local experiences mattered to the formation of national agreements and policies of the 1930s is outlined in A.O. Johansson, 'Arbetarklassen och Saltsjöbaden 1938: perspektiv ovan- och underifrån' in S. Edlund et al. (eds.), *Saltsjöbadsavtalet 50 år. Forskare och parter begrundar en epok 1938-1988,* Arbetslivscentrum (1989) Stockholm, pp72-94; M. Isacson, 'Från strid till samarbete: samförståndets framväxt under mellankrigstiden' in *Arbetarhistoria* 43 (1987), pp4-8; Isacson, *Verkstadsindustrins arbetsmiljö: Hedemora Verkstäder under 1900-talet* Arkiv (1990) Lund, pp54-101.
25. A.O. Johansson, *The Swedish road to Affluence 1800-1990 - and then? From self-sufficiency to dependent specialisation.* Uppsala University Economic History Department (1994) (mimeo); for the LO and the SAF see Johansson, *Tillväxt*, chap. 3; also, J. Fulcher, *Labour Movements, Employers and the State. Conflict and Co-operation in Britain and Sweden* Oxford University Press (1991) Oxford, pp131-53. More specific industrial studies include M. Isacson, *Verkstadsarbete under 1900-talet: Hedemora verkstäder före 1950* Arkiv (1987) Lund, p54 and passim; and H. Glimstedt, *Mellan teknik och samhälle - stat, marknad och produktion i svensk bilindustri 1930-1960* Gothenburg University, History Department (1993), p149.
26. N. Unga, *Socialdemokratin och arbetslöshetsfrågan 1912-34.* Arkiv (1976) Lund, pp121-46; K. Östberg, *Hur genomfördes den lokala demokratin i Sverige?*, (1993) [Mimeo]; R. Svensson,

'Socialdemokratisk arbetslöshetspolitik - Diskussion och praktik i Västerås 1921-1933'. C-paper: Uppsala University Economic History Department (1989).
27. A.L Johansson, 'Saltsjöbadspolitikens förhistoria' in Sten Edlund et al., *Saltsjöbadsavtalet* pp19-28; B. Simonsson, 'Den långa vägen till Saltsjöbaden' in Edlund et al. (eds.), *Saltsjöbadsavtalet* pp41-45.
28. Johansson, *Tillväxt*, pp99-124; P.-E. Back,. Svenska Metallindustriarbetareförbundets historia: Band III 1925-1940 Tiden (1963) Stockholm, p218; T. Svensson, *Från ackord till månadslön. En studie av lönepolitiken, fackföreningarna och rationaliseringarna inom svensk varvsindustri under 1900-talet* Svenska Varv (1983) Kungalv, pp194-200.
29. S. Edlund, 'Saltsjöbadsavtalet i närbild' in Edlund, et al. (eds.), *Saltsjöbadsavtalet* pp53-69.
30. Johansson, *Tillväxt*, chap. 4; S.A. Söderpalm, *Arbetsgivarna och Saltsjöbadspolitiken. En historisk studie i samarbetet på svensk arbetsmarknad.* SAF:s förlag (1980) Stockholm, pp38-45. For contemporary reactions to the Basic Agreement, R. Carsparsson, *Saltsjöbadsavtalet i historisk belysning* Tiden (1966) Stockholm, pp196-230.
31. Korpi, *Arbetarklassen*, p103.
32. Olsen, *Struggle*, p54; S. A. Söderpalm, *Direktörsklubben: storindustrin i svensk politik under 1930- och 1940-talen.* Rabén and Sjögren (1976) Stockholm, pp14-20.
33. L. Mjöset (ed.), *Norden dagen derpå. De nordiske ökonomisk-politiske modellene og deres problemer på 70- og 80-tallet* Universitetsforlaget (1986) Oslo, pp56-61, gives a brief account of the political alliances in the Nordic countries in the 1930s. The political compromises between the workers and farmers in the 1930s is presented in a long-term historical context by C-E. Odhner, 'Workers and farmers shape the Swedish Model: Social Democracy and Agricultural Policy' in K. Misgeld, K. Molin and K. Åmark (eds.), *Creating Social Democracy. A Century of the Social Democratic Labour Party in Sweden* Pennsylvania State University Press (1992), pp175-212.
34. Johansson, 'Arbetarklassen', p74.
35. Svensson, *Från ackord*, pp200-203; B. Persson, *Skogens skördemän. Skogs-och flottningsarbetareförbundets kamp för arbete och kollektivavtal* Arkiv (1991) Lund, p158-67; L. Ekdahl and M. Börjeson, *Norstedts Grafiska Personalklubb. En lokal fackklubbs historia 1902-1992* Norstedts (1992) Stockholm, p54-55.
36. F. Kupferberg, 'Byggnadsarbetarstrejken 1933-34' in *Arkiv för studier i arbetarrörelsens historia* 2 (1972); Swenson, *Fair Shares* pp42-53; Johansson, *Tillväxt* pp191-95; Johansson, 'Arbetarklassen', pp78-85; J. Ullenhag, *Den solidariska lönepolitiken. Debatt och verklighet* Uppsala Studies in Economic History: Läromedelsförlagen (1971) Stockholm.
37. Swenson, *Fair shares*, pp42-53, and 'Bringing capital', pp513-44.
38. Casparsson, *Saltsjöbadsavtalet*, pp188-92, 196-212; K. Åmark, *Facklig makt och fackligt medlemskap. De svenska fackförbundens medlemsutveckling 1890-1940* Arkiv (1986) Lund, pp153-154; B. Björklund, *Svenska Typografförbundet. Studier rörande Sveriges äldsta fackförbund* Tiden (1965) Stockholm, pp287-98.
39. Söderpalm, *Arbetsgivarna*, pp53-62.
40. L. Lewin, *Planhushållningsdebatten* Almqvist and Wiksell (1967) Stockholm, pp213-34; K. Åmark, 'Social Democracy and the trade union movement: solidarity and the politics of self-interest' in Misgeld, et al. (eds.), *Creating Social Democracy*, pp76-83.
41. *Arbetarrörelsens efterkrigsprogram* LO and SAP (1945) Stockholm, pp3-5, 30. On the post-war programme see V. Bergström, 'Party program and economic policy: The Social Democrats in government' in Misgeld, et al. (eds.), *Creating Social Democracy*, pp144-152.
42. Söderpalm, *Direktörsklubben*, pp103-38.
43. Bergström, 'Party program', pp144-82; Lewin, *Planhushållningsdebatten*, pp348-422.
44. R. Meidner, *I arbetets tjänst* Arbetslivscentrum (1984) Stockholm, pp141-78; Johansson and Melling, 'The roots', pp359-68.
45. P-E. Back, *Svenska Metallindustriarbetareförbundets historia 1940-1956. Band IV.* Tiden (1977) Stockholm, pp132-85; Korpi, *Arbetarklassen*, pp277-89; Johansson, *Tillväxt*, pp321-26; Svensson,

Från ackord, pp275-79; T. Svensson, *Socialdemokratins dominans. En studie av den svenska socialdemokratins partistrategi* Acta Universitatis Upsaliensis (1994) Uppsala, pp54-75.

46. For an overview of central negotiations and agreements in the 1940s, see Johansson, *Tillväxt,* chaps. 7-10.

47. L. Ekdahl, *Facket, makten och demokratin. Grafiska Personalklubben på DN/Expressen 75 år* Dagens Nyheter (1990) Stockholm, p130, and 'Industrial democracy on the agenda? The Swedish labour movement and local union power during the post-war period'. Paper presented at the conference 'Management, Production and Politics', Glasgow (1992).

48. I. Janérus, 'Företagsnämnderna - en parentes' in Edlund et al. (eds.), *Saltsjöbadsavtalet,* pp168-175; Johansson, *Tillväxt,* chap.9; Isacson, *Verkstadsindustrins,* p117-32.

49. Johansson, *Tillväxt,* chap.10; P. Sundgren, 'Införandet av MTM-metoden i svensk verkstadsindustri 1950-56' in *Arkiv för studier i arbetarrörelsens historia* 13-14 (1978), pp3-33.

50. A. Booth and J. Melling, 'Institutions and economic growth: trade unions and the politics of productivity in West Germany, Sweden and the U.K. 1945-1955'. [Mimeo] Department of Economic and Social History, University of Exeter (1994).

51. P.S. Andersen and J. Åkerblom, 'Scandinavia' in A. Boltho (ed.), *The European Economy. Growth and Crisis* Oxford University Press (1988) Oxford, pp618-19, 631; A. Johansson and L. Ekdahl, 'Labour Market Institutions and Productivity in Post-war Swedish Industry'. Paper presented at 'CEPR Workshop Institutions and Economic Growth', (1992) London.

52. R. Meidner, *I arbetets,* pp147-79.

53. Olsen, *Struggle,* pp57-8; 'Workers and farmers', pp200-06; Söderpalm, *Arbetsgivarna,* pp101-07.

54. Fulcher, *Labour movements,* p262; O. Svenning, *Socialdemokratin och näringslivet* Tiden (1972) Stockholm, pp43-47.

55. Söderpalm, *Direktorsklubben,* pp150-53.

56. A. Martin, 'Trade unions in Sweden; Strategic respons to change and crisis' in P. Gourevitch et al. (eds), *Unions and economic crisis. Britain, West Germany, and Sweden* Allen and Unwin (1984) London, pp203-11; Mjöset (ed.), *Norden dagen,* pp132-35; L. Erixon, 'En svensk ekonomisk politik. Rehn-Meidnermodellens teori, historia och aktualitet' *Häften för Kritiska Studier* 2-3 (1994), pp67-104; R. Meidner, *Samordning och solidarisk lönepolitik* Prisma (1974) Stockholm; R. Meidner and G. Rehn et al., *Trade unions and full employment* LO (1953) Stockholm.

57. Meidner, *I arbetets,* pp179-202.

58. Meidner, *I arbetets,* pp431-33; Mjöset (ed.), *Norden dagen,* p133; Erixon, 'En svensk', p84-93.

59. G. Esping-Andersen, 'The making of a Social Democratic welfare state' in Misgeld, et al. (eds.), *Creating Social Democracy,* pp35-66; Ekdahl, 'Industrial democracy'; A. Elmér, *Från Fattigsverige till välfärdsstaten. Sociala förhållanden och socialpolitik i Sverige under 1900-talet* Aldus (1975) Stockholm.

60. Ekdahl, 'Industrial democracy'; Ekdahl and Börjeson, *Norstedts,* pp63-84; E. Giertz, *Människor i Scania under 100 år. Industri, arbetsliv och samhälle i förändring* Norstedts (1991) Stockholm. pp341-45.

61. E. Mindus, *Arbete och mental hälsa* Folksam (1968) Stockholm; T. Björkman and K. Lundqvist, *Från MAX till PIA. Reformstrategier inom arbetsmiljöområdet* Arkiv (1981) Lund, pp48-54; G. Fredriksson, 'Om arbetskraftsforskning' *Häften för Kritiska Studier* 5 (1970), pp30-41.

62. R. Molin, *Organisationen inom facket. Organisationsutvecklingen inom de till Landsorganisationen anslutna förbunden* Carlssons (1991) Stockholm, pp9-17, 153-59; for a systematic analysis see A. Hadenius, *Facklig organisationsutveckling. En studie av Landsorganisationen i Sverige* Rabén and Sjögren (1976) Stockholm, and L. Lewin, *'Hur styrs facket?' Om demokrati inom fackföreningsrörelsen* Rabén and Sjögren (1977).

63. Svensson, *Socialdemokratins,* pp58-75; T. Kanger and J. Gummesson, *Kommunistjägarna: socialdemokraternas politiska spioneri mot svenska folket* Ordfront (1990) Stockholm.

64. U Eriksson, *Gruva och arbete. Kiirunavaara 1890-1990. Avsnitt III 1950-1970* Uppsala University (1991) Uppsala, pp293-371.

106   *Management, labour and industrial politics*

65. S.E. Olsson, 'Hamnarbetarna och Transportarbetareförbundet 1897-1972' *Arkiv för studier i arbetarrörelsens historia* 7-8 (1975), pp3-68; C. Thörnqvist, *Arbetarna lämnar fabriken. Strejkrörelser i Sverige under efterkrigstiden, deras bakgrund, förlopp och följder* Gothenburg University, Department of History (1994).

66. B. Shiller, *Samarbete eller konflikt* Arbetsmiljöfonden (1988) Stockholm, pp57-65; B. Simonson, *Arbetarmakt och näringspolitik. LO och inflytandefrågorna 1961-1982* Arbetsmiljöfonden (1988) Stockholm, pp51-87.

67. On the reorientation of the large employers in favour of non-Fordist production concepts and decentralised bargaining systems, J. Pontusson and P. Swenson, 'Varför har arbetsgivarna övergivit den svenska modellen?' *Arkiv för studier i arbetarrörelsens historia* 53-54 (1992), pp37-66; R. Mahon, 'From Fordism to...? New Technology, Labour Markets and Unions' and 'From Solidaristic Wages to Solidaristic Work. A Post-Fordist Historical Compromise for Sweden?' in Clement and Mahon (eds.), *Swedish Social Democracy*, pp 83-136 and 285-314.

68. Pontusson and Swenson, 'Varför'. The growing concern among employers about productivity and the search for new forms of piecewages and organization of work was foreshadowed in a series of reports made by SAF in the early 1970s. For example, J. Edgren, *Med växlande framgång - ett försök till förnyelse av lönesystem och arbetsformer* SAF (1973) Stockholm.

69. Swedish Commission on Low Income: *The 1968 Level of Living Survey*; Olsen, *Struggle*, p16; Meidner, *I arbetets*, p430.

70. B.Furåker, *Stat och arbetsmarknad. Studier i svensk rörlighetspolitik* Arkiv (1976) Lund, pp169-75.

71. Meidner, *I arbetets*, pp429-31; Olsen, *Struggle*, pp64-66; Svenning, *Socialdemokratin*, pp132-36.

72. B. Swedenborg, G. Johansson-Grahn and M. Kinnwall, *Den svenska industrins utlandsinvesteringar 1960-1988* IUI (1988) and C.H. Hermansson, *Sverige i imperialismens nät* Arbetarkultur (1986) Stockholm.

73. Svenning, *Socialdemokratin*, pp114-21.

74. Mjöset (ed.), *Norden dagen*, pp256-69; Pontusson, *Limits*, pp138-42.

75. Pontusson and Swenson, 'Varför'; C. Berggren, 'Marché du travail, l, l'exception Suédoise (1970-1990)' in Jean-Pierre Durand, *La fin du modèle suédois* Syros 1994, pp 184-209. See also C. Berggren, *Det nya bilarbetet. Konkurrens mellan olika produktionskoncept i svensk bilindustri 1970-1990* Arkiv (1990) Lund.

76. Mahon, 'From solidaristic wages', pp285-314.

77. Erixon, 'En svensk'; Olsen, *Struggle*, p66; Meidner, *I arbetets*, pp431-37; E. Lundberg, 'The Rise and Fall of the Swedish Model' in *Journal of Economic Literature* XXIII (1985), p25.

78. *Svenskt näringsliv och näringspolitik 1991* Industridepartementet [Department of Industry] (1991) Stockholm, pp48-61.

79. H. Heclo and H. Madsen, *Policy and Politics in Sweden. Principled Pragmatism* Temple University Press (1987) Philadelphia, pp51-53; G. Ahrne, H. Ekervald and H. Leiulfsrud, *Klassamhällets förändring* Arkiv (1985) Lund.

80. Esping-Andersen, 'The making', pp54-62.

81. Pontusson, *Limits*, chap.6.

82. R. Meidner, *Employee Investments Funds. An approach to Collective Capital Formation* Allen and Unwin (1978) London; E. Åsard, *LO och löntagarfondsfrågan. En studie i facklig politik och strategi* Rabén and Sjögren (1978) Stockholm; Pontusson, *Limits*, chap. 7.

83. S. Edlund and B. Nyström, *Developments in Swedish Labour Law* Swedish Institute (1988); Martin, 'Trade unions', p260.

84. Fulcher, *Labour movements*, pp274-79; M. Elam and M. Börjeson, 'Workplace Reform and the Stabilization of Flexible Production in Sweden' in B. Jessop, H. Kastendieck, K. Nielsen and O. Pedersen, *The politics of flexibility. Restructuring state and industry in Britain, Germany and Scandinavia* Edward Elgar (1991) Aldershot, p322.

85. E. Åsard, *Kampen om löntagarfonderna. Fondutredningen från samtal till sammanbrott* Norstedts (1985) Stockholm, pp37-54.

86. Quoted in Åsard, *Kampen*, p34.

87. R. Meidner, et al., *Löntagarfonder* Tiden (1975), Stockholm, p107; Olsen, *Struggle*.

88. Meidner, *Employee Investments*, pp15, 76-93.

89. Heclo and Madsen, *Policy and politics*, pp271-72; Åsard, *Kampen*, pp27-45; K-O. Feldt, *Alla dessa dagar...I regeringen 1982-1990* Norstedts (1991) Stockholm, pp26-30.

90. Olsen *Struggle*, pp78-83; Åsard, *Kampen*, pp65-134.

91. Åsard, *Kampen*, pp102-22; Shiller, *Samarbete*, pp96-100. T. Bresky, J. Scherman and I. Schmid, *Med SAF vid rodret. Granskning av en kamporganisation* Liber (1981) Stockholm, pp109-115.

92. Fulcher, *Labour movements*, pp283-85; Pontusson, *Limits*, pp196-98.

93. *Om avveckling av löntagarfonderna* [Government proposal to Parliament] (1991) 92:36

94. H. De Geer, *I vänstervind och högervåg. SAF under 1970-talet* Publica (1989) Stockholm, pp117, 278; H. De Geer, *Arbetsgivarna. SAF i tio decennier* SAF (1992) Stockholm, pp176-95; S. O. Hansson, *SAF i politiken* Tiden (1984) Stockholm.

95. J. Lönnroth, 'Fallet Grassman och vänsterns svåra förnyelse' *Ord and Bild* 3 (1994), pp74-86.

96. Olsen, *Struggle*, pp107-12; M. Micheletti, *Organizing interest and organized protest. Difficulties of member representation for the Swedish Central Organization of Salaried Employees (TCO)* University of Stockholm, Department of Political Science, (1985), p143.

97. See A. Kjellberg, 'Sweden: Can the model survive?' in A. Ferner and R.Hyman (eds.), *Industrial relations in the new Europe* Blackwell (1992) Oxford, pp88-142; N. Elvander, *Lokal lönemarknad. Lönebildning i Sverige och Storbritannien* SNS (1991) Stockholm, pp15-55, 226-42.

98. Pontusson, *Limits*, p198.

99. F.W. Scharpf, *Crisis and Choice in European Social Democracy* Cornell University Press (1991) Ithaca, pp108-13; Olsen, *Struggle*, pp117-20; Fulcher, *Labour movements*, pp301-03.

100. SAF-statutes decided by an extra SAF meeting 29 June 1982. N. Elvander, *Den svenska modellen. Löneförhandlingar och inkomstpolitik 1982-1986* Publica (1988) Stockholm, pp83-5.

101. Elvander, *Den svenska modellen*, pp83-4.

102. Kjellberg, 'Sweden', pp105-112; Elvander, *Den svenska modellen*, pp79-89.

103. *Farväl till korporatismen* Svenska Arbetsgivaref Foreningen (SAF) (1991) Stockholm; Kjellberg, 'Sweden', p100; De Geer, *Arbetsgivarna*, pp167-69, 173-75.

104. *Det goda arbetet* Metall (1985) Stockholm; *Solidarisk arbetspolitik för det goda arbetet* Metall Gotab (1989) Stockholm; *Det utvecklande arbetet. En rapport till LO-kongressen 1991* LO (1990) Stockholm.

105. B. Swedenborg, 'Svenska multinationella företag' in *Sveriges Industri* Industriförbundet (1994) Stockholm, pp.87-98.

106. *Dagens Nyheter*, 14-15 November 1994.

6. Industrial relations and crisis management in the coal mines of the Ruhr, 1945-1968

Werner Abelshauser

Introduction

Twice during the twentieth century the new order in Germany's economy and society has been decided in the 'Revier', the industrial region of the Rhine and Ruhr. After each world war the political and economic significance of this industrial cradle was demonstrated as the district tipped the balance of forces towards a moderate and anti-revolutionary solution to Germany's political problems. The centre of this material power can be found in the region's mining industry, with the coalmining sector occupying a strategic role in both politics and industrial relations. Germany's coal mines have served both as an indicator and a precipitator of social stability. Further, the industry itself provided a model during the 1960s of how Germany might manage the industrial decline of a major region and contain the crises of a troubled sector in transition.[1] The emergence of co-determinatio, or *Mitbestimmung*, is of historic importance in German industrial relations. Co-determination has become the underlying principle of capital-labour relations in Germany, even beyond the heavy industries where labour achieved parity representation with management in the management of the iron and steel works. This spirit of *paritaetische Mitbestimmung* spread from the Ruhr to almost every corner of large-scale production. The remarkable success of co-determination must be attributed not only to the transparent bias in favour of labour interests within the practice of the industrial relations courts (the *Arbeitsgerichte*), but also to a longer tradition of co-operation between capital and labour on the shop floor of German industry which had been evolving since the First World War. This tradition had been perverted by the compulsory 'co-operation' of employers and workers after the Nazi accession to power and was finally shattered by the collapse of the Third Reich. *Mitbestimmung* as developed by the British occupation authorities provided an opportunity, therefore, to continue relations on the path of co-operation liberated from the burden of Nazi ideology.

For German labour the key issue was not how to control the workplace but rather how to occupy the commanding positions within large companies and industry itself. Yet it should be recognised that the practical implications of co-determination did affect the position of workers on the shop floor, as co-determination gave the unions more room for manoeuvre in dealing with changes in working practices. Concessions in such circumstances of change were no longer confined to wages questions since *Mitbestimmung* allowed organised labour the opportunity to engage in discussions on the social policy of private firms, working time allowances and such matters as job guarantees. Control of the shop floor was now more effectively shared between employers and labour and in consequence the information available to both parties facilitated longer-term investment decisions affecting the mining industry and the region.

The success of the campaign for co-determination has to be understood in the context of the conditions which prevailed in 1951 in the field of domestic and foreign policy, which gave the unions extraordinary bargaining strength for a brief period. Adenauer as Federal Chancellor was ready to offer parity of representation in the heavy industries as the price for the support of the unions in surmounting the difficulties associated with the Schumann Plan, the Korean Crisis, and so on. Within a year, when the Works Constitution Act (Betriebsverfassungsgesetz) was on the Federal political agenda, by which the general scope of *Mitbestimmung* was regulated for industry as a whole, these peculiar conditions no longer obtained and Parliament was able to confine the model of qualified co-determination to the heavy industries. The remainder of the industrial workforce were to comply with a much reduced version of *Mitbestimmung*, leaving only one third of the seats on the board of supervisors to labour nominees. The influence of workers' representatives (or *Betriebsraete*) on the shop floor was nonetheless significant. Even where the principle of parity was not present, therefore, co-determination can still be viewed as the foundation stone of the new order in industrial relations.

The implementation of co-determination in the coal and steel industries

The demand for co-determination 'from the single factory upwards to the highest echelons of economic organisation in order to democratise the economy' was a salient feature of the new constitution of the *Industrieverband Bergbau* (IVB) or Mining Industry Union.[2] There were no profound differences of opinion amongst the mining unions as to how this might be achieved since it was assumed that nationalisation would open the door to full co-determination rights for miners in the coalfield. This view, embodied in the resolution of the Ruhr-Revier-Konferenz, was cited on numerous occasions and in consequence the struggle for co-determination was subsumed beneath the campaign for nationalisation which implicitly promised full rights of participation to industrial labour.[3] In 1947-48, as the realisation of the nationalisation goal receded, the IG-Bergbau mineworkers' union sought to secure at least the basic right of co-determination which was envisaged by the Occupying Powers which were reorganising the

mining industry. Following the reform of the *Deutsche Kohlenbergbauleitung*
(DKBL) or German Central Coal Mining Bureau in the Summer of 1949, this
became a plausible and tangible strategy for organised labour, even if the IG-
Bergbau also endorsed the distinctive model of equal representation which was
propagated by the *Deutsche Gewerkschaftsbund* (DGB) or West German Trade
Union Congress, at this time. The miners' union gave greater priority to the
DKBL's plan of reorganisation (in which it had participated) and as a result the
drive for co-determination at company level did not become a major issue of
concern for the union until 1951.

   This Mining Union (IVB) was known under the title of IG-Bergbau after
1948 and secured representation in the DKBL at two levels. Two of the eight
departmental directors (those dealing with 'workers' issues' and 'housing and
social work') were appointed on the recommendation of the IVB. Secondly, the
IVB was allocated six of the twelve places on the advisory committee, though this
was of much less practical significance. The main thrust of the union's criticism
was directed at the organisation of the DKBL and the composition of the main
committee. The IVB argued that it lacked proper representation at each level. It
is significant that the Union advocated the unified control of the whole coal
industry and acknowledged the progress which the creation of the DKBL
represented, noting that:

> For the first time in the history of German coal mining a central directive
> administrative body for mining in the Rhine and Ruhr areas had been created.
> Production, sale of coal, central purchasing, finance, administration including
> personnel issues, as well as social concerns, were regulated on an industry-wide basis
> by a unified management.[4]

The first priority of the DKBL was to increase the support for, and the efficiency
of, both the hard and brown coal mining sectors, as well as to direct the output,
refining and distribution of the product. These responsibilities steadily returned
to the control of the individual mining companies, particularly following the
currency reforms, whilst the DKBL discovered a new task after 1948: the
reorganisation of the Revier itself.

   In response to this challenge the Union strongly reaffirmed its commitment to
an independent and reasonably centralised mining industry which could forge an
equal partnership with the iron industry. The IGB wanted the continued
existence of the DKBL, reorganised around optimal business units for coal
production in the region and fought strongly for the continuation of a mutual
marketing organisation for the sale of Ruhr coal. With this policy the IGB had
developed a coherent principle but had still to discover a platform on which to
base its contribution to the reorganisation debate in the post-war era. This was to
change in mid-1949, after the unions threatened to withdraw from the advisory
committee which had been set up under the chairmanship of Ernest Hellmut Vits,

president of the Vereinigte Glanzstoff AG, by the Combined Coal Control Group (CCCG). This advisory committee was to prepare the reorganisation of the industry, though the IGB were given limited representation and in response to the withdrawal of the unions, the Allies decided to commission the DKBL, in consultation with the advisory committee, to take overall responsibility for the formulation of a plan of reorganisation. At this point the DKBL itself was reconstituted, against the opposition of Vits, with six equal departments under the new post of General Secretary. The new organisation was led by Dr. Hans Korsch, the justiciary of the DGB and Dr. Theobald Keyser, chief of the mining board and representative of the mining companies. Seven committees of experts began work in September 1949 under the general control of the General Secretary. The new committees were largely chaired by members of the earlier advisory committee though they were now working under the brief that they should meet the 'interests of the workforce as far as was possible'.[5] After a year of consultation the General Secretary of the DKBL presented in September 1950 a German plan for reorganisation which both unions and employers endorsed, providing for industrial co-determination, though the plan was rejected as a result of American opposition. The Americans remained hostile to a centralised coal industry, even if power at the branch or plant level was to be balanced by the representation of organised labour.

The origins of co-determination can be found in the management-labour relations of the iron and steel industry, where practical forms of co-operation developed between management and works councils soon after the fall of the Third Reich. The chairman of the board of the Kloeckner Works, Karl Jarres, agreed with the head of the firm's works council to the representation of the union on the executive and supervisory boards of his company, beginning at the start of 1946. This supervisory board accepted 'the involvement of employees in the rebuilding [of the industry]', whilst rejecting arrangements reached for any individual mine.[6] The announcement by the British 'North German Iron and Steel Control' (NGISC) authority in December 1946 of the break-up and reorganisation of the industry, provided an opening for the introduction of co-determination within the iron and steel sector. The leader of the unified trade union (*Einheitsgewerkschaft*) in the British zone, Hans Boeckler, persuaded the unions to reach a common policy on dismantling the combines and the creation of 'unified companies' which required employee representation on their executive and supervisory boards. Trade unionists received an assurance that this would be implemented at the end of 1946 when the NGISC and the director of the German Trust Administration, Heinrich Dinkelbach (previously director of Vereinigte Stahlwerke), approved this principle. The employers were also anxious to promote such policies to secure labour support in their resistance to the radical dismantling projects of the Allied Forces, leading Karl Jarres, Hermann Reusch and Heinrich Hehemann to lobby both the trade unions and the Head of the Administration Office for the Economy, Viktor Agartz, in support of co-determination. Jarres proposed that the supervisory board of the Kloeckner Works should be reorganised on the basis of equal representation for capital and labour, with the representatives of the employees and of central or local government being given a majority of seats.[7]   The industrialists declared themselves in favour of co-determination, noting that: 'We have no desire to shut ourselves off from the challenges of a new age.' They accepted the participation of employees in the planning and directing, as well as on the supervisory bodies, of the largest concerns in the iron and steel industry.[8]

The introduction of co-determination can therefore be dated from 1 March 1947 when the first four iron works were taken out of the old combine and reformed as independent *Aktiengesellschaften* or joint-stock companies. Personnel directors moved to the executive board room and the representatives of capital and labour sat across the table from each other in the eleven-person supervisory board, chaired by a neutral member of the Trustee Administration. This form of co-determination foreshadowed the model subsequently adopted in the coal and steel industry, and was also adopted in the reorganisation process (which already encompassed twenty-five companies by April 1947), throughout the iron and steel plants. During the Autumn and Winter of 1950 the discussions of a European Community for Coal and Steel (the Schumann Plan) were progressing, when the question of the transfer of responsibility for the break-up of the iron and steel combines from the Allies to the German Government arose. At this point there emerged the first signs of serious conflict between the unions and the Ministry of Trade and Commerce under Erhard. The Minister took the view that until the introduction of the German Works Constitution Act (i.e. Works Council law), only German legal provisions and not the rules established under the British occupation, should be implemented in factories which had been reorganised. Existing German law provided no ruling for equal representation and neither did the new Works Constitution measure, administered by Anton Storch at the Employment Ministry. The Federal Government was hostile to increasing employee representation on supervisory boards beyond a maximum of one third, even in the coal and steel industry.[9] In Spring 1950 the Employment Minister had failed to bring employers and unions to an agreement on co-determination, thereby setting the scene for the industrial conflicts which followed.[10] The IG-Bergbau had not taken part in either the discussions with the employers nor those at the Ministry for Trade and Commerce and during 1950 it fought for the maintenance and extension of co-determination where it had been introduced within the DKBL's framework. The mineworkers expressed solidarity with the steel employees but wished to retain their own concept of industrial reorganisation. This explains the position of the IGB during the disputes between the DGB (German TUC), IG-Metall and the Government, where the IGB combined support for the DGB with a demand for the distribution of property within the mining industry.

In January 1951 the board and advisory committee of IG-Metall resolved to call for strikes if no solution to the co-determination issue could be found by the beginning of February. In response the IGB balloted its members on co-determination and more importantly on the question of reorganisation in the mining industry.[11] In November 1950, 96 per cent of iron and steel workers voted in favour of strike action as an ultimate weapon, whilst 93 per cent of mineworkers subsequently supported industrial action in support of co-determination. The DGB withdrew from its participation in plans for the break-up of the iron and steel industry when the Employment Minister rejected a proposal for reorganisation with co-determination.[12] This forced the Chancellor himself to declare a position on co-determination. Against a background of severe coal and steel shortages as well as internal and external political turbulence, Adenauer needed to avoid a conflict with the unions and particularly with the striking miners and steelworkers. In these conditions it was a *necessity* to resolve the dispute in favour of the unions, but labour's bargaining power was not a *sufficient* reason for a decisive breakthrough on issues of industrial organisation. It was the extraordinary domestic and foreign political conditions at the start of 1951 which explains the outcome of the struggle. The Federal Government had weathered the crisis of 1950-51 and reached a decisive phase of economic growth in the Korean War boom, with the support of the trade unions. By the Spring of 1951 the goodwill of organised labour could no longer be taken for granted. Co-determination in coal and steel was to be the first step in its introduction throughout heavy industry. The unions assumed that their capacity to secure co-determination would prevent the misuse of economic power, which reduced much of the controversy around the nationalisation question. It is important to recognise that neither the abandonment of the ownership question nor the unions' participation in the Schumann Plan discussions for European co-operation on iron and steel production, were preconditions for the successful negotiation of co-determination. Nationalisation plans had foundered in 1947-8 when conditions favoured organised labour and their revival could not be realistically expected from the conservative majority of the first German parliament. The Bundestag's decision in May 1951 to approve the law providing for 'equal representation of employees' on supervisory and executive boards of mining and iron and steel companies was widely regarded as a substantial triumph for the trade unions.

The new legislation followed existing co-determination practices in the dismantled iron and steel concerns and provided for the introduction of similar rules throughout the industry by the end of 1951, though in fact the first case of reorganisation, the 'Gewerkschaft Rheinpreussen', was not achieved until October 1951 and the whole process continued until 1954. Those twenty or so mining firms which employed less than one thousand people, along with the 220 smallest mining and tunnelling enterprises, were not covered by the co-determination agreement, though by early 1954 a total of thirty-three hard coal companies had complied with the legislation, with equal representation on the supervisory board and a personnel director serving on the executive board. Of the sixty-one serving personnel directors in the mining industry, sixteen had come from the works councils, twenty-one from the technical grades, and sixteen from sales staff, with four others having both administrative and practical experience of mining. One director had been a full-time union official. The recruitment pattern of the IGB was to change little for the second generation of personnel directors. One of the most difficult questions which the advocates of co-determination faced was the implementation of these rules in firms controlled by holding companies, since the creation of such entities after the dismantling of the industrial combines effectively excluded them from the terms of the legislation. This loophole was closed by parliament in 1956, though there remained a need to reach voluntary arrangements between unions and managers since the legal requirement to enforce co-determination ceased when a company rearranged its portfolio. The most significant of these agreements, the 'Luedenscheider Abkommen' of 1959, secured the continuation of co-determination in the formerly separate coal and steel subsidiaries of the Hoesch, Ilseder Huette and Kloeckner companies. By the close of the 1950s it was generally agreed that qualified co-determination represented one of the most important innovations in the reorganisation of the Revier during the post-war era. These practices were to undergo substantial change following the formation of the unified Ruhrkohle AG company.

Expansion

During the early 1950s the region's coalminers had shared in the very favourable market conditions seen in Germany, as miners restored their relatively high position in the occupational hierarchy during the 1950-51 energy crisis. In 1950 itself the IGB secured pay rises of 9 per cent and 10 per cent for the mineworkers, placing them briefly at the peak of the pay hierarchy before being overtaken by the iron workers. Face workers continued to command a high position in the wages league and by 1957 their monthly earnings were 61 per cent above the 1950 level, whilst the rest of heavy industry had risen by 42 per cent in this period. Shift times were also cut in 1953 from 8 to 7.5 hours and in 1956 the Ruhr managers and workers accepted a plan to reduce monthly hours in stages, even though the relative pay differentials of the mineworkers were reduced as wages elsewhere climbed at a steady rate.

These boom conditions were abruptly halted in the coal crisis of 1958 and by June 1958 the IG-Bergbau was facing almost a million cancelled shifts, prompting the union to demand an institutional strategy to deal with the situation.[13] The union called for the formation of both an energy council and a coal council as well as the amalgamation of the collieries into a single nationalised venture. Here the IGB was appropriating the principle identified in the early 1950s within the DKBL with the co-operation of the mining firms, though the aim was now to consolidate production units rather than to rejuvenate the German economy. Parallels can be drawn between the two periods of radical demands: as in the chaotic conditions of the immediate post-war period, German mineworkers were again being asked to carry a significant burden during the overproduction and structural crisis of 1958. In calling for a coal council to represent the interests of owners, unions and consumers, the IGB argued that a coherent energy policy was required which involved the nationalisation of the coal mines. The union was convinced that rationalisation would be obstructed by the existing distribution of assets and interests amongst some forty collieries at this period, hence the IGB view that an optimal scale of production and enterprise would only be reached under public ownership.

Attempts to explore these arguments in talks between organised labour and the Federal Chancellor, representatives of the 'hohe Behoerdc' (i.e. 'High Authority'), the Ministry of Trade and Commerce, and with the Association of Ruhr Mineowners, did not prove fruitful even though the Chancellor and the High Authority supported the proposal to appoint an energy council. Opposition from the Ministry of Trade and Commerce and the mineowners ensured that this channel of communication was closed for the foreseeable future. Self-regulation was fatally hindered by the lack of consensus between the parties on the evolution of energy policy, as was apparent when the union called for the preservation of the coalfield's capacity whilst the Ministry advocated a programme of cheap energy to secure economic growth. The Mineowners' Association proved incapable of formulating a coherent response to these conditions for a significant period, with the result that the IGB reverted to its traditional role of defending the interests of its members. It appears paradoxical that in these circumstances the practical relations between capital and labour in the German mining industry remained relatively good, arising out of the mentality of 'social partnership' which had been facilitated by the experience of co-determination during the 1950s. Sections of the Association of Mining Companies (UVR), more particularly the managing Committee and the Committee of Experts functioned along with the personnel directors as mediators between the organised industrialists and the unions. There had also been regular informal meetings between the executives of employers and labour in Essen since the early part of the decade, where relations of trust were built up even if the two sides rarely agreed about the common interests of their industry. There *was* greater consensus on the need to raise the social status of the mineworker, claiming a level of pay and insurance benefits which placed him at the summit of the league table.[14] This gave the two sides a common interest in ensuring that the financial position of the employee should be improved with minimal costs to the mining industry and could best be funded with public money.

The formation of Ruhrkohle AG

It was another looming crisis on the Ruhr which provided the context for the reappraisal of the industrial organisation issue and for the union (now the Mining and Energy Trade Union or IGBE), proposal that the employers should join them on a new commission to be chaired by the Chancellor himself. The purpose of the new commission was to find 'possible solutions for the reorganisation of hard coal mining', though the IGBE claimed for itself the right to participate in the drafting of a plan of rationalisation and to have an equal share 'in its implementation'.[15] In doing so, the union pushed the issue of public ownership into the background and emphasised that the ownership question did not 'need to be given priority treatment'. This move towards an organisational and political pragmatism had been signalled as early as the eighth trade union conference of the IGBE in September 1964, when the deputy chairman, Heinz Kegel, told the delegates that mixed economy solutions were a viable 'interim solution' and that the preservation of the coal stock should be the basis of a common energy policy for Federal Germany.[16] The Government was initially reluctant to seize the initiative on concerted action, convinced that the creation of a tripartite commission would lead (in the words of one commentator) to 'a state super-dirigisme, which would intervene strongly in the distribution of property',[17] the state believing that the present relationship between owners and miners would yield better results 'than a new institutional framework'.[18] The Minister of Trade agreed that the optimal size of undertaking would be a decisive factor in the future of German coalmining, though the Government's primary commitment was to preserving 'the basic order of the private economic sector' and of encouraging the private owners to work towards the 'optimal business size and industry-wide rationalisation'.[19]

The Ministry was to reverse this policy in the Spring of 1966 as the crisis in the industry mounted and the national and regional governments found themselves confronted by a series of demands to resolve the problems of reorganisation. The matter had become an unavoidable political priority.[20] Having failed to secure its goal of 'longer term planned co-operation', the Ministry now wanted to promote a private concentration of the industry under a single management structure to serve as 'an instrument to create, without nationalisation, a plenipotentiary entrepreneurial partner for the Federal Government's coal policy'. Erhard's Government therefore changed the direction of its coal policy on the eve of its fall from office, though the shift arrived too late to avert this political collapse - precipitated in part by the failure of its market economy strategy for the crisis-torn Ruhr.

The deepening crisis also forced the Ruhr industrialists to attempt a more imaginative and flexible response to the structural problems of the region. Senior figures in German industry became involved in the search for solutions to the problem and in doing so helped to undermine the position of the regional

Mineowners' Association (UVR) which was forced to hand over the responsibility for representing the mining industry to the powerful Federal Association of German Industry (BDI). From the outset the UVR had failed to devise a coherent plan of action and even its four-point programme for centralising business decision-making in the industry carried little weight. The business interests organised in the commercial associations and firms in the iron and steel trade were much more effectively mobilised, representing the most significant Ruhr mining interests in their ranks. Germany's steel industry was at this point engaged in a strenuous bid to protect its share of international markets, investing heavily in modernisation of plant and therefore receptive to proposals which would entail selling off its loss-making mines and improve its liquidity in so doing. It is therefore not surprising that all of the suggestions for a unified mining corporation had arisen in the steel industry. The interests of the steel industry can be contrasted with the anxiety of German industry more generally to secure a cheap energy supply whilst maintaining a minimum supply from native mines in line with pricing policy. A proposal for a campaign of self-help across the whole German economy to overcome the coal crisis, which bore fruit in the form of the Action Group of German Hard Coal Mines (ADS), was actually grounded on a tacit agreement that neither the Government nor the mineowners would seek restrictions in the use of heating oil.[21] The ADS funds of 64 million Marks gave the leading associations of German industry not only control over the further industrialisation of the Ruhr but also access to the reorganisation process for the region. The banker Hermann J. Abs (of Deutsche Bank AG), the president of the BDI, Fritz Berg, and the president of the German Trade and Industry Congress, Ernst Schneider, joined with leading steel industrialists (Henle, Sohl, Funcke and Kemper) to create the 'entrepreneurial partner' envisaged by the Erhard Government in its dying days. The IGBE union responded to this clear change in the political climate by reaffirming their demand for a unitary company.

This new departure in coalmining policy was co-ordinated and underwritten by the government of the Grand Coalition between the Christian Democrats (CDU) and the Social Democrats (SPD) which had taken over from the CDU-Liberal coalition of Erhard. The new Minister of Trade, Karl Schiller, was an SPD politician who conceived of economic policy-making as a process of corporatist consultation where the major organised interests would agree guidelines for the Keynesian management of the economy. This principle of involving the interested parties in the formulation and implementation of economic policy as a deliberate strategy for social accommodation is also apparent in such measures as the 'Stability Law' of 1967, though the practice of 'Concerted Action' should be understood as an elaboration of the corporate market economy model developed in the Republic during the early 1950s rather than a radical innovation in corporatist management of Germany's economy.[22] In March 1967 the first in a series of 'Concerted Action' meetings for the coal industry took place under Schiller's chairmanship in Bonn, bringing together the representatives of the coalowners' associations, the IGBE union, and the governments of North Rhine Westphalia and Saarland along with various economic institutions. In May the Federal Cabinet passed the draft law for the adaptation of the coal industry and the mining districts, granting the German state far-reaching powers and threatening the mining firms with a cessation of subsidies as a lever to force the conflicting parties to reach a consensus.

The initiative was again seized by the so-called Rhine Steel Guild of Steelmakers, who needed a stabilisation of the coal industry, along with representatives of the large banks and other business groups. The Steel Guild set up a committee structure, including a co-determination committee on which the chair of the IGBE union sat, whilst the union also discussed the question of Ruhr rationalisation with the Bonn Government. A decisive breakthrough which led to the formation of the Ruhrkohle AG occurred when it was resolved to appoint a 'personnel and social concerns manager' at the works level in the proposed unitary company. The PS-Manager was subordinate to the works director but superior to all other staff grades and was appointed by the company board on the nomination of the personnel director, who in turn enjoyed the confidence of the trade union. In this way a new political institution was created around the function of co-determination in the iron and steel industry. Previously the IGBE held 150 positions on the supervisory and executive boards of the mining companies by virtue of the co-determination rule. Unless the fifty-two works units of the new unified company were brought under the terms of the iron and steel co-determination agreement, the representation of employees on the supervisory and executive boards of the mining concerns would have been cut to a third of the previous level. IGBE was not merely anxious to retain its proportion of representation on the boards but was also conscious of the increased influence of these figures as a result of the concentration process, as well as their growing distance from the co-determination concerns of the shop floor. The PS Manager was supposedly filling a gap in the line of communication which had opened as a result of the very business structure which the union had itself advocated.

The existence of briefly favourable economic conditions during October 1968, as sales rose and stockpiles of coal fell, meant that the mining companies found it difficult to reach agreement on the Rhine Steel Plan. Representatives from twenty-two companies who had already decided in principle to fuse together finally agreed to the formation of a unified enterprise in early November. They also rejected the IGBE's demand for equal representation on both the supervisory and executive boards, and nineteen of the original companies (responsible for 73 per cent of Ruhr output) joined the new Ruhrkohle AG. A six-member executive was appointed under the chairmanship of Hans Helmut Kuhnke, who had a Kloeckner pedigree, and the staff pattern followed the established lines familiar to the iron and steel industry. The Personnel Director, Heinz Kegel, was solely the nominee of the IGBE and whilst three other Board members were recruited from the Revier, the Finance Director (Hubert Gruenewald) was new to the region, having worked previously in the finance department of the city of Frankfurt and at the Hesse Ministry of Finance. Grunewald's appointment was suggested by the IGBE members, Arendt, Vetter and van Berk, sat across the table from Funcke, Kemper and Sohl on the supervisory board.

The creation of the Ruhrkohle AG confronted the IGBE union with an unfamiliar situation. The union had advocated the unified company and was now well represented in its management and executive structures, as the IGBE itself proudly boasted when claiming credit for the reconstruction of the industry.[23] Having sponsored the new enterprise, the union was now closely associated with the performance of the business and in a firm where labour costs amounted to almost half the turnover, there was obvious scope for a conflict of interests between the health of the firm and the interests of its employees. In the first year of the firm's operation the union sought to clarify its relationship to the business, acknowledging that the Ruhrkohle AG was 'certainly a result of a political initiative of the IG-Bergbau und Energie, but is not an enterprise of the IG-Bergbau und Energie'. The union argued that as a private company the enterprise inevitably existed 'in a relationship of tension' with union interests.[24] Such statements could not avoid the reality that the representatives of the labour force were now directly involved in commercial decisions affecting the whole enterprise. These tensions have to be understood in terms of a specific reformation of German industrial capitalism in the post-war period. The merging of twenty-five mining firms had been encouraged by the State and by the trade unions but the real context for the reconstruction of the Ruhr coal industry was the awareness of the social and regional costs of decline. Never before had a whole section of German industry, and its regional base, been threatened with rapid and catastrophic collapse. The economic, social and political consequences of such disintegration were difficult to assess. The solution reached was one which allowed for an ordered process of adaptation and employment decline in a region where every second job in the Ruhr had been located in the coal and steel industry during the 1960s and where some towns were wholly dependent on coalworking. The achievement of the 1967 settlement was to spare a region, rich in cultural traditions and political sensibilities as well as resources, from sliding into conditions of economic and political crisis which bordered on a state of emergency.

Conclusions

The qualified co-determination which eventually emerged in the coal and steel industry was not the achievement which the labour unions originally contemplated. The IGB had initially sought co-determination in industry under the terms of the arrangements made by the German Coal Mining Bureau (DKBL) from mid-1949. In the early days the coal miners had offered only tepid support for the steelworkers in their struggles for co-determination at company level, and then only to offer solidarity with the German DGB. In the event, co-determination became a significant substitute for the failed nationalisation plans of the union under the terms outlined by the DKBL. During the 1950s, co-determination appears to have assisted the successful transfer of new technology and rising productivity in conditions of coal shortages which characterised the post-war years. Co-determination enabled the industry to find a common voice in its dealings with the federal government and with the senior reaches of German business. The coal crisis of 1958 was to expose the strains and limitations of the co-determination machinery as different parties struggled to find a common solution to the problems of changing market demand for energy and employment. The crisis promoted new forms of interest inter-mediation which went far beyond the earlier scope of co-determination and which were rooted in older traditions of corporatist, national interest policy-formation.

Overcoming the coal crisis and the subsequent formation of the Ruhrkohle AG in 1968 was the result of the intervention of wider non-coal German business interests, which formed an unspoken coalition with the Government and the trade unions. This business nexus was dominated by the big banks and was concerned to prevent the coal mining industry from damaging the development of a thriving national economy. With the emergence of the new unified company in coalmining, the character of co-determination was altered as the miners' union gained greater power and influence. The inevitable consequence of this engagement with a new business venture was that the union also shared responsibility for the company's economic success. The union became enmeshed in the process of planned decline which has marked the history of the Ruhrkohle AG since its foundation.

At the end of the 1960s co-determination in its most substantial form was faced with a challenge which went far beyond the difficulties of German coal and steel. At stake were the interests of the national economy as the twin goals of social stability and fast economic growth were threatened. The crisis provoked a response of 'concerted action' from the major interests, though the resolution of the problems facing German production and society derived from the spirit of co-determination which had impressed itself on the different groups. For a few years the parity version of co-determination became, under the leadership of the Social Democrats, a general model of industrial relations in the Federal Republic. Only in the mid-1970s did it become apparent that the alignment of political forces in West Germany precluded a further expansion of parity co-determination. In these specific circumstances *paritatische Mitbestimmung* was confined to the peculiar conditions of German heavy industries.

Notes

1. See W. Abelshauser, *Der Ruhrkohlenbergbau seit 1945. Wiederaufbau, Krise, Anpassung* (1984) Munich.
2. Minutes of first General Meeting, p139.
3. Decision of the Ruhr-Rhine-Conference of the IVB, 1 March 1947 in Bochum, printed in G. Berger, *Die Sozialisierung der Bergbauwirtschaft* (1947) Bochum, p22.
4. The task of the DKBL in Essen and its significance for the reorganisation of German hard coal mining was discussed in a paper by Dr. A. Menstel at the second meeting of the IGB Committee 'Neuordnung der deutschen Bergbauwirtschaft' on 9 May 1963 in Bochum. Archives of IGBE Central Office, file 'Neuordnung'.
5. *Die Bergbauindustrie*, publication of the IGB, 15 September 1949.
6. *Montanmitbestimmung: Dokumente ihrer Entstehung*, edited by J. Peters (1979) Cologne, p16.
7. Letter 18 January 1947 printed in ibidem, Dokument 15, p79f.
8. Letter 21 January 1947 to the leader of the VAW, printed in ibidem, Dokument 17, p85.
9. Compare Deutscher Bundestag 1. Wahlperiode, circular 1546, 31 October 1950.
10. Compare H. Thum, *Mitbestimmung in der Montanindustrie. Der Mythos vom Sieg der Gewerkschaften* (1982) Stuttgart, p40.
11. See M. Martiny and H.J. Schneider (eds.), *Deutsche Energiepolitik seit 1945* (1981) Cologne, p84.
12. Information and news service of Bundespressestelle des DGB, II (1951) p32ff. Archives of the Board of the DGB.
13. H. Gutermuth, 'Bergbauwirtschaftspolitik heute und morgen', Seminar paper at the Sixth General Meeting of the IGB on 8-13 June 1958 in Munich. Printed in Martiny and Schneider, *Energiepolitik*, Dok. 29, p125.
14. Note in the minutes of Board Meeting of UVR and IGBE, 15 February 1965, in Kaiserhof, Essen, enclosure to TOP2: Regelung der Beziehungen zwischen UVR und IGBE, Archive of Board of the IGBE, file 'UVR'.
15. Enclosure to letter of 8 June 1965: Die Stellungnahme der Industriegewerkschaft Bergbau und Energie zur Neuordnung des Steinkohlenbergbaus, Bochum, 8 June 1965. Archives of IGBE Board, file 'BMWi'.
16. H. Kegel, 'Die wirschaftlichen Probleme des Bergbaus und ihre Bedeutung fuer die Arbeitnehmer', Lecture at the eight conference of IGBE 13-18 September 1964 in Wiesbaden Minutes Bochum 1965, p98.
17. Speaker of Federal Government quoted in *Westdeutsche Allgemeine Zeitung* Nr.132, 9 June 1965.
18. Permanent Secretary, Dr. Neff (BMWi) to board of IGBE, 19 July 1965, Archives of IGBE board, file 'BMWi'.
19. Neff (BMWi) to board of IGBE, 1 July 1965.
20. Record of Permanent Secretary Dr. Neef regarding the present situation in hard coal mining, Bonn, 21 November 1966. Archives of IGBE Board, file 'BMWi'.
21. Permanent Secretary, Dr. Neef to representatives of Mining Associations of the Ruhr, Aachen and Saar. Observations about the briefing in the Federal Ministry for Trade and Commerce, 21 January 1967, Archives of the IGBE Board, file 'BMWi'.
22. See W. Abelshauser, 'The first post-Liberal Nation: stages in the development of modern corporatism in Germany', *European History Quarterly* 14, 3 (July 1984), pp285-318.
23. Paper of the Board of IGBE, detailing its position on the unified company, Bochum 18 April 1969, Archives of the IGBE Board, file 'Einheitsgesellschaft'.
24. 'Einheit', 15 November 1969.

7. Production, politics and technological development: British coal mining in the twentieth century

Jonathan and Ruth Winterton

Introduction

For over two centuries the coal industry provided the energy for Britain's industrial development. Coal mining has also been the setting of major labour confrontations against a continual background of frequent local conflicts. The industry was once vast, employing over one million miners, and, in the view of the Samuel Commission exhibited such diversity as to make generalisation impossible.[1] Its strategic significance and traditions of conflict partly explain why the coal industry has so frequently been a subject of inquiry.[2] During the twentieth century, coal mining methods changed from those which had remained virtually unaltered since Roman times to modern automated production, making the British coal industry the most technologically-advanced in the world. Each transformation of work (for there were several stages in this process) was closely bound up with the politics of production at the coal face. This essay offers an historical review of technological developments in coal mining and analyses the relationship between technology and the social relations of production.

Different phases of coal-face work in British deep mining may be distinguished by considering three dimensions. First, there is the *material technical base,* the physical instruments of labour, or hardware, employed. Secondly, there is the *technique of production,* the way in which work is undertaken or particular tasks carried out. These two dimensions can be thought of as the constituents of 'technology'. Thirdly, there is *work organisation*, a collective term for social aspects such as the division of labour, skill and autonomy. At the point of production these three dimensions, each of which constrains the others, allow a simple typology of coal-face work to be developed.

It is self evident that contexts have a significant influence on the labour process. The *physical context*, largely a function of variations in the *subject of labour* (depth, thickness, geology and quality of the coal measures), constrains the technology and work organisation adopted, and has been one explanatory factor for spatial differences in the politics of the coalfields.[3] The *power context*, in terms of the balance of power between labour and management (influenced by economic, political and social factors) has had a major impact on strategies of management and labour at the point of production. While the struggle for control over the labour process has been central to developments in technology and work organisation, so technological and social transformations of work have affected the politics of workplace control.

It is conventional wisdom that coal-face work in Britain passed through four phases: hand-getting; mechanised mining; power-loading; and advanced technology mining.[4] However, this is an over-simplification because both hand-getting and mechanised mining could employ two alternative techniques of production: shortwall mining, working a number of small areas of coal; or longwall mining, getting coal from the entire length of a coal face, and these different techniques profoundly influenced the politics of production. There were several different routes between the six phases of the labour process at the coal face, distinguished in Figure 7.1.[5] While hand-getting generally gave way to mechanised mining and shortwall mining was replaced by longwall, the process of development was uneven and not unidirectional. New collieries would generally adopt the most modern mining practices, but distinctions between coalfields, companies and collieries, created variations within each of the phases of the coal-face labour process as a result of different geological conditions and historical traditions. It is therefore impossible to offer a precise periodisation of each phase for the whole industry, although it is necessary to identify the periods with which each was associated in order to relate the labour process to broader developments in the political economy of the coal industry.

Hand-got shortwall mining (HGSW) was the earliest method, which has survived in some small mines to the present day, and which was dominant at least until 1910. Although coal cutting machines were developed in the late nineteenth century, machine-cut shortwall mining (MCSW) was only significant during the period 1890-1920 and never became a dominant method. Hand-got longwall mining (HGLW) began as early as 1880 and persisted up to nationalisation in some collieries, being the dominant method during the period 1910-39. Machine-cut longwall mining (MCLW) may have developed before the turn of the century, was still being practised in Yorkshire as late as the 1970s, and was the dominant method from 1939 to 1961. Powerloading machinery was introduced in 1947 and especially after 1957, forming the dominant method during the period 1961-84. Advanced technology mining, a sophistication of powerloading, was introduced from 1978 and since 1985 has been the dominant method. Given these difficulties of periodisation, each phase of coal-face work is considered below and related to the political economy and politics of production associated with its period of dominance.

Figure 7.1 Phases of the Labour Process at the Coal Face

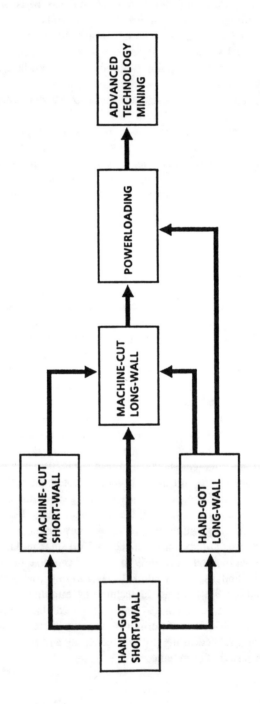

Source: J. Winterton, 'Social and technological characteristics of coal-face work' *Human Relations* 47 (1994), 1.

Hand-got shortwall mining

The earliest deep mining employed a variety of HGSW methods known variously as pillar and stall, bord and pillar or room and pillar. A parallel series of narrow headings driven into the seam would be connected by perpendicular cross-headings, removing about 25 per cent of the coal and leaving panels of coal fifty to one hundred metres square. Then roads or bords would be driven from the cross headings, opening up stalls or rooms, typically ten metres wide and ten metres apart, to work the coal from the pillars, leaving some intact for safety reasons and to control subsidence. Two operations were involved: colliers got the coal at the face, and trammers or putters dealt with haulage. The coal was customarily worked by a hewer and his mate, who would undercut the coal with a pick, supporting the face with sprags (props set at an angle to the face). The supports were then removed and the coal was hacked from the face with a pick, broken away using wedges, or blasted down with explosives, depending on the nature of the seam. The loosened coal would then be shovelled by the colliers into tubs pushed to the working place by trammers.

Sets of between two and four colliers and trammers worked together, building stone packs to support the gob (the waste area previously worked) when they had advanced a particular distance. Each miner needed to possess all face skills and the division of labour was minimal: trammers would normally become colliers when opportunities arose to move to the face. Work proceeded continuously, but variations in seam conditions prevented any fixed time schedule for the cycle of operations so each shift continued where the previous shift had left off. There was no division of labour between miner and machine under HGSW so the manual skills required were extensive. In addition to being able to wield a pick in a confined space, colliers also needed to possess mental skills in order to work the coal safely. Opportunities for supervision were limited by the remoteness of working places, but miners also rejected the supervision of the overman, as the essay by Melling below indicates.[6]

Miners were undoubtedly skilled and enjoyed considerable control over the labour process, but not as a result of craft control. The detailed, tacit knowledge of miners at work in their respective rooms was less holistic than the knowledge of mine managers, who were required by statute to hold a certificate in mining engineering, and were familiar with conditions in all the seams worked by a colliery. It was the relative *invisibility* of miners, rather than the mysteries of the craft, which maintained their job control. Moreover, control over the labour process was not necessarily replicated in the labour market, where the 'independent colliers' of one district coexisted alongside the 'degraded slaves' of another.[7]

Given the inability to exert direct control, managers introduced indirect control in the form of payment by results. Colliers were paid according to the tonnage of coal filled, and contracts usually stipulated that deductions would be made for dirt or slack (fine coal, unsuitable for burning). Other work was either incorporated in the contract or paid for explicitly in the form of supplementary allowances. Miners argued that they had the right to determine their own pace of work because they were only paid for what they did, and the resultant 'internalised supervision' was described as *responsible autonomy* by Trist and Bamforth in their seminal study of coalface work in the early years of nationalisation.[8]   In Durham, work teams (or 'marra' groups) were formed by the system of 'cavilling', or mutual self-selection, and members were paid according to group performance,[9] but this practice was not widespread outside of the Durham coalfield.[10]   Moreover, payment by results still created divisions between trammers and colliers in the North East,[11] just as it did in Lancashire,[12] and South Yorkshire[13] where cavilling was absent.

Variations in the method of payment influenced the forms and levels of internal and external supervision as well as work organisation. In the negotiation of Price Lists, management used power over the *whole* process of production, and since different seams in the same colliery had separate Price Lists, the miners were inhibited in generalising issues to challenge piecework prices or methods of work beyond a particular seam. The relative invisibility of the miners' work therefore both facilitated autonomy and prompted management to use payment by results to combat the physical difficulties of supervision. The indirect control of payment systems was inherently divisive but the development of effective resistance by the miners reinforced their cohesion. There was, in other words, a *dialectical* process in which the miners experienced contradictory pressures towards solidarity and sectionalism, and towards both adversity and responsibility, a situation comparable with Burawoy's notion of consent.[14]

The initial expansion of the coal industry was achieved through increasing the numbers employed as the owners maintained profits through the pursuit of absolute surplus value. Profits were largely determined by wages and prices; the sliding scale was used to link wages to prices so that if prices fell surplus value could be maintained. To offset the effect of diminishing returns (a result of working out the best seams and the increased haulage as workings became more remote from the pit bottom), employers extended hours and cut wages. The passage of the Coal Mines Regulation Act in 1908 and its implementation of a maximum shift length of 8 hours from 1910 constrained mine owners from lengthening the working day, while the minimum wage established in 1912 made wage cuts more difficult. These developments were followed by the First World War, which led to the further loss of export markets and an acute manpower shortage. The Coal Mining Organisation Committee was established to sustain output, and had the effect of encouraging the exploitation of easily-won coal and the neglect of development work which damaged the infrastructure of the industry.[15]

Machine-cut shortwall mining

The first coal-cutting machine was manufactured around 1780 and several different models were developed later,[16] including disc cutters, bar cutters and percussion cutters, which were the most manoeuvrable. Machine holing, where such machines were introduced to existing faces, never became widespread in Britain; by 1913 only 8 per cent of coal was machine cut in Britain, and part of that was from longwall faces.[17] Although miners were occasionally hostile to the introduction of coal-cutting machines,[18] more protracted stoppages concerned *payment* for machine-holed coal,[19] not the new technology per se. The employers' reluctance to adopt machine mining was more significant than the miners' resistance.[20] The machines were difficult to manoeuvre in confined working places and had to be constantly moved to cut a short face of coal. The Reid Committee believed that, compared with HGSW, mechanised pillar and stall working demanded higher skills, which the employers regarded as a disadvantage.[21] Capital costs per ton of output were also high because each working place needed its own machine, and such capital expenditure was impossible for the proliferation of small collieries operating beyond their peak efficiency and unwarranted given the abundance of cheap labour which sustained them. While MCSW mining was relatively unimportant in Britain, the evidence from America, where it was the predominant form of mining in very thick, shallow seams suggests that despite a diminution in manual skills,[22] task discretion and autonomy increased.[23] As with HGSW, autonomy under MCSW was a function of the relative invisibility of miners in shortwall working places and the solidaristic character of the primary work group.

Hand-got longwall mining

Longwall mining had to be adopted in Britain as deeper seams were accessed and intensified pressure from the overlying strata made it impossible to work a shortwall face. The longwall technique was widespread in Britain before mechanised mining, although its adoption inevitably facilitated mechanisation. As mines were sunk deeper, longwall techniques were adopted without any change in the material technical base or even work organisation. Management recognised the advantages of the longwall technique and introduced changes in work organisation affecting firstly the miners' autonomy and later their skills, changes which themselves led to new developments in the material technical base. At first HGLW maintained the work organisation associated with HGSW, and along a face of 200 metres, separate sets of colliers worked their individual places. However, the altered physical layout made the miners' work more visible to management and opened it up to greater supervision. Under shortwall mining management faced the problems of exerting control over miners in many separate workplaces hundreds of metres underground and a long distance from the pit bottom. In HGLW the miners were still in separate work groups but in one workplace, which was more accessible to management because longwall mining effectively removed the walls of the colliers' rooms. Mining engineers noted that with HGLW there is 'easier supervision of workmen and a greater number of men can be set to work in a given length of face than in bord and pillar stalls'.[24] Conditions became more uniform along the longwall face, allowing managers to transfer colliers between workplaces more easily. However, colliers also found it easier to make comparisons among themselves along a face, between different faces and seams within a colliery and between different pits working the same seam, which created opportunities for further cohesion in workplace bargaining.

The colliers were more easily supervised under HGLW but their skills were intact and inroads into their autonomy were limited to the extent that they retained discretion over task elements. The move to HGLW, however, made possible a change in work organisation which entailed a new division of labour. Miners were divided into holers (the most skilled), who undercut the coal, getters (whose work was more akin to that of the hewers), and fillers, who loaded the coal into tubs. Mining manuals from around the turn of the century recommended division of labour and specialisation at the coal face, so that miners would become 'proficient in their respective classes of work and therefore do it well and cheaply'.[25] The division of labour reduced the breadth of each individual's skill, eroded job autonomy and facilitated more close direction and supervision of work. Although HGLW was more productive and profitable, it required more packing and ripping than in HGSW. If faces were not worked for any length of time, the pressure on workings would damage mine roads, but if the coal was mined continuously there was an uplift in the seam which made successive coal-getting from the face easier. Shift working, introduced to gain the geological advantages of continuous mining, was easier under longwall mining because working conditions were more uniform, enabling more than one set of miners to work in the same place. Irrespective of mechanisation, therefore, longwall mining facilitated increased supervision, division of labour and the introduction of shift work. Compared with shortwall mining, HGLW represented a spatial concentration and temporal intensification of work at the coal face. The intensification of face work demanded improvements 'outbye' to cope with increased production, while its spatial concentration made such improvements in haulage possible. Conveyors were impractical under shortwall mining, but their use at the face under HGLW, an apparently small change in the material technical base, had a dramatic effect in association with other innovations in work organisation and proved the key to effective face mechanisation.

Work intensification arose from the end of the post-war coal boom, when the Government announced its intention to decontrol the industry in 1921 after holding private negotiations with the coal owners.[26] The owners immediately introduced drastic wage cuts and lack of support for the miners led to the disastrous National Coal Wages Agreement of July 1921 which made coal mining one of the worst paid trades and increased the owners' profits. By 1924 trade revived, with output and exports the highest they had been for a decade, and the miners successfully pressed for increased wages. The Buckmaster Court of Enquiry ruled that minimum wages should be increased, but in June 1925, when the export market had fallen by 18 million tons, the coal owners gave notice to terminate the 1924 agreement, effecting immediate wage cuts. The Government granted a subsidy to maintain wages at the 1924 level until 1926 to avert an immediate crisis, while the Samuel Commission was established to investigate the industry's economic situation.   The Samuel Commission recommended that the subsidy should come to an end and that there should be immediate wage cuts. The owners reduced wages and obtained Government approval to re-introduce underground shifts of 8 hours under the Coal Mines Act 1926, passed while the lockout was still in progress. The miners' defeat demonstrated the change in the balance of power between labour and capital, but also resolved a division within capital in favour of the faction which opposed intervention to reorganise the industry.

Machine-cut longwall mining

Mechanised longwall mining entailed a material technical base of coal cutting machines and face conveyors, accompanied by a rigid work organization and an extreme division of labour involving a cycle of operations spread over three shifts. On the *preparation shift* cuttermen used coal cutters along the entire length of the face to make an undercut, which was cleared out by gummers who followed the machine. Borers drilled holes into which explosives were placed at intervals along the face, and the coal was shot off the face by shotfirers. On the *coaling shift*, the loosened coal was filled onto the conveyor by fillers, who were required to shovel however much coal had been loosened, to avoid delaying work on the following shift.   On the *repair shift*, conveyormen dismantled the conveyor, and moved it forwards and re-assembled it on the new face line. Packers built stone packs to absorb the shock and protect the headings when the roof was collapsed, set new props to support the new working area and removed the old supports to collapse the previous working area into the gob. Rippers removed the rock at the junction of the gates to the face in order to maintain the height of the headings. The cycle then recommenced with the preparation shift. Under MCLW mining the coal cutters remained on the face and were more heavily utilised, so capital costs per ton were lower than under MCSW. Larger, more powerful chainsaw machines were also developed for the longer runs of coal cutting under MCLW.   The rate of mechanisation differed between coalfields, so coal cutters were used to access thin seams in Scotland (see Melling's essay),[29] but were seldom employed in the faulted coal of South Wales.[30]   In general, however, even with the widespread move to longwall mining, mechanisation proceeded slowly. The owners of a large number of small, labour-intensive collieries responded to unstable market conditions for coal by varying wages, working hours or the numbers employed, and would not invest in mechanisation when successful in adjusting labour costs. Mining journals and manuals advised managers to introduce coal cutters into longwall mining only if coal could be produced more cheaply than with hand-got methods.[31]

Labour shortages and fuel demands of the first world war, along with the Coal Mines Regulation Act of 1908 and the Coal Mines Act 1919, which limited the length of the working day, had done little to stimulate mechanization and by 1925 only 20 per cent of output came from mechanised faces. The miners' defeat in the 1926 lockout and the passage of the Coal Mines Act 1926 allowed coal owners to continue primitive forms of production based on the pursuit of absolute surplus value.[32]   It was the Coal Mines Act 1931, which restricted hours indefinitely to seven and a half hours, which induced employers to introduce new methods to raise relative surplus value, and by 1938 mechanised faces were producing 59 per cent of British coal.[33]   Increased mechanised output between the wars was a consequence of intensifying the use of existing cutting machines, principally through employing more conveyors. The number of face conveyors increased three-fold, from 2,078 in 1927 to 5,859 in 1939,[34]   while the total number of conveyors increased from 2,185 in 1927 to 7,826 in 1938,[35] so the number of *tail-gate* conveyors increased by a factor of eighteen.   Tail-gate conveyors allowed more coal to be cleared from the face, facilitating further intensification of face work, 'speeding up' as Page Arnot described it.[36]

Face work was intensified, deskilled and dehumanised under MCLW. Ebby Edwards, President of the Miners' Federation of Great Britain, told the 1931 Conference 'it is not a process adapted to meet the human needs of the workers'.[37] The miner 'was still involved in considerable effort with little scope for the exercise of the skill he had acquired through the old system',[38] and 'the machine eliminated the most skilled part of the work ... the holing or undercutting of the coal'.[39] The extreme division of labour made it difficult for one worker to substitute for another on the same shift, and work left from one shift was not completed by the next. As tasks became more specialised, they required only a fraction of the old hewer's skills. The social effects of MCLW mining became manifest in accident rates, particularly from roof falls,[40] and in deteriorating health, especially coal dust pneumoconiosis, which HM Inspectorate of Mines linked to mechanisation.[41] In Scotland, where 60 per cent of coal came from mechanised faces by 1928, there was a fourfold increase among underground workers in nystagmus, an eye disease attributed to poor luminosity and stress,[42] while Halliday discovered an epidemic of stress-related illness among Scottish miners, and noted the prevalence of stress-related illness among skilled miners and their wives.[43] Unemployment inevitably contributed to ill health in mining communities; in 1932 unemployment among mineworkers reached 42 per cent nationally, while some localities in Scotland, Durham and South Wales recorded levels of 66 per cent. However, the differential impact upon the households of *skilled* miners suggests that changes in the labour process were also implicated in the patterns of ill health.

Economic recovery, followed by the Second World War, altered the balance of power between labour and capital. In addition to internal, individual responses in the form of stress-related illness, miners began to exhibit external and collective responses to the negative social effects of the labour process under MCLW mining. Under wartime control, but particularly after nationalisation in 1947, absenteeism became endemic to the British coal industry,[44] and unofficial strikes were similarly widespread,[45] especially on the coaling shift, where fillers bargained allowances from management to compensate for failure to complete the task under adverse conditions.[46]

The nationalised era and power loading

Lack of capital investment by the coal owners during the inter-war years was exacerbated by the exigencies of war-time control. When the National Coal Board (NCB, renamed British Coal in 1987) was established as a public enterprise in 1947, it was charged with the duties of producing and supplying coal and with securing the efficient development of the coal mining industry. The first decade of nationalisation was marked by attempts to increase coal supply to fuel post-war reconstruction as well as measures to reduce coal demand by substituting alternative fuels. A vital part of the strategy to raise the industry's efficiency depended upon securing the commitment and co-operation of the workforce. The Morrisonian model of nationalisation involved neither democratic control nor worker involvement, but was founded upon corporatism, where collaboration between state, employer and union blurred their distinct economic interests. The resultant pluralist structures, highly-regulated institutional arrangements for collective bargaining and conciliation which co-existed with consultative arrangements in which managerial unitary philosophy was dominant, continued with only minor modifications until the 1984-85 strike.[47]

In September 1944 the Ministry of Fuel and Power had appointed a Technical Advisory Committee under Charles Reid to advise on technical changes to raise the efficiency of the coal industry. Productivity under MCLW mining was constrained by hand filling and the discontinuities of the three-shifts system. The Reid Committee advocated the adoption of power-loading machines, like those then used in Continental Europe, which cut and loaded the coal, eliminating hand filling and allowing continuous mining.[48] The technical base of power loading comprised a shearer, which traversed the coal face, breaking away the coal with a series of picks ranged round a rotating drum, and an armoured flexible conveyor (AFC), which could be advanced with the face line without being dismantled.   Hydraulic pit props offered more stable roof support in the working environment subject to vibration from power loading machinery, and were later modified to ram over the conveyor. The Anderton Shearer Loader (ASL), developed with the involvement of face workers and craftsmen, was available from 1957,[49] and the success of power loading was largely due to its rapid adoption in preference to other machines like the Meco Moore, Trepanner and Huwood Slicer.[50]

The technique of mining under power loading involves continuous operations: as the shearer traverses the coal face, the conveyor is pushed over towards the face behind the machine and the supports are advanced to the position formerly occupied by the conveyor. In this way, the face line advances just behind the shearer, allowing the machine to be reversed for the next cut when it has reached the gate at the end of the face. Ripping operations are similar to under MCLW, but are continuous. The same coal-winning techniques are employed in reverse with retreat mining, where the face is established at the extreme end of the panel of coal and worked back towards the roadway. On a retreat face, however, all the development work of the headings is completed before the face is established. Fine, O'Donnell and Prevezer argued that power loading 'did not by itself radically transform conditions of control over the labour process',[51] while Douglass noted that power loading led to increased supervision.[52]   However, the labour process was clearly different under power loading because instead of an extreme division of labour, each shift now performed the same tasks, and while workers were specialised as craftsmen, machine men, rippers, and so on, they were interdependent members of a *team*, so regained some of the former social cohesion characteristic of face workers under HGSW. Power loading eliminated the skills of undercutting but demanded new skills of faceworkers and craftsmen; manual skills associated with guiding the shearer along the face and knowledge-based skills akin to those of the hewers under hand getting. Moreover, this applied to face workers on *every* shift. Craft workers increased as a proportion of the number employed, and needed specialist skills to install and maintain the power loading machinery. Power loading had a direct and profound effect on work organisation: it reunified tasks, required new skills, and returned a degree of autonomy to face teams. The reskilling of face work and craft work made management control over the labour process more difficult, and since the rate of production on one shift was independent of the work of the previous shift, power loading was conducive to workers regaining control over the pace of work and timing of natural breaks.

The restoration of miners' control over the labour process was in marked contrast to their position in the labour market. The introduction of power loading, from 1957 to 1970, coincided with a steady fall in demand for labour. Coal consumption was reduced by 22 per cent, largely as a result of increased oil burning in electricity generation, while technological improvements and rationalisation raised productivity by 77 per cent over the same period. From the time when the NCB began to plan for permanent reductions in output, from the *Revised Plan for Coal 1959*, the corporatist approach came under increasing strain. By the mid 1970s, almost half a million jobs, two thirds of the total, had disappeared. These labour market changes altered the balance of power in favour of management, who attempted to introduce new working arrangements to counteract the miners' increased control over the labour process.

Under power loading, indirect control via piecework was inappropriate because output was no longer dependent upon physical effort, and because management wished to avoid the disruption associated with fragmented bargaining at the coal face. From 1948, when the earliest power-loading machines were introduced, divisional power loading agreements were negotiated.[53] Most divisional agreements introduced measured daywork, although some retained an element of payment by results. The agreement negotiated in 1966, which is normally referred to as the National Power Loading Agreement (NPLA),[54] introduced standard shift rates in place of piece rates for all workers on power-loaded faces, with task norms and manning levels to be established by method study at pit level.[55] To combat the reskilling associated with power loading, the NCB sought to make workers more interchangeable under the NPLA, replacing specific jobs, such as chockman or ripper, with 'taskworker'.[56] The objective of increasing flexibility was a conscious attempt by the NCB to avoid the disruption of production caused by the division of labour under MCLW mining. While flexibility supported the reunification of face work, it was accompanied by more direct instruction by management, effectively separating conception and execution and reducing workers' discretion. Face production plans under the NPLA detailed management responsibility to 'check the exact time the men arrive at and leave the face ... [and] check the actual speed of the machine against the planned speed'.[57] The greater emphasis on direct control represented an effort to distinguish between workers restricting output and diverse geological and operational problems, in order to raise actual output closer to the potential output of the machines. A higher proportion of underground officials was employed to increase supervision and the NCB reported that 'intensive efforts continued at collieries to extend the running times of power loading machines, particularly by the use of method study techniques and by the appointment of officials at each colliery as delay shooters'.[58]

The product- and labour-market changes which reduced the miners' bargaining power were institutionalised in power loading agreements, which made inroads into the miners' control over the labour process and removed opportunities for fragmented bargaining over pay. Although miners' relative earnings declined substantially,[59] their control over work was evident both in autonomy at the point of production and in the power retained by local NUM branches over pit issues.[60] With wages no longer dependent upon output, miners were able to use their control over work to restrict output in response to declining relative earnings, even in the face of increased supervision. In Yorkshire, for example, the achievement of task norms under the NPLA brought earnings only marginally above the Comprehensive Power Loading Agreement fallback rate, so face workers were content to economise on effort in difficult conditions and accept fall-back rates.[61] The removal of piece work and elevation of collective bargaining, allied to the miners' weakened bargaining position, led to a substantial decline in strike proneness from 1958, and particularly after 1966. While the proportion of strikes over pay issues fell, working arrangements, particularly manning levels, became a focus of conflict.[62] This change in strike issues reflected both management attempts to reduce task discretion while intensifying the pace of work and the miners' willingness to defend their control over the labour process.

The Third Daywage Structure Agreement of 1971 completed the move towards industry-wide pay bargaining, the miners' union became more unified behind national wage claims,[63] and a militant rank-and-file movement brought to power left-wing leaders committed to arresting the decline of miners' earnings.[64] The success of the 1972 strike, the first national stoppage since 1926, restored some of the miners' bargaining power, and this was reinforced by the 1973 oil shock. Management sought further productivity growth in the 1970s, without further change in the material technical base, and considered ways of combating the emergent left leadership of the NUM and limiting miners' control at the point of production. In a secret report to the NCB chairman in December 1973, Board member Wilfred Miron recommended the reintroduction of payment by results, to be negotiated at area level, in order to restore influence to moderate union leaders, and the development of new technologies to limit miners' control at the point of production.[65] A 'high-powered confidential group' was to be established at headquarters to implement the strategies, and ultimately influenced the technological decisions made under *Plan for Coal*, the corporatist settlement of the 1974 strike.

Advanced technology mining (ATM)

The most recent phase of coal-face work represents a refinement of the material technical base of power loading with the use of computer automation and more powerful face machinery. Productivity was to be raised in line with the objectives of *Plan for Coal* through the application of systems engineering, which involved the development of automation and monitoring rather than new machinery. Mining Research and Development Establishment (MRDE) expenditure between 1975 and 1982 therefore moved away from coal-face projects to computer-based comprehensive monitoring.[66] The MINOS (Mine Operating System) package developed out of this programme is shown schematically in Figure 7.2, and has been analysed extensively elsewhere.[67]

Figure 7.2 The **MINOS** *Hierarchy*

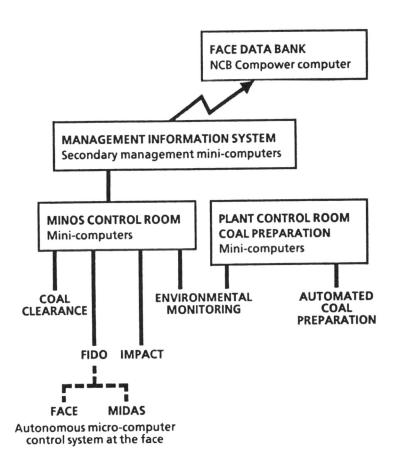

Source: A. Burns, et. al., 'The miners and new technology' *Industrial Relations Journal* 14 (1983), 4.

Before outlining the salient features, three design principles should be noted. First, MINOS was designed on a modular basis, which enabled the separate subsystems to be evaluated in a variety of situations, but which also facilitated the piecemeal introduction of new technology without opposition from the workforce.[68]   Second, the system is hierarchical and centralised; it mirrors the existing management structure but is designed to bring accurate, detailed information from all areas of the pit to the highest levels of management on a continuous basis, thereby increasing managerial control.[69]   Thirdly, as many functions as possible are subject to closed-loop automatic computer control, thereby increasing labour productivity,[70] and return on capital,[71] and deskilling work.[72]   The technical papers make clear these design principles and betray a Taylorist approach to work organisation.

MINOS is a computer system for centralised monitoring and control of colliery activities, comprising various automated subsystems devoted to particular functions such as coal clearance, face delays and coal preparation, all of which are overseen by computers in a surface control room. Work measurement during the 1970s had shown that of the available shift time at the coal face, approximately one third was lost in 'operational delays' (breakdowns, etc.) and a further third on 'avoidable delays' (natural breaks). A key objective of the MINOS programme was therefore to increase machine running time. Operational delays were to be reduced by the Machine Information Display and Automation System (MIDAS) and In-built Machine Performance and Condition Testing (IMPACT) which monitor the health of plant and machinery to predict and report on breakdowns. Man-made delays were to be reduced by recording stoppages through Face Information Digested On-line (FIDO), a worker surveillance system at the coal face. Incentive payments were reintroduced to support computer-based work monitoring: delays of less than twenty minutes would adversely affect bonus earnings, whereas a contingency rate was paid for genuine operational delays lasting at least twenty minutes, penalising miners for unscheduled breaks. In addition to increasing machine running time at the coal face, by reducing operational delays and unscheduled breaks, MINOS facilities intensify the rate of production in other ways. The automated steering function of MIDAS increases the rate of extraction, while the availability of coal clearance to the face is raised by automation and co-ordination of belts and bunkers. Machine monitoring improves the reliability of ancillary machinery, reducing down-time due to failures of fans and pumps. The increased rate of extraction made possible by remote control and monitoring through MINOS therefore necessitated the development of heavy-duty face equipment (HDFE) capable of sustained operation at high levels of output. HDFE involves a more powerful shearer-loader, banks of self-advancing roof supports with face shields, heavy duty conveyors and up-rated gate-end electrical equipment to convey sufficient power to the coal face.

Advanced Technology Mining (ATM) refers to the marriage of HDFE with MIDAS automated steering, a combination capable of producing a daily face output of 4,000 tonnes with two men on the face line. According to the former head of MRDE, the parallel application of HDFE and microelectronic control systems brought a 'huge reduction in downtime due to machine failure'.[73]   The demands imposed on development work by such a dramatic increase in the pace of production also led to a change in the technique of production, from longwall advancing to retreat faces, both double-entry longwall and single-entry shortwall. The impact of the new technologies can be assessed from the Selby mine complex, which was designed from the outset to employ ATM and retreat mining methods.   In 1990, the value of a conventional coalface was in the range £3-4 million, the value of an average heavy-duty face was £6.5 million, while the average value of coalfaces in the Selby complex was £9 million. During 1988/89 Selby productivity averaged 8.35 tonnes per manshift (compared with a national average of 4.14 tonnes), while in 1991/92 Selby productivity was over 12 tonnes per manshift (compared with a national average of 5.36 tonnes) and individual mines in the complex achieved performances far superior to those achieved in any other European deep mine.

The new technologies were developed, tested and quite extensively installed prior to 1984, and according to Sir Ian MacGregor,[74] who had been appointed NCB Chairman in September 1983, would bring about a transformation of the industry from a labour-intensive to a capital-intensive one.[75]   Management argued that reformed working practices were required in order to liberate the true productive potential of the new technologies. A number of proposed changes had been formulated by the mid-1980s, including: the extension of direct production time through multi-shift working, which was designed to increase the time for which machinery was available for production; the development of localised, highly-flexible forms of payment systems (including *ad hoc* payments); the fusion of the roles of fitters and electricians into a single 'electro-mechanic' (reflecting changed maintenance needs); and the transfer of certain maintenance functions to machine operators. According to the NCB, the coal industry would be smaller as a result of the changes, but for those who remained a high-wage/high-productivity scenario was envisaged.

Despite indications of managerial objectives and predictions of changes to come, there were few significant changes in work organisation before 1984. It was the defeat of the 1984-85 miners' strike which provided a permissive environment in which management could unilaterally restructure work organisation and reconstruct industrial relations in order to extract the maximum return from ATM.[76]   The privatisation of electricity supply, and the prospect of privatising coal, intensified pressures on management to adopt new commercial perspectives along with the new corporate name, British Coal. Stringent cost objectives were established in the Moses Strategy in 1985,[77] while the means of attaining these, including controversial temporal flexibility, were outlined in the

Wheeler Plan.[78] The new technologies have affected skill requirements, and management have referred explicitly to deskilling strategies, but these have not been overwhelming.   Some skills of face work were eroded by ATM, since automatic computer guidance of the shearer embodies the machine drivers' skills in the system, just as computer-based machine monitoring incorporates the diagnostic skills of craft workers in the system software. Condition monitoring facilitated a reduction in the number of craft workers, a routinisation of their work, and the merger of fitters and electricians into 'multi-skilled' electro-mechanics who undertake the replacement of faulty modules rather than fault finding and repair. A few craft workers gained new skills in maintaining the new systems, although mostly this involved sub-contractors. Surplus craftsmen were re-deployed as machine drivers, with the intention of having them undertake nuisance breakdown repairs. Attempts by management at Selby to introduce the practice of machine operators conducting certain maintenance functions were initially abandoned in the face of union opposition, although demarcations between craft groups were eroded to a greater degree than in the older mining areas.[79]   This may be a function of technological requirements, as the electrical and mechanical technologies converge. The motives for seeking multiskilling are common to the whole coal mining industry but more acute at Selby because of its technological infrastructure. Management describe the need for a higher return on capital investment through fuller utilisation of assets, while union branch officials see this in terms of reducing manpower and intensifying work in order to increase profitability.

What has been more significant, and increasingly apparent in the decade since the 1984-85 strike, is the degree to which work has become more intensive and tasks have become more extensive. The effects of work intensification were distinctively apparent in the North-east coal mines in the period after the miners' strike, where there was little investment in new technologies. The rapid and unprecedented increase in productivity was frequently referred to by management and the press as a 'miracle'. Despite being in apparent terminal decline and having production difficulties associated with undersea mining, productivity increased by 87 per cent between 1982/83 (the last year of normal production before the 1984-85 strike) and 1988/89. The number of collieries was reduced by 61 per cent and employment by 47 per cent, while output fell by less than 18 per cent. At Westoe Colliery, for example, employment fell from 2,380 in 1983 to 1,536 in 1990, while productivity rose from 2.71 tonnes to 4.36 tonnes per manshift over the same period.[80] In the coastal pits of the north-east, the coal-face workings had become remote from the shaft bottom, several miles out under the North Sea. As a consequence, an increasing proportion of the total shift time was spent in travelling to the coal face and a correspondingly reduced proportion of time was spent in coal cutting, since the Coal Mines Regulation Act 1908 stipulates that a miner can only be required to work a shift of 7.5 hours. In the long term, management attempted to overcome this problem of diminishing productive time by campaigning for a relaxation of the legal restrictions. In the short term, and in the face of NUM opposition to legal changes, management in the north-east instituted the practice of coal production during 'voluntary' overtime. Despite formal Union opposition to any extension of the working day and to the practice of coal production during overtime on grounds of health and safety, by late 1989 management had established coal production in overtime as the norm at every colliery in the north-east, allowing improved machine utilisation rates and greater continuity of production.

Far-reaching changes to working practices have involved extending the range of tasks for virtually all categories of worker, both underground and on the surface. Examples include abolishing the position of fork-lift operator and requiring surface craft workers to operate the machines in addition to their existing tasks. Below-ground craft workers have been made responsible for maintaining a wider range of equipment. The operators of coal-getting and development machinery are now expected to undertake a wider range of ancillary tasks that were previously the responsibility of other workers, but these responsibilities do not extend to the area of maintenance. The assignment of extra responsibilities does not amount to the meaningful acquisition of additional skills. Such developments are experienced overwhelmingly by workers as a process of work intensification. In addition to these developments, there has been a major increase in the use of external contractors to perform tasks formerly undertaken internally. As measures to increase the rate of working and task flexibility were introduced after the 1984-85 strike, productivity grew substantially. From the year ended March 1984 to the year ended March 1989, overall output per manshift (OMS) increased by 70 per cent, representing an average increase (ignoring the strike-affected year) of 14 per cent per annum. Over the next three years, productivity growth slowed to an average annual increase of 9 per cent. From the year ended March 1992, productivity increased at the fastest rate of any period in the history of the industry: 34 per cent in the year to end March 1993 and 25 per cent in the year to end March 1994. Moreover, OMS is projected to grow by a further 60 per cent over the next four years with the further application of ATM, the use of new technologies such as roof bolting, single-entry retreat faces and continuous miners, and further changes in working methods.[81]

Conclusions

This essay has distinguished six phases of technology at the coal face and in identifying the associated periods of predominance of five of them, demonstrates the complex inter-relationship between technology and work organisation, and the impact of the wider context of the labour process, especially in relation to the balance of power between labour and capital. While it would be wrong to romanticise the HGSW era, colliers nevertheless had considerable autonomy and control over their work, largely as a result of their invisibility and the inaccessibility of working places. This autonomy was contested by management through the use of payment by results, which had paradoxical effects of creating divisions within the miners' ranks and strengthening their resistance to such indirect control.   The move to longwall mining enabled management to restructure work organisation even though the material technical base and technique of production of HGLW was little different from HGSW. The greater accessibility of the working places to management and increased visibility of the miners enabled more direct supervision and weakened the miners' control over the labour process, irrespective of any changes in the skills deployed at the face. Longwall mining encouraged the adoption of mechanisation and with MCLW, changes in the material technical base and technique of production led to even more profound changes in work organisation. The labour market changes which accompanied the 1926 defeat and the depressed state of the industry between the wars, enabled the employers to effect changes in the labour process which intensified work and had a detrimental impact upon miners' health. The market changes after the Second World War, when coal was needed for industrial reconstruction, had a more significant impact than nationalisation itself. In the new context, miners reacted to the work situation with absenteeism and unofficial stoppages, and the NCB engaged the Tavistock researchers to develop alternative forms of work organisation to alleviate the apparent social dislocations of the MCLW 'three shifts' system.

When power loading became dominant in the 1960s, the changes in the technique of production and work organisation restored some of the miners' control over the labour process, but the demand-deficiency which accompanied these developments reduced the miners' bargaining power. Management sought further ways of exerting control through increasing coal-face supervision and moving to a measured daywork payment system, but miners retained much of their control at the point of production. The development of ATM was profoundly influenced by management strategies which attempted to counter three developments: the miners' control over the labour process; the restoration of the miners' power in the labour market as a result of the 1973 oil shock; and the ascendancy of the left-wing leadership of the NUM. Management attempted to re-establish indirect supervision through the use of incentive schemes introduced in 1977, and these were designed alongside computer-based work monitoring under the automation programme. Changes in work organisation, which can be traced to management strategies developed in the late 1970s, have only been implemented since the miners' defeat in 1984-85, and especially since the October 1992 crisis,[82] when the power context has been more permissive of managerial prerogative.

Notes

1. H.L. Samuel, Report of the Royal Commission on the Coal Industry (1925), [hereafter Samuel Report] : HMSO, Cmd.2600, (1926), p44.
2. J. Benson, R.G. Neville and C.H. Thompson, *Bibliography of the British Coal Industry* Oxford University Press (1981) Oxford.
3. R.J. Waller, *The Dukeries Transformed: The Social and Political Development of a 20th Century Coalfield* Clarendon (1983) Oxford.
4. A. Burns, M. Newby and J. Winterton, *Second Report on MINOS*, Report no. 6 (1984), Working Environment Research Group, University of Bradford; R. Penn and R. Simpson, 'The development of skilled work in the British coal mining industry, 1870-1985' *Industrial Relations Journal*, 17, no.4, (1987), pp339-49.
5. J. Winterton, 'Social and technological characteristics of coal-face work: a temporal and spatial analysis' *Human Relations* 47, 1 (1994), pp89-118.
6. C. Goodrich, *The Frontier of Control* (1920) Bell, pp137-8.
7. R. Harrison (ed.), *Independent Collier: the Coal Miner as Archetypal Proletarian Reconsidered*, Harvester (1978) Hassocks.
8. E.L. Trist, and K.W. Bamforth, 'Some social and psychological consequences of the longwall method of coal getting' *Human Relations*, vol.4, no.1, 1951, p6.
9. E.L. Trist, G.W. Higgin, H. Murray and A.B. Pollock, *Organizational Choice* Tavistock (1963), p.33.
10. Douglass, D., 'The Durham pitman', in R. Samuel (ed.), *Miners, Quarrymen and Saltworkers*, Routledge (1977), pp221-46; J. Krieger, *Undermining Capitalism: State Ownership and the Dialectic of Control in the British Coal Industry* Princeton University Press (1983) Princeton, N.J., pp80-90.
11. B. Williamson, *Class, Culture and Community: a Biographical Study of Social Change in Mining* Routledge (1982).
12. C. Forman, *Industrial Town* Granada (1979)..
13. S. Heycock, 'Effects of collective bargaining structures on the nature of industrial conflict', Ph D thesis, University of Leeds (1986).
14. M. Burawoy, *Manufacturing Consent,* University of Chicago Press (1979) Chicago.
15. R.A.S. Redmayne, *The British Coal-Mining Industry During the War* Oxford University Press (1923) Oxford, p20.
16. A.J. Taylor, 'Labour productivity and technological innovation in the British coal industry, 1850-1914', *Economic History Review* 14, no.1, (1961), p58.
17. C. Reid, *Coal Mining: Report of the Techincal Advisory Committee on Coal Mining* [hereafter *Reid Report*] London: HMSO, Cmd.6610, (1945) p4.
18. Taylor, 'Labour productivity', p59; A.R. Griffin, *The Miners of Nottinghamshire* Nottingham Printers Ltd (1955) Nottingham, pp150, 198.
19. Griffin, *Miners*, p158.
20. Griffin, *Miners*, p177; Taylor, 'Labour productivity', p63.
21. *Reid Report*, p40.
22. K. Dix, 'Work relations in the coal industry: the handloading era 1880-1930', in A. Zimbalist (ed.), *Case Studies on the Labor Process* Monthly Review Press, (1979) New York, p164.
23. M. Yarrow, 'The labour process in coal mining: struggle for control', in Zimbalist (ed.), *Case Studies*, p185.
24. C.M. Bailes (ed.), *Modern Mining Practice: A Practical Work of Reference in Mining Engineering* Bennett, (1906) Sheffield, p28.
25. R. Peel, *An Elementary Text Book of Coal Mining* Blackie (1893) London, p129.
26. R. Page Arnot, *The General Strike May 1926: Its Origin and History* Labour Research Department (1926) London, p74.
27. J.R. Raynes, *Coal and its Conflicts: A Brief Record of the Disputes between Capital and Labour in the Coal Mining Industry of Great Britain* Benn (1928) London, p198.
28. B. Fine, K. O'Donnell and M. Prevezer *Coal before Nationalisation*, Discussion Paper No.128, Department of Economics, Birkbeck College (1982), p33.

29. Taylor, 'Labour productivity', p60.
30. Reid, op.cit., p.11.
31. W.S. Boulton, *Practical Coal Mining* Graham, (1907) London; G.L. Kerr, *Practical Coal Mining: A Manual for Managers, Undermanagers, Colliery Engineers and others* Griffin (1921) .
32. Fine, et. al., *Coal before*, p33.
33. R. Page Arnot, *The Miners: Years of Struggle from 1910 Onwards* Allen and Unwin (1953) London, p528.
34. *Reid Report*, p6.
35. Page Arnot, *Years of Struggle*, p528.
36. Page Arnot, *Years of Struggle*, p528.
37. R. Page Arnot, *The Miners in Crisis and War, from 1930 Onwards* Allen and Unwin (1961) London, p60.
38. *Reid Report*, p6.
39. W.D. Stewart, *Mines, Machines and Men* King (1935) London, pp35-6.
40. Stewart, *Mines*, pp45-6.
41. A. Meikeljohn, 'History of lung diseases of coal miners in Great Britain: part III, 1920-1952', *British Journal of Industrial Medicine* 9, no.3 (1952), pp208-20.
42. J.H. Wilson, *New Deal for Coal* Contact Publications (1945) London, p41.
43. J.L. Halliday, *Psychosocial Medicine: A Study of the Sick Society* Heinemann (1948) London.
44. F.D.K. Liddell, 'Attendance in the coal-mining industry', *British Journal of Sociology* 5, 1 (1954), pp78-86; L.J. Handy, 'Absenteeism and attendance in the British coalmining industry: an examination of post-war trends', *British Journal of Industrial Relations* 6, 1 (1968), pp27-50.
45. S.K. Saxena, *Nationalisation and Industrial Conflict: the Example of British Coal Mining* Nijhoff (1955) The Hague.
46. J. Winterton, 'The trend of strikes in British coal mining, 1949-79' *Industrial Relations Journal* 12, 6 (1981), p14.
47. J. Winterton, 'The demise of collective bargaining in the British coal mining industry', *Revue du Nord*, Hors série, Collection Histoire 8 (1994), pp179-92.
48. *Reid Report*, p54.
49. J.F. Townsend, *Innovation in Coal Mining Machinery: the Anderton Shearer Loader*, Occasional Paper No.3, Science Policy Research Unit (1976), Brighton: University of Sussex, p11.
50. D.M. Kelly, 'The process of mechanisation in British coal mining since 1945', *Economic Studies*, Vol.4, (1969), p136; National Coal Board, *Mechanisation Profile* NCB (1971) London.
51. B. Fine, K. O'Donnell and M. Prevezer, *Coal after Nationalisation*, Discussion Paper No.138, Department of Economics, Birkbeck College (March 1983), p16.
52. D. Douglass, *Pit Life in County Durham*, Oxford University Press (1972) Oxford, p1.
53. Winterton, 'The trend of strikes', pp14-15.
54. *Supplemental Agreement to the Revision of the Wages Structure Agreement of 20th April 1955. Coal Faces Operated by Power Loading Machinery* (usually referred to as the National Power Loading Agreement 1966).
55. R.G. Searle-Barnes, *Pay and Productivity Bargaining: A Study of the Effect of National Wage Agreements in the Nottinghamshire Coalfield* Manchester University Press (1969) Manchester; L.J. Handy, *Wages Policy in the British Coalmining Industry*, Cambridge University Press (1981) Cambridge.
56. R.H. Heath, 'The National Power Loading Agreement in the coal industry and some aspects of workers' control', *Trade Union Register* (1969), p187.
57. Heath, 'National Power Loading', p189.
58. National Coal Board, *Report and Accounts 1967/68* NCB (1968) London.
59. J. Hughes and R. Moore (eds.), *A Special Case? Social Justice and the Miners* Penguin (1972) Harmondsworth.
60. C. Edwards and E. Heery, *Management Control and Union Power, A Study of Labour Relations in Coal Mining* Clarendon (1989) Oxford, pp32-3.
61. R. Hepworth, et al., 'The effects of technological change in the Yorkshire coalfield 1960-1965', in D.M. Kelly and D.J.C.Forsyth (eds.), *Studies in the British Coal Industry* Pergamon (1969) Oxford, pp221-37.

62. Winterton, 'The trend of strikes', p15.
63. I. Rutledge, 'Changes in the mode of production and the growth of 'mass militancy' in the British mining industry 1954-1974', *Science and Society* 41 (1977), pp410-29.
64. V.L. Allen, *The Militancy of British Miners* Moor Press (1981) Shipley.
65. J. Winterton and R. Winterton, *Coal, Crisis and Conflict: The 1984-85 Miners' Strike in Yorkshire* Manchester University Press (1989) Manchester, pp9-12.
66. A.D.W. Jones, J.J. Quinn and K.M. Woolley, *Evaluation of Coal Winning Technology*, London: Technical Change Centre (1984), pp65-69.
67. A. Burns, D. Feickert, M. Newby and J. Winterton, *An Interim Assessment of MINOS*, Report 4, Working Environment Research Group, University of Bradford (1982), and 'The miners and new technology', *Industrial Relations Journal* 14, no. 4 (1983), pp7-20; A. Burns, M. Newby and J. Winterton, *Second Report on MINOS*, Report no.6, Working Environment Research Group, University of Bradford (1984), and 'The restructuring of the British coal industry', *Cambridge Journal of Economics* 9, 1 (1985), pp93-110.
68. J. Winterton, 'Computerised coal, new technology in the mines', in Beynon, H. (ed.), *Digging Deeper: Issues in the Miners' Strike* Verso (1985) London, pp231-43.
69. K.W. Chandler, 'MINOS - A computer system for control at collieries', Second International Conference on Centralized Control Systems, London (March 1978); J. Cleary, 'FIDO (Face Information Digested On-line) at Bold colliery', *The Mining Engineer* (November 1981), pp281-9.
70. E. Horton, 'Mining techniques in the 1980s', *COMMIT 82* Computer-based Mine Management Information Technology Exhibition and Symposium, Harrogate (8-10 December 1982).
71. C.C. Cooper, 'Improving machine utilization and reliability', *COMMIT 82.*
72. J.J. Bates, 'Inbuilt Machine Performance and Condition Testing - IMPACT', *The Mining Engineer* (July 1981), pp31-7; F. Fennelly, 'Coalface machine health', *COMMIT 82.*
73. P. Tregelles, Memorandum No.59, House of Commons Select Committee on Energy, *The Coal Industry*, Vol.II, HMSO (1986), pp312-14.
74. I. MacGregor, *The Enemies Within, The Story of the Miners' Strike 1984-5* Collins (1986) London.
75. D. Feickert, 'The midwife of mining', *Capital and Class* 31 (1987), pp7-15.
76. National Union of Mineworkers, 'The attack on union organisation in the British deep coal mining industry', Industrial Relations Department, Sheffield: NUM (1989) [mimeo]; S. Leman and J. Winterton, 'New technology and the restructuring of pit-level industrial relations in the British coal industry' *New Technology, Work and Employment* 6, 1, (1991), pp54-64.
77. National Coal Board, 'New Strategy for Coal', Joint Policy Advisory Committee (15 October 1985); J. Winterton, 'Private power and public relations, the effects of privatisation upon industrial relations in British Coal' in G. Jenkins and M. Poole (eds.), *New Forms of Ownership* Routledge (1990) London, pp134-50.
78. National Union of Mineworkers, 'New proposed working practices in the British deep coal mining industry' and 'Flexibility in the British deep coal mining industry', Industrial Relations Department, Sheffield: NUM (1987) [mimeo].
79. J. Winterton, 'Flexibility, new technology and British Coal', in P. Blyton and J. Morris (eds.), *A Flexible Future ? Prospects for Employment and Organization* de Gruyter (1991) Berlin, pp275-94, and 'Human factors and reliability in colliery maintenance', *International Journal of Quality and Reliability Management* 8, no. 2 (1991), pp52-7.
80. J. Tomaney and J. Winterton, 'Technological change and work relations in the British coal mining industry', in W. Littek and T. Charles (eds.), *The New Division of Labour* de Gruyter (1995) Berlin.
81. J. Winterton, *The Effects of New Technologies on the Productivity and Production Costs of the British Coal Mining Industry* Report no. 12, University of Bradford Working Environment Research Group (1988); J. Winterton and R. Winterton, *Productivity and its Impact on Employment and Labour Relations in the Coal Mining Industry in the United Kingdom*, Report to the International Labour Office, University of Bradford Work Organisation Research Unit (1994).
82. J. Winterton and R. Winterton, *Strategic Implications of Proposed Colliery Closures* University of Bradford Work Organisation Research Unit (1992) and 'Coal', in A. Pendleton and J. Winterton (eds.), *Public Enterprise in Transition: Industrial Relations in State and Privatized Industries* Routledge (1993) London, pp69-99. It is worth drawing a direct comparison with the relatively high levels of cooperation and reciprocity which Abelshauser's essay in this collection outlines, and the

frictions and conflicts which we have documented in the British coal industry. The absence of consensus is, of course, the key point which our essay is concerned to document.

8. Safety, supervision and the politics of productivity in the British coalmining industry, 1900-1960 *

Joseph Melling

Introduction

The British coalmining industry has attracted some of the most vivid mythologies in labour history. Not only the conflicts between miners and coalowners but also the confrontations between mining communities and the state have defined the key moments in the development of the British coalfields. The importance of these struggles in the formation of class politics during the nineteenth and twentieth centuries helps to explain the enormous scholarship which has been devoted to the evolution of mining and the distinctive mining communities. At different moments the collier has appeared to carry the whole burden of class leadership on his shoulders. It is this historical role which remains the subject of vigorous debate amongst economic and social historians seeking to trace the origins of industrial and political loyalties amongst British coalminers' in the past century. Not only have scholars recently questioned the assertion that industrial and political radicalism flows from the 'natural' environment of the workplace or the mining communities, but the impact of mineworkers' attitudes on the performance and long term decline of coalmining has formed an important part of the wider debate on the mediocre rates of productivity growth reached in British industry. The remarkable shrinkage of the workforce in the post-war era until the mines were a marginal employer of labour in former coalfield districts has been interpreted by some as the inevitable cost of militancy and political confrontation in earlier decades.

This essay reviews the recent literature on labour relations in coalmining and more particularly the impact of changing work technologies on relationships at the coalface and on workplace bargaining. Recent research by Roy Church and others has offered a reinterpretation of both production and industrial conflict in the industry during the past century, challenging the familiar Marxist portrait of coalminers' struggles as a class project. The revisionist writers seek to deconstruct colliery conflicts as the product of a complex array of peculiar

historical conditions which varied over space and time. There is therefore no
necessary or fundamental connection between the structure of production and the
pattern of industrial relations found in coalmining, which should be seen as the
product of institutional arrangements between organised employers, labour and
the state rather than the expression of inherent antagonisms within the workplace
or class society. Such an approach introduces a basic discontinuity between the
politics of production and the wider programme of class politics in modern
Britain.

Whilst these debates have raised important questions about the impact of
industrial politics on the performance of coalmining in the past century,
surprisingly little attention has been given to the management of safety
underground and its place in the formation and conduct of labour relations within
the industry. Much is known about methods of production in the heroic age of
hand-got mining and transition to mechanised techniques after 1900 though we
still possess only sketchy impressions of practical nexus between managers and
men below ground. This is an important omission since it is increasingly clear
that we cannot adequately explain the path of productivity growth or the course
of labour relations in the industry until we have a more precise understanding of
the methods of labour management. Safety considerations were central to the
practices of mining management and became the focus of controversy and
conflict in periods when production techniques were being altered. The
prevention of accidents was also a defining principle of the state's regulation of
the coalmining industry from at least the 1840s and formed one of the
institutional boundaries within which bargaining took place. Mining
management was itself the subject of statutory certification rules which reached
down to shotfiring level.

This essay examines the issue of safety in coalmines during the twentieth
century as a way of exploring the influences on productivity growth in the pits.
More particularly the concern is to consider how changes in production methods
and the drive for increased output per miner affected the relations between
management and labour in the industry and how these labour relations in turn
affected the employers' capacity to control production. It will be argued that the
discussions of safety within the mining industry have to be read as part of a wider
discourse on the responsibilities of management and the duties of the state. This
discourse itself defined the relationship of employers, labour and the state as well
as providing a basic frame of reference for bargaining within the industry. The
exercise of power and autonomy within production was therefore dependent in
large part on the different actors' capacity to present certain working practices as
safe or unsafe. There was no absolute measure of safety and different groups
interpreted or manipulated statutory requirements according to their various
needs and interests. Perceptions and discussions of safety formed one of the most
significant issues in management-labour relations and workplace bargaining in
the pits. The significance of these everyday debates is that they involved, of

necessity, basic principles of authority in the production process and the limits which managers, supervisors and mineworkers could reach in their efforts to control output to their own advantage.

In this continuing engagement the role of the colliery deputies and overmen, responsible for the supervision of production below ground, was to be critical. For it was the capacity of some grades of supervisors to invoke their statutory responsibilities for safety which helped to insulate them against the drives by colliery management to impose tighter controls over production whilst the deputies were also able to resist the attempts of mineworkers to soften and blur the 'frontier of control' at the coalface. Such experiences call into question the arguments made by Church and others that the struggles over production methods and workplace authority had little significant impact·on the labour relations of the coalfields. For it can be seen that the institutional relations between employers, labour and the state were nowhere more evident than in the regulation of colliery safety and yet it was precisely such issues which formed the battleground for fundamental struggles at work. The politics of safety underground were complex and diverse. We need to distinguish the 'low politics' of safety and workplace bargaining from the formal policies of the main institutions involved in the industry. It is significant that safety went unreformed throughout the early years of nationalisation and it was the deterioration of working conditions in the 1950s that brought the matter once again to the public domain. The existence of such distinct levels of conflict indicates that even major institutional change can have relatively little impact on key areas of production and labour relations, whilst periods of innovation in technology and work organisation could generate both controversy and collusion in matters affecting the safety of colliers.

The following section offers a brief review of some recent literature on the evolution of production systems in British coalmining from the end of the nineteenth century.

Production, productivity and the pattern of conflict in modern coalmining

The vitality of business leadership during the decades of private ownership in the British coal industry remains a matter of vigorous debate, though there is less dispute about the course of productivity growth since the late nineteenth century. Roy Church has recently challenged the accepted view that the industry reached a watershed in the 1880s as the rising productivity gave way to falling output when the numbers of mineworkers employed increased more rapidly than their average product.[1] His research casts doubt on Mitchell's conclusion that there was sustained productivity growth in the first six decades of the nineteenth century, achieved by improvements in haulage, the use of gunpowder for shotfiring and improved ventilation from the 1830s.[2] Church argues for a more even rate of growth following a relative decline in productivity during the mid-century with a sharp fall in the Edwardian years caused by the Eight Hours Act of 1909.[3] Yet Church's findings appear to confirm the 'unmistakable trend' of decline in output from the 1880s, even if his explanation differs from that of some earlier scholars. In contrast to Mitchell's emphasis on diminishing returns from ageing collieries with thinner seams and longer haulage routes, Church points to the adverse impact of legislation and diminished labour effort in the period.[4] In his earlier research, Church also underlined Mitchell's assessment of lengthening roadways and the effect of explosives in raising productivity whilst abundant labour limited the introduction of new machine cutters.[5] The growing popularity of longwall working reduced the need for powder blasting of the coal seam though it was only in the thinner, harder seams of ageing coalfields in Scotland and elsewhere that cutters offered an advantage over blasting in proving the larger valuable coals which customers demanded before 1914.[6]

The introduction of mechanical cutters in such areas helped to offset the falls in productivity which undoubtedly set in from the 1880s, a decline in output per hour which accelerated between 1906 and 1914 across the major coalfields.[7] Output stagnated between the outbreak of war and 1923, though less seriously at the coalface than in the workforce as a whole. Every major study of the industry stressed the great diversity in the physical conditions and working methods which persisted in the twentieth century.[8] The industry as a whole suffered from diminishing returns and ageing collieries, which provided a major impetus to the introduction of robust coal cutters and the adoption of advancing longwall methods in some older districts such as Scotland.[9] Paradoxically it appears that the hewers were most productive in those ageing pits where they shouldered the burden of longer haulage roads and more oncost labour.[10] After 1923 the pace of productivity growth quickened as pre-war production levels were regained and surpassed until by 1938 output per hour was 37 per cent above that of 1914.[11] The spread of mechanised longwall working was undoubtedly increasing from less than 20 per cent of coal in 1924 to about half in 1935, with 43 per cent being conveyed mechanically in the latter year.[12] At the same time the workforce shrank from some 1.13 million employees in 1913 to 780,000 by 1935 and whilst the total product of the industry fell by a quarter in these years, there were significant gains in output amongst face workers during the 1930s.[13] There was some concentration in the amount of output controlled by larger enterprises but as Supple has observed, the structure of the coal industry was remarkably resilient despite the rise of large firms in old and new fields.[14]

Scholars have differed in the assessment of the scale and sources of productivity growth in this period. Whereas Buxton emphasised the strong performance of British entrepreneurs in the introduction of cutting machines at this time, other writers have called into question the standards of business strategy and the significance of mechanical cutters in raising output. Dintenfass takes issue with Buxton's claim that within the bounds imposed by industrial structure and fixed wage costs, colliery firms performed creditably as they introduced cutters and raised productivity in the face of tough European competition.[15]   Research undertaken on a number of enterprises suggests to Dintenfass that successful companies could carry wages significantly higher even than the industrial average (equivalent to two thirds of production costs) by adopting imaginative policies for the extraction, processing and marketing of their product.[16]   Equally apparent is the argument that it was mechanical *conveying* of coal rather than cutting which held the key to productivity growth in the interwar years.[17]   It was the failure of sufficient numbers of coalowners to recognise the importance of investment opportunities and the need for organisational reform which consigned even many large companies to poor growth and profitability in these years.[18]

This pessimistic appraisal by Dintenfass can be balanced by studies of such successful producers as the giant Powell Duffryn Company which controlled one third of South Wales output and was the largest coal firm in Britain by the 1940s. Here the pursuit of a coherent and deliberate strategy of expansion and new investment enabled the employers to consolidate their grip on core reserves and rationalise output as well as reaping economies of scale without jeopardising their financial base.[19]   Even such achievements should not obscure the basic point that in comparative European terms Britain's productivity growth in the interwar years was modest if not mediocre.   This was the conclusion reached by the Reid Committee in their assessment of the technical standards in the industry in 1945, noting that output per shift increased by only 11 per cent overall in the years 1927-39 compared to over 50 per cent in the Ruhr and Poland.[20]   Reid also argued that the surge in underground productivity which occurred in British pits during the decade after 1927 was due primarily to the spread of conveyors as well as the growth of mechanised longwall working at coalfaces.[21]   More soberly, there was a fall in productivity growth in British and European coalfields after 1936, evident in the output of haulage rather than face workers underground.[22] This emphasis on the importance of haulage costs and efficient winding is also found in many recent accounts of productivity in the interwar coal industry, including Greasley's assessment of the role of integrated machine mining in the growth of output.[23]   As Greasley notes, it is difficult to explain the continuing variation in productivity growth across the coalfields without some analysis of working practices and the labour environment as well as the geology of the mine and the pace of mechanisation.

Although doubts have been raised about the importance of industrial structure in determining productivity growth, there is abundant evidence that a combination of physical and enterprise structures served to impede rapid output in many pits. At the end of the Second World War Britain possessed almost five hundred mines which employed no more than thirty workers whilst 2 per cent of firms employed a little less than one quarter of the whole workforce - which totalled 700,000.[24]   Scotland had extended its programme of mechanical cutting before 1939 to 80 per cent of coal produced but was unable to complete offset falling productivity at the same time.[25] Following nationalisation of the industry in 1946 output per shift increased 13 per cent in 1947-51 but then slowed with an improvement of a mere 1 per cent in the years 1953-57, though as in earlier decades faceworkers performed well above the workforce average.[26] Much of the gain probably accrued from the closure of older and less productive collieries following state ownership, though impressive variations in output growth between the coalfields continued with Scotland emerging with a persistent record of poor productivity. Only in the mid-1950s did the National Coal Board (NCB) embark on a programme of investment to fund the new phase of mechanisation which power loading made possible.

Whilst there is a fair measure of agreement on the path of productivity growth in the British coal industry before 1960, there is much less consensus on the growth of labour relations in coalmining or their impact on output at the coalface. Recent research on the industry documents the importance of workplace bargaining over effort and rewards during much of the nineteenth and twentieth centuries as the mineowners relied on piecework wages to drive the hewers in conditions where close surveillance of labour was virtually impossible. Prices were usually set for particular coal seams and the cutters and fillers rewarded for the number of tubs loaded with reasonably clean and solid coal. The basic method of extracting the mineral by hand changed very little in the nineteenth century though the division of tasks between groups of workers and the amount of specialisation at the coal face varied across the coalfields and over time. Intense disputes could occur when new seams were opened up and prices being fixed and where there was a transition from the pillar and stall method of working very short coalfaces to the larger groups found on the longwall faces. Even where prices were well known there were persistent appeals for allowances and indulgences when unforeseen or abnormal conditions were uncovered by the miners. The success with which labour could press these claims depended on their local bargaining strength and the owners' perception of the trade. In order to avoid the numerous problems of labour management and even the risks of development, coal firms continued to use a variety of sub-contracting practices throughout the nineteenth and early twentieth centuries. It is true that the 'butty' was in much more powerful in the Midlands and some peripheral fields than in expanding coalfields with stronger unions, though there were still numerous districts and even new seams where sub-contracting remained an important feature of colliery life even in the interwar years.[27]

The fact that the coalface was always moving and constantly changing as the miners followed the seam inevitably led to constant bargaining over the opportunities for better rewards. In some coalfields the access to different working places was regulated by customary rules of drawing lots or establishing seniority ladders, whilst in others there were contracts issued to butties who led work groups and acted as pace setters rather than merely exploiting those in their charge. It is therefore unsurprising that the bulk of labour disputes involved the payment of hewers, whatever system of payment was in place at the time.[28] There is also little doubt that the mineworkers were able to increase their real wages substantially in the decades before 1914 when the productivity of labour was falling, even though they possessed few obvious defences against wage cuts in periods of depression. Some scholars have argued that the growing unionisation of the mineworkers after 1889 and their capacity to restrict the introduction of new technologies whilst promoting legislation which limited their working hours and wage cuts served to weaken the competitive strength of British coalmining before 1914.[29] Church argues that the reticence of the state and the reluctance of coalowners to maximise their bargaining strength after 1926 meant that the opportunity for a radical overhaul of industrial relations and working practices was missed in the interwar years.[30] The mechanisation of the coalface did not alter the division of labour or deskill labour and nor (claims Church) did changes in work organisation play any central role in the evolution of industrial relations.[31] In the post-1945 era management struggled to reform piecework practices and bargaining by the introduction of national wage scales, though the eventual agreement of 1966 failed to secure the control over earnings, tasks and production teams that the NCB expected would follow.[32]

Throughout their recent discussion on conflict within the coal industry, Church and his collaborators have emphasised the limits of any general social model for explaining the pattern of disputes and the importance of changing local circumstances in both communities and workplace.[33] At the same time Church seems to be concerned to show *both* that broad social and class factors are less important than local and peculiar conditions in the making of industrial disputes, and also that changes in the working and social environment were less important to the evolution of labour relations than institutional policies and formal agreements. Whilst disputes over piecework wages explains the persistence of conflict in the industry, the removal of this source of friction in the reforms of the 1950s and 1960s shifted attention to the level of effort and manning in the collieries which intensified the 'politics of productivity' as miners resisted further encroachments of managerial prerogatives over their working lives.[34]

The following section examines these claims by considering the forms of workplace management which developed in the industry after 1900. In contrast to the interpretation offered by Church, it will be suggested that there was a vigorous politics of productivity in the interwar coal industry and that the role of the supervisor arguably the most important issue facing colliery management. The terrain on which owners and employees struggled to promote the interests was the discussion of safety underground. This aspect of the pursuit of productivity in the industry has previously been all but ignored. Since it is clear that mechanisation went further in Scotland whilst at the same time output per shift declined slightly, particular attention is paid to developments in the Scottish pits. This also provides some insight into the tensions apparent within the bargaining process in these decades.

Whilst there is an important distinction to be drawn between the procedures or relations created by national institutions and the practices of workplace bargaining, it was the manipulation of such issues as safety at different levels as well as the ability to dramatise the dangers of the coalmine which were so important to the promotion of different interests. It can be argued that the distinction made in recent literature between these struggles and the class politics of the mining industry is, in practice, an artificial one. For the creation of solidarity within a mining community, across a coalfield or a national industry must always be an act of social construction which cannot derive naturally from the working conditions or the social disposition of a colliery. The period under review is one in which the institutions of bargaining (from the district unions and Miners' Federation to the creation of a National Union of Mineworkers [NUM] in 1945) were evolving at the same time that class and political identities were being constructed. To assert their separate development is to misunderstand the politics of production in coalmining.

Safety and supervision in the coalmines, 1900-1960

In their assessment of the pace of change in the British coal industry before 1945 scholars have relied heavily on the observations of the Reid Committee which reported on technical standards in the industry at the end of the war. Presented as an exercise in brutal realism, the *Reid Report* castigated the whole mining strategy of driving roadways to follow the coal seam and insisted that the undulations in the transport passages which resulted from this method seriously inhibited the capacity of the mine operators to move the cut coal rapidly away from the face. Whilst productivity at the face increased with mechanisation, the traditional roadway system could not cope with the output produced - as was evidenced by the fall in the amount of tons hauled per worker at the end of the 1930s and during the war.[35] Reid also criticised the rigidity of the longwall advancing system, with its triple shift cycle of operations by which cutting, filling and ripping was undertaken in turn and each shift dependent on the capacity of their predecessors to complete the work on time.[36] The Committee was composed of business leaders who represented those large companies which had taken a lead in advancing technical innovations during the interwar period. They were highly critical of the limitations of technical training in the industry and of the customary resistance amongst the mineworkers to rationalisation of working methods, which had 'put a brake on the modernisation of the industry' and retarded productivity growth. Payment systems as well as workplace attitudes needed to be reformed if the future of coal was to be secured.[37]

Another feature of the *Report* which deserves emphasis is the weaknesses which the Reid group of employers identified in the training and promotion of management itself, observing that it was impossible to exploit the full potential of the new technologies until those who operated and managed them had the technical expertise required.[38]   They concluded that it was the supervisors themselves who were most in need of preparation and support, since:

> The most important, yet at the same time the weakest link in the chain, at the moment, is the selection and training of the deputies and overmen. Indeed, a progressive improvement in the quality of these grades would make an outstanding contribution to the efficiency of the Industry as regards both production and safety.[39]

Standing on the threshold of an era when 'the human factor' in production was to become as important a theme in the productivity debate as the virtues of mechanisation and American manufacturing practices, the Reid group acknowledged that their first line managers had to demonstrate a capacity for leadership as well as an awareness of technical problems in mining coal.[40]

It is possible to read into such sombre assessments that formidable impediments to productivity growth had persisted throughout the earlier decades and that the division of labour and industrial relations were little changed by management policies before 1939.[41]   Yet from the *Report* and *Minutes of Evidence* collected by the important (if neglected) Royal Commission on Safety in Coal Mines, published immediate before the outbreak of war, we receive a very different impression of rapid workplace change which had transformed workplace relations in the interwar period.[42]   The Rockley Commission found that the employers had developed a portfolio of policies in the interwar period to defend their market position and raise output without incurring the heavy debts that sank a number of firms in the late 1920s as profits declined disastrously. Existing accounts suggest that it was the inability of owners to work thin seams economically with hand picks and explosives which prompted the application of machine cutters in growing numbers from the turn of the century, rather than the opportunity to substitute capital equipment for expensive manual labour. The certainty of losses on thin and faulted seams where rapid holing of the dirt and firing of explosive shots could not yield sufficient marketable coal to justify piece rates and reap profit for the firm left the owners with the alternative of abandoning the seams or finding a way of raising productivity. The static capital:labour ratio in the late nineteenth century indicates that the growth in the coal market was met by roughly equal inputs of invest and workers even though the productivity of the pits was falling significantly.[43]

Yorkshire led the industry in mechanised pits in 1900 but by 1914 Scotland had surpassed all others and cut more than one fifth of its coal with machines.[44] Whilst there seems little doubt of the owners' reluctance to invest in cutting machines at this period, it is difficult to explain the surge in Scottish usage without some reference to the peculiarities of Scottish labour relations before 1914. In some other districts, owners responded to the exhaustion of thicker seams and accessible workings by passing the responsibility for working the coal to butty masters whose only concern was to drive labour with little regard for the

long term future of the pit or the workforce.[45] Scotland was clearly a weaker area
of unionisation for much of the nineteenth century, along with Yorkshire and
South Wales, with truck shops operated by butty masters and deputies still
common in Ayrshire later in the century. Yet Scotland shared with other weak
fields a strong momentum for unionisation after the foundation of the Miners'
Federation in 1889 and particularly in the immediate pre-1914 period.[46] The
capacity of the owners to drive labour in Scotland was circumscribed by the
growing strength of unionism, even though profits were squeezed in the western
coalfields at this time.[47] What is not often appreciated is that the Scottish owners
actively sought to exploit the new technology under a system, of extended sub-
contracting, rather than viewing the capital investment as the basis for a more
rigorous system of colliery management. Such policies can be more easily
understood in terms of the wider capital-labour relations in west Scotland than
the narrow rationale of investment calculation with which conventional
scholarship struggles to explain the investment strategies of coal entrepreneurs at
this time. Whilst the *Colliery Guardian* accused miners of opposing the new
machinery, with little evidence in support, it seems more likely that it was the
employers' recognition of growing labour resistance to price cuts and driving
which explains the growing interest in new technology after 1900.[48] It was in
west Scotland that the first two generations of cutting machines had been
developed and where Bairds and other employers faced serious conflicts over
their use in the 1890s.[49]

Central to the Lanarkshire coalmasters' strategy of early mechanisation was a
system of incentive wages and driving supervision, with piecework and sub-
contracting in machine mining emerging as major issues of contention before
1914.[50] Originally restricted to difficult working places in Lanarkshire, by 1908
the owners were arguing that butty contracts should be put out to tender for the
major seams as well as driving and ripping work, where mining could be
controlled by the contractor 'to much greater advantage than every man having
his own place.'[51] Before the First World War, sub-contracting was spreading in
west Scotland with some pits cutting one third of their coal with machines
operated under sub-contracts, though the coalowners denied that they wanted to
introduce butties throughout the coal-getting process.[52] The Lanarkshire
machine policy followed that of such firms as Dixons in promoting the practice
of sub-contracting and piecework on longwall cutting and for deadwork, rather
than continuing with bord and pillar mining at their pits.[53] These strategies were
quite deliberately designed to sustain a long-term campaign in areas such as
Lanarkshire against customary restrictions on output or the 'darg' at their pits.
The general concern of the coal masters was to tighten their grip over working
methods and the labour market as a means of sustaining productivity and
profitability in west Scotland.[54]

In these conditions the colliery 'firemen' (deputies) faced intense pressure
from the Lanarkshire Miners' Union to join the miners in resisting the employers

by joining their ranks, though a separate Firemen's Association was formed to represent the supervisors.[55] After the retreats of the pre-1914 period the miners were able to exploit their stronger position during the war years to restrain unpopular business strategies and also to force their acknowledgement that the deputies could be unionised, even though this meant representation by the manual unions more often than autonomous associations.[56] The coalminers' unions also continued their fight against sub-contracting, insisting that the employment of three quarters of the workforce by contractors in some collieries was unacceptable.[57] It is interesting that there was little overt resistance to mechanisation in the Scottish mines and that the owners increased their investment in new machines to sustain output as labour shortages were felt. The point of contention appears to have been the effort bargain extracted by sub-contractors using machines rather than mechanisation or deskilling as such. Indeed, the logic of the unions' policies was to promote a standard contractual arrangement between owners and labour and an end to butty working. Therefore it is true that the First World War period marked an important stage in the state's growing regulation of the industry, though it is difficult to see that government control of wages and profits formed the beginning of any a radical departure in industrial relations.[58] Even the mining legislation of 1921 and 1930 appear to have a limited impact on the conduct of coal enterprises or the management of labour and little direct influence over labour relations. Those writers who focus on the institutional reforms initiated by peak organisations and the state tend to obscure the importance of shifts in the organisation of production and the bargaining power of capital and labour.

For it was rather the serious decline in profits after 1923 which forced coalowners to reappraise their management practices and pursue a range of policies to reduce the labour costs which represented two thirds of production charges at this time. Some enterprises even in the developing coalfields such as Nottingham reverted to the use of sub-contracting and butty masters to raise output, in the haulage as well as the cutting of coal.[59] After the defeat of the miners in the great strike of 1926 it was also possible to cut wages, reduce piecerates and impose systematic overtime working in the coalfields as bargaining became more important at workplace and local levels. More significant for the management of production, however, was the creation of a new grade of taskmasters who were integrated into the structure of colliery management and were responsible for exploiting the opportunities of mechanisation and labour's weakened bargaining position. One aspect of this drive for increased productivity was the *increasing* use of explosive shots to bring down the undercut face and accelerate the ripping of new strata and roadways in the mines.[60]

The growing use of explosives and the accidents which resulted both from firing explosive shots and from the intensified pace of machine mining, which provided one of the main points of controversy during the interwar years. The safety aspects of machine mining was the basis of the criticism of employers' policies levelled by the Miners' Federation of Great Britain (MFGB) in the evidence presented to the Rockley Commission in 1936, where the Federation argued for stricter controls over shotfiring and machine mining.[61] Shots were placed rapidly along the extended longwall face, with as many as forty shots a day under machine mining conditions, intensifying during the early 1930s and a factor in the maintenance of the accident rate underground.[62]

Serious accidents resulted both from the blast itself and the ignition of firedamp in gassy mines worked by machines (including those where contractors were used), even if the general trend was for fatal explosions to decline.[63] The Federation leadership insisted that these pressures for increased output had jeopardised safety in the pit. They criticised both the systems of piecework and sub-contracting as well as the intensification of work pace which came with the system of a rapidly advancing longwall.[64] The unions reserved their strongest attacks for the growing army of overmen who were frequently recruited from younger miners and promoted specifically to assist the undermanager in raising output from each shift of workers.[65]

The rise of the overman was a point of bitter controversy in the interwar industry. Although there was some reference to overmen in the 1887 Mines Act, their role was extended into that of a senior shift supervisor only after the First World War. Unlike other mine officials the overmen were not clearly classified in the statutory provisions for the certification of mining officials and by 1930 the Holland Committee was recommending a more precise definition of the overman's role and proposed they should hold the second-class certificates required for appointment as under-manager.[66] These recommendations were firmly opposed by the coal owners, who argued that the primary qualification for the post was personality - irrespective of the age of the deputy who was promoted to overman.[67] There was also disquiet amongst the ranks of the traditional supervisory grades in the coal industry as well as the working miners. Colliery supervision was traditionally placed in the hands of deputies (known as firemen in Scotland), whose primary responsibility for maintaining safety standards in the mine was clearly stated in the important Coal Mines Act of 1911. This position was emphasised by the Rockley Commission, who observed that:

> They are, as it were, the non-commissioned officers of the mine; it is on them that falls the immediate responsibility for seeing that many of the requirements of the law are observed and that discipline is maintained, and it is mainly through them that most of the instructions of the management in regard to safety are carried out. They form the chief connecting link between the workmen and the senior officials of the mine, and their principal duty is to see to the safety of the districts of the mine assigned to them.[68]

This definition of the deputies' role in terms of statutory safety provisions helps to explain why their responsibilities had become a contested terrain in the decades after 1911. For the owners relied on deputies to ensure that production was organised effectively and more particularly that the haulage system was arranged so as to carry the tubs or corves which were used to bring the increasing amounts of coal away from the faces. It was to deputies that miners had to appeal for allowances for wet, difficult or other abnormal conditions, including the issue of the celebrated 'water notes' allowing miners time to change wet clothes. Workplace bargaining therefore gravitated around the deputy who had to balance the maintenance of safe working conditions against the pressures from both employers and miners to raise the value of the product from the mine.

As the drive for increased output gathered pace after 1923, so the deputies were placed under growing pressures to facilitate mechanisation and raise output whilst attending to their statutory safety duties.[69] The growing emphasis which colliery operators placed on production supervisors rather than safety officials was reflected in the employment of the different grades. Whereas the numbers of overmen increased in the 1930s, the ranks of the deputies shrank from 28,000 in 1930 to less than 18,000 five years later.[70] Not only was the ratio of overmen to deputies increasing and pressures placed on the lower officials by the overmen mounting, but the colliery deputies found that increasing numbers of colliery managers were appointing younger men with some technical training to the post of deputy, before quickly moving them up to the rank of overman. This marked something of a break with the traditional culture of the industry and a growing emphasis on formal technical training rather than the 'pit sense' gained by colliery experience as younger entrants to the supervisors' ranks were imbued with an ethos of high output rather than a primary regard for either customary methods or safety.[71]

This placed the deputies in an awkward relationship to both miners and management during the interwar period. During the nineteenth and early twentieth centuries deputies were responsible for ensuring that colliers did not work in areas where gas or firedamp was suspected and that the firing of shots occurred only when certain safety rules were respected. Even when the full butty system was in place and the charter master was the virtual employer of underground labour, safety standards and shotfiring remained the province of the certificated deputy. The shotfirer was himself assumed to be a responsible miner who drilled holes or at least placed and fired the explosive charge correctly. Shotfiring was undertaken in some districts by deputies themselves and these officials remained responsible for ensuring that dangerous practices were minimised.[72] Since explosives were readily accessible the control over the firing of charges was difficult to achieve and was considered less critical where mines were free of gas and damp, whether seeping from the face or from the waste material (the goaf) which could be ignited by a spark. The introduction of electrical machinery and the limited use of pneumatic picks to bring down the coal face made for more rather than less responsibilities on the shoulders of the deputy from the turn of the century given the dangers of electric sparks, the hazards of the machines themselves, and the difficulties in averting the wrecking of lighting systems by the blasts themselves. In their tours of inspection - usually at the beginning and end of the shifts - deputies were expected to ensure that no naked lights were used and that safety helmets were secured as well as providing for adequate working conditions and dealing with any disputes over opportunities for coal cutting and hauling. Since the hewers on piecerates were often as anxious as the colliery manager to rip out and raise the coal as quickly as they could, underground officials often faced the collusion of both sides to avoid strict safety checks.

The relationship with the miners was strained by the growing strength of unionism in the coalfields from the 1880s and the rise in the shift earnings of hewers (increasing by more than 80 per cent in many districts by 1914), which left deputies earning less than the men for whom they were responsible.[73] These circumstances as well as the statutory status of the supervisors helps to explain the emergence of distinct deputies' unions at this period. It is significant that the unionisation of deputies and shotfirers remained strong in the interwar period, even after the defeat of the miners led to a decline in their organisation after 1927. The deputies were recruited to the various district associations and represented nationally by a Federation, which claimed 14,000-15,000 members from the various deputies' associations assembled in its ranks by 1936.[74] These bodies provided the main lines of defence against what the unions perceived as the bullying tactics of the colliery overmen, whose ranks were swelled as the numbers of deputies declined along with the mining workforce between the wars. Faced with the pressures to drive up output, the deputies depended on their associations to take the most serious cases of harassment to the Mines Department on the grounds that their safety responsibilities should take precedence over the pressure for production.[75]

It was in Scotland that many of the most serious abuses were reported and Scottish conditions offer an important example of workplace change and industrial conflict in the period 1900-1939. The thin, wet and often badly faulted seams found in many Scottish mines meant difficult working conditions and an early push for mechanisation to extract the coal rapidly. By 1914 at least one fifth of Scottish coal was cut with the aid of machines with impressive results in terms of productivity growth. In line with the pattern of British coalmining, there was little structural change in the industry between the wars. There was a large number of small mines with only five collieries employing over one thousand men in 1936, though there *were* significant output gains taking the interwar period as a whole.[76] This was achieved in large part by a reduction of one third in the underground workforce whilst mechanisation was pushed ahead. By 1934 three quarters of Scottish coal was being cut by machines and almost half was mechanically conveyed - substantially above the national average.[77]

There is little doubt that Scottish coalmasters, led by such firms as the Fife Coal Company (under Nimmo), adopted a strategy of progressive mechanisation as a means of maintaining their competitiveness when faced with unpromising and diminishing opportunities for hand-cut mining.[78]

Scottish Coalowners used wartime coal and labour shortages to press their case for mechanisation and improved output, both of which seem to have increased significantly in the war years.[79] The coalowners avoided confronting the miners directly on issues of sub-contracting or unionisation, which included allowing their firemen to be pressed back into the miners' union during the post-war years. It was from 1922 onwards that the employers under the powerful Adam Nimmo (later a member of the Reid Committee) exploited the widening gulf between miners and firemen, until the General Strike provided the opportunity for a recognition of a separate association of firemen.[80] Nimmo pushed forward the policy of *raising* the status of firemen as a means of increasing efficiency in the mines and weakening the miners' union.[81] Before the coalmasters could engage in such a policy, however, they needed to cement their relations with the colliery managers who were responsible for coal production throughout the pit. The bonds of loyalty between owners and managers had been seriously weakened during and immediately after the First World War. Not only overmen and undermanagers but even colliery managers were recruited to staff and manual unions during this period. Faced with the rise of the National Association of Colliery Masters (NACM) in 1920, the Scottish owners finally discussed with them methods of improving salaries and superannuation as well as strategies for increasing output in the coalfields.[82]

It is interesting that Nimmo and the Lanarkshire coal leaders faced fierce resistance from their own constituents to even considering the NACM's demand for a minimum wage for undermanagers.[83] Such firms argued that the introduction of a superannuation scheme with the NACM would strengthen trade unionism amongst their managers.[84] Although the Mining Association of Great Britain had developed a national policy on representation and superannuation, the Lanarkshire Masters strongly opposed any collective strategy for wages or pensions and pushed through individual wage reductions in 1922.[85] A similar pattern was apparent in their dealings with the under managers and overmen, who organised in a Scottish Association (SUMA) to present a series of demands in 1920.[86] With some difficulty, Nimmo persuaded the Lanarkshire firms to avoid a confrontation which would force the Association into the arms of the miners' union.[87] Their patience was vindicated during the 1921 coal strike, when under managers and overmen remained on active service to keep the mines operating.[88] From 1922 onwards there was a powerful movement amongst Lanarkshire (and Scottish) coalowners for a return to individual bargaining with all their managerial grades and a decline in the membership and influence of both management and supervisors' associations.[89] The employers were able to identify activists amongst their firemen and overmen during major strikes in the years 1921-26 and were able to exploit the decline in supervisory numbers to remove the more prominent unionists from their collieries. At the same time the miners' unions in Scotland continued their own efforts to recruit deputies within the union rather than accept independent associations.[90] The capacity of the miners to resist such policies was severely weakened by the sustained contraction of the industry in the interwar period, particularly in the Lanarkshire coalfield, whilst at the same time the owners were forced by squeezed profits to pursue output growth by any means available to them.[91]

The evidence suggests that it was the declining strength of both manual and non-manual unionism during the early 1920s which enabled coalmasters in Scotland and other regions to press ahead with their efforts to restore and surpass pre-war output levels.   Such policies were significantly extended after the decisive defeat of the miners in the great strike of 1926 and Scottish masters were particularly determined to maintain the output and profitability of their pits in the worsening market conditions of the 1920s.   This involved not only increased mechanisation and the continued use of piecework (as well as sub-contracting for deadwork), but also a longer working day as systematic overtime was imposed on miners and supervisors alike.   Mechanisation was not an alternative to more intensive working but rather an accessory to it.   One enquiry revealed that an excessive amount of overtime was worked in Scotland, with the worst offenders found in pits practising mechanised cutting and conveying in Lanarkshire and east Scotland.[92]   Unauthorised overtime working was particularly heavy amongst firemen, with as much as a quarter or even a third of all the overtime worked at some collieries undertaken by supervisors.[93]   The spread of the mechanised three-shift system and the need to leave the face clean for the cutters and the track clear for conveyors placed great pressure on supervisors to extend working hours.[94]

Another feature of the intensification of work in Scottish collieries was the increased use of explosives to fire down the coal after holing or under-cutting. There was a general trend for shotfiring to increase in the early 1930s, as coalowners were less concerned with winning larger coals as price differentials for smaller coals (which was inevitably the result of using explosives) declined.[95] At least *part* of the productivity gains of the 1930s were achieved by using significantly more, if lighter, shots on the coalface itself.[96]   Scotland was particularly prominent in the use of explosives, with most of the authorised firing carried out by firemen and shotfirers.   Employers appear to have used large numbers of young men to fire shots, whilst the firemen themselves were expected to assume overall responsibility for the safety of conditions where and when explosives were being used.   It was also the Scottish and Northern fields, where both mechanisation and shot-firing was most prevalent that recorded the highest proportion of explosives casualties.[97]   Whilst the Northern district (Durham and Northumberland) fired a larger number of shots by 1935, Scottish pits had by far the greatest amount of non-permitted shots fired.[98]

This was clearly one of the most sensitive areas of the debate on the supervisor's responsibilities and vividly exposed the strains between his statutory duties and his role as a co-ordinator of mineworkers. The miners' unions and the Mines Inspector for Scotland, Frazer, argued for the strict limitation, if not abolition, of shot-firing and more reliance on manual and pneumatic picks.[99] Although the coalowners had little scope for restricting the safety duties of the firemen, they rejected the Inspector's views on firing and insisted that the supervisors were able to oversee or undertake shotfiring without prejudice to their statutory obligations.[100] The employers also dismissed Frazer's contention that Scottish overmen bullied the deputies when their concern for safety conflicted with the drive for output. Coalmasters suggested that the great increase in shot-firing was actually the result of a growing preference amongst hewers and getters for the use of explosives rather than hand pick work on thin seams.[101]

The conflicting claims are difficult to assess though it appears that the tendency of Scottish miners to use increasing amounts of explosives on the face and in deadwork was the product of growing pressure from overmen to work quickly and sufficient collusion from management to ensure that shotfirers and miners were able to acquire, handle and place large numbers of charges near the face. The majority of shots seem to have been fired using non-permitted explosives (possibly because the wet conditions of Scottish mines made their use less hazardous than elsewhere), which contravened current best practice of applying sheathed and permitted charges underground. The whole question of safety became highly politicised during the 1930s, as the miners' unions struggled to regain some advantage by organising workmen's inspections of unpopular pits and appealing to the inspectorate for support in resisting the rise of the overman as a dominant figure in production. In practice the Scottish Inspector was willing to defend deputies against overt intimidation by overmen, but objected to the union using the workmen's inspections 'for the purpose of propaganda and just coloured with safety'.[102] The importance of the safety issue in what were both production struggles and contests between bargaining institutions for advantage can hardly be underestimated. In emphasising the 'political reasons at the back of these inspections', Frazer (the Scottish Inspector) illuminated not only the vigorous politics of the miners' unions but also the role of the safety question in defining the relations between employers, labour and the state.[103]

This continued controversy over safety cannot be adequately explained in terms of the greater hazards of Scottish mining, since in some respects (such as fatalities and serious injury from roof falls) these mines recorded below-average accident rates.[104] Rather, it was the rapid pace of change in Scotland, implemented by aggressive employers against the stubborn opposition of strong unions, which explains the intense scrutiny of safety questions during these years. A key element in the drive to increase productivity was the creation of a loyal stratum of production supervisors who were primarily concerned with output.

The coalowners saw the labour policies and their collective response to supervisory trade unionism as part of the same process of strengthening the bonds of loyalty amongst their deputies and overmen. In the early 1920s the Scottish coalowners abandoned the policy of recognising supervisory unionism and sought to foster their loyalties to the employers by a collaborative welfare programme, though their main efforts went into providing tied welfare benefits for managers and undermanagers on an individual company basis. Such business policies became a source of grievance which continued to sour relations between colliery managers and firemen in the interwar years and was criticised by the Royal Commission on Safety in Mines as short-sighted and damaging.[105] Meanwhile the overmen, who served as the linchpin in the new managerialist regime, were bitterly resented by miners and deputies alike in many coalfields. This grade of supervisor remained poorly unionised even in north England and appears to have been completely unorganised in Scotland before the Second World War.[106]

Although there were a number of official investigations into these conditions, including the Holland Committee of 1930, it is interesting that the state made no serious attempt to legislate for safety before the Rockley Commission reported in 1938. In terms of statutory provisions, the deputy remained the key figure in the conduct of the mine his authority had been seriously compromised (though not destroyed) by the introduction of a new production system which marginalised his role in the drive for output. The miners were able to weaken the autonomy of the firemen and press them more firmly into their unions once recognition of supervisory associations was refused by the employers. Unfortunately, the consequence was to confirm an erosion of the firemen's position and persuade the owners of the need for a new strategy on appointments and promotions which overturned the customary recruitment of older, skilled colliers to the ranks of the deputies and introduced a new breed of younger, ambitious individuals who saw their tasks less in terms of strict safety standards and more in terms of co-operating with the demands of the overman. In their anxiety to defend the 'independent collier' as the guardian of safe working practices at the coalface, the miners' unions failed to respond quickly to the new division of labour or to insulate the supervisor against the pressures placed on him by management.[107]

The impact of these policies on productivity growth are difficult to assess given the complexities of output measurement and the wide diversity in colliery performance. The evidence available to the Reid Committee suggested that in spite of the continued mechanisation of the cutting and conveying process, productivity underground declined slightly after 1936 and continued to falter during the Second World War. By 1939 four fifths of Scottish coal was cut by machine and three fifths was conveyed by machines, though output at the face had fallen fractionally since 1927.[108] The more recent Fife field was very productive in conveying as well as cutting, though the older districts were clearly facing serious problems of diminishing returns by the 1940s.[109] The general trend for diminishing productivity growth was registered not only in the British coalfields but also in Europe which suggests that a number of factors associated with the increased demand and output of the late 1930s were combining to constrain output growth.[110] In the British coalfields the resurgence of trade unionism and increased bargaining power of mineworkers in the late 1930s would suggest that labour relations altered in favour of the cutters and conveyors even though mechanisation continued at this time. Although mechanisation progressed rapidly to 1943 the tonnage handled by haulage workers actually fell as the numbers of faceworkers diminished and 'discipline problems' arose.[111] Whilst the Reid Committee propagandised for its own vision of the future needs of the industry, the sustained criticisms of the poor quality of technical training for supervisory and management grades as well as the primitive conditions in which miners travelled to the face and worked their day appear to be well founded.[112]

It is significant that Reid says very little about safety provisions and accident rates in the industry and bargaining concerns of 1945 as well as the policy agenda of capital and labour appears to have moved away from the issues raised before the Rockley Commission in 1936-38.[113] By 1945 almost three quarters of British coal was cut by machines and virtually the same amount was mechanically conveyed, though it was not until the late 1950s that the power loading of coal was introduced on a large scale.[114] By 1957 a quarter of all coal was cut and mechanically loaded at the same time and a decade later the success of the Anderton Shearer loader (ASL) dominated the great bulk of coalmining activities in Britain.[115] Although the market environment for the nationalised coal industry was considerably more favourable than that which had faced many private firms in the interwar period, there was actually only a limited programme of new investment in the industry before 1953 and only in 1956-57 was a new phase of reconstruction noticeable in the coalfields.[116] This appears surprising in view of the 1950 *Plan for Coal*, which estimated a growth of demand of 18 per cent by the early 1960s whilst manpower was set to decline by more than 10 per cent in the same period.[117] Output per shift rose quite significantly (by 13 per cent) between 1947 and 1951, though reached a plateau and did not rise noticeably again until the new programme of innovation in 1957. The fact that the productivity of face workers was much better than that of the workforce overall in the 1950s seems to vindicate the conclusions of both the Reid Report and also the *Fleck Report* of 1955 on weaknesses in management quality and organisation.[118] Ashworth notes that the decline in the productivity and performance of the Scottish coalfield was one of the most notable features of the post-war years, including the 'disastrous transformation' in the fortunes of the Fife collieries from profit to serious loss-making in the decade after 1948. The official historian of the nationalised industry notes that geological and technical difficulties burdened the Scottish district, though these were compounded by 'notoriously difficult labour relations'.[119]

The troubled character of industrial relations in the post-war coalmining industry is one of the enduring mythologies of labour history and has often obscured the complexities of bargaining and conflict within the coalfields. The great wage struggles of the 1970s and 1980s revived debates on the militancy of British miners and their contribution to industrial costs which continues with the recent work of Church and others on the patterns of conflict in modern mining. These scholars suggest that, far from enjoying any broad social or political coherence, miners' strikes were almost invariably confined to a small core of pits (varying over time) and overwhelmingly concerned with wage questions until the introduction of national day wages turned the attention of miners to productivity issues in the 1960s.[120] Institutional arrangements appear to have largely dictated the politics of productivity in the post-war era.

Yet if we focus on the problem of output and safety in the 1940s and 1950s a rather more complicated picture of production struggles and labour politics emerges. The recommendations of the Rockley Commission had been overtaken by the outbreak of war and remained in obscurity during the post-war period of nationalisation as the legislation of 1911 continued to provide the industry's safety rules until the Mines and Quarries Act of 1954.[121] Fatalities in mines did not decline in the early years of the NCB and rose to a peak in 1947, with a noticeable fall only in the mid-1950s. There was also a rise in non-fatal serious accidents as pressure for output continued in the late 1940s and these began to rise again in the later 1950s before declining only in the 1960s. There was an even sharper increase in non-serious accidents from 1958 onwards which rose over 60 per cent on the previous decade.[122] When we compare this pattern with that of wage disputes in the post-war years there is a rough parallel between the conflicts over rewards in the industry and the trend in accident rates. The common denominator appears to be the drive for output in the late 1940s and the late 1950s which involved pressures on mineworkers to produce more coal as part of a general NCB (and government) strategy for industry. In contrast to the pre-war period, however, safety provisions did not become an arena of conflict - despite the severity of accident rates - mainly (it seems) because the NCB was able to secure the support of both miners and the managerial grades for the programme of reforms which were introduced in the 1950s. This achievement was not merely the product of the National Union of Mineworkers' co-option within the aims of the *Plans for Coal*, but arose out of a series of struggles that occurred in the industry itself.

The pervasive use of piecework incentives for faceworkers and rippers of various kinds meant that workplace bargaining persisted under the nationalised corporation, as well as constant struggles between different grades in the enormously complex grading structure of the industry where numerous titles and variations in duties even amongst the supervisory grades continued after 1946. Strikes over job appraisals as well as payment systems and even pit closures marked the early years of nationalisation, though it is apparent that industrial relations improved markedly over the last years of private ownership.[123] Only in the later 1950s did a significant rise in disputes occur as the era of 'coal at any price' closed and the drive for efficiencies in production and new investment really began. By 1955 the NCB had begun the arduous task of standardising day wages for its oncost staff and initiated a process that culminated in the National Power Loading Agreement (NPLA) of 1966. Part of this process was the resolution of grievances and anomalies amongst its supervisory grades from shotfirers who engaged on a major strike in 1948 to supervisory staff covered by the 1956 agreement on job titles and pay rates across the industry.[124] This transition to a new staffing and wages structure occurred at a time when strikes (measured in terms of tonnage lost) were peaking in the British coal industry before the decline in disputes of 1958-68, even though absences from work caused by illness and accidents continued to rise.[125]

The absence of these accident rates from the public agenda of the industry must surely be understood not simply in terms of a declining sensitivity to miners' health in the industry, but as an expression of the quite different concerns of the working miners and their unions. In the 1930s the safety question had been the means by which both miners and supervisors could dramatise the costs of the drive for increased output whilst invoking the statutory responsibilities of the state for the protection of those employed in the industry. The miners and their unions used safety (as housing conditions had been used in the time of Sankey) as an instrument to demonstrate the iniquities of private ownership. The nationalisation of the industry and the massive institutional reorganisation hardly affected the bargaining machinery until the mid-1950s when there were signs of growing friction at the workplace and union leaders were anxious to consolidate their authority within the industry. Unpopular overmen and sub-contractors no longer drove the work teams on longwalls though it would seem that the combination of a semi-mechanised extractive process, where coal was still hand-filled, and a traditional piecework system for the cutters and rippers, was no longer yielding the output gains that the management required.[126] Once again the deputy was at the centre of the transition in working methods and bargaining practices. Under the system inherited from the interwar period the deputies and overmen were responsible for ensuring discipline on the haulage system, which was much more tightly supervised than facework, and also for bargaining with the coal getters as to piecework allowances. Pressures mounted as the technical and human system designed in the pre-war era was placed under strain and these pressures were communicated to the supervisors. The new phase of mechanisation that arrived in the later 1950s removed some of these frictions by extending power loading and phasing out piecework, though the deputies themselves were now held responsible for the maintenance of the work cycle in the absence of incentive wages.[127] It could be argued that the transition first to nationalisation and then to the era of power loading and standard wages actually reduced the earlier

emphasis on the safety responsibilities of the deputies in the pit. This presents
the paradox that the officials were less motivated to publicise the safety problems
of the post-war years when legislation was unsatisfactory and accident rates rose,
than in the pre-war period when safety was improving though controversial
policies were being pursued in the coalmines.

Conclusions

This essay provides only a preliminary survey of supervision and safety in the
British coal industry during the years 1900-1960. It has attempted to show that
safety was no more a neutral phenomenon in British coalmines than it was in the
mining industry of South Africa.[128] Therefore the attempts of some scholars to
demonstrate that mining trade unions are more concerned with wages than with
the safety of their members rather misses the point.[129] For safety was a
consciousness of hazards which was constructed in specific historical
circumstances for particular purposes. Unions are clearly concerned with
promoting their own ends, though these ends are not predetermined by the
structure of the organisation. This seems to be the flawed assumption beneath
the institutionalist interpretation of labour relations which Church and others
provide. Such scholars criticise Marxist accounts which attribute class interests
to workers engaged in workplace struggles and which frequently portray unions
as bureaucratic impediments to class militancy. In these recent accounts it is the
formal bargaining institutions which figure most prominently and the unintended
consequences of shifting strategies which dominate the scene (such writers argue)
far more clearly than any coherent pattern of membership interests or class
conflict.[130] The concern to emphasise institutional politics over workplace
conflicts leads to arguments that mechanisation was not central to changes in
work organisation or industrial relations between the wars.[131]

Yet the arguments offered by the institutionalists provide a parallel analysis of
workers' and union interests in which the imperatives for conflict are held to be
specific to particular industries at the time and where the political concerns of
union officers and activists are held to be the capture of power within the union
structure.[132] Church, for example, is concerned to demolish the myth of miners'
class militancy as well as documenting the vitality of entrepreneurship in the
private era. His findings indicate not only the peculiar circumstances of local
disputes throughout the twentieth century but also the overriding importance of
national institutional arrangements to the bargaining practices which developed
in this period. There was no substantial politics of productivity at the workplace
until the piecework system was reformed and attention turned to effort levels in
the late 1950s.[133] Up to this period miners' disputes were almost exclusively
concerned with wage questions.

Such a perspective on labour relations in the coalmining industry provides a
valuable corrective to the heroic mythologies of class struggles in the coalfield

which were generated by Communist and socialist chronicles of the period. The difficulty with such revisionist assessments is that they impose a formal distinction between 'wage militancy' and 'political motivation' which trivialises the complexities of industrial relations and the different discourses which are engaged in both labour management and the conduct of disputes. Nor can the relations of the state with capital and labour be adequately encompassed within such terms as 'tripartism' or even 'institutional stalemate'. The evolution of safety legislation from the mid-nineteenth century to the 1950s reveals the different forms of state intervention which existed and the capacity of the inspectorate to defend lower management even when the government favoured modernisation of production. Finally, the institutionalist assessment of labour relations provided by Church ignores the importance of conflicts within and throughout the hierarchical division of labour in the industry and in particular the pivotal position occupied by colliery supervisors in the structure of management and authority. The pattern of conflicts and their impact on the management of labour can only be fully appreciated if we consider the distribution of power with the workplace and the bargaining arena as well as the role of institutions in the exercise of power.

The debates on safety standards in coal mines reflected the transitions in production and in labour relations throughout the period. Safety was the terrain on which methods of production were scrutinised. Mechanisation itself did not provoke widespread resistance from labour and the use of explosives continued to be commonly used (and even increased) with the coming of the machines. Miners and masters colluded in the growth of shooting as the premium for larger coals began to diminish with the use of smaller coals by power stations and other major customers from the end of the nineteenth century. The statutory responsibilities of both managers and supervisors led to a strained identity as they sought to achieve maximum output whilst ensuring the safety of those working underground. Such strains were particularly noticeable in the duties of the deputies at moments of conflict between employers and labour as these officials endeavoured to maintain safety standards in pits even when they were laid idle by strikes. The key periods of transition from hand mining to machine mining also created conditions where the loyalties of the safety officials were placed under intense scrutiny. Controversy arose when the coalowners in Scotland and some other districts sought to exploit the new technology by placing it in the hands of sub-contractors at the pits. It was more common for haulage and other oncost labour to be employed under a butty master but even then deputies oversaw the working conditions of the hauliers. With the arrival of the contractor at the workface the deputy's own role in relation to workplace bargaining was eroded and tensions clearly increased throughout the workforce before 1914 and again after 1923.

The interplay between management policies, workplace bargaining and institutional policies dominated the discussions of safety in the 1920s and 1930s.

Miners appear to have quickly adapted to the pressures from owners for mechanisation and output. The increased firing of shots in districts such as Scotland may have been, in part, an attempt by the coal getters to satisfy the demand for increased output and reduced costs as prices fell and pits closed around them. Miners and deputies were pressed into working systematic overtime to maintain the steady rhythm of the cutting, filling and ripping cycle. Evidence suggests that managers favoured younger men on piecework to cut, shoot down, load, and even supervise the coal face as overmen. In these terms the coalowners were able to isolate and defeat not only the miners' unions in the great set-piece battle of 1926 but had already crushed the challenge from the supervisory and managerial associations during the early 1920s. Faced with disaffection amongst the deputies, the owners established the overman as the key official on the shift with responsibility solely for achieving output. Deputies found their numbers shrank rapidly in the 1930s as they were marginalised in the drive for coal. The policy of the miners in forcing the Scottish firemen into their union actually served to weaken the autonomy of the supervisors and arguably weakened their capacity to resist the management. In these conditions the deputies appealed to the state inspectorate to protect them from managerial intimidation and the expanding power of the overman, whilst both the manual and the supervisory unions sought to increase statutory safety regulations on the production process as a means of controlling workloads. The stagnation of productivity growth after 1936 may be partly due to the resistance which the aggressive drive for output had provoked amongst miners and deputies alike by this period.

Nationalisation and the increased co-operation evident after wartime wage anomalies were resolved in 1947-48 probably contributed to the improvement in productivity growth before 1957, even though major new investment was not undertaken until the later 1950s. The NCB then faced diminishing returns not only from ageing collieries but from the technical organisation of work and the payment structure which had been inherited from the interwar years. The Scottish coalfield, including the productive Fife district, went into serious decline during the 1950s. Mounting tensions were evident before the industry moved to standardised day wages between 1955 and 1966. Although the accident rate remained stable in the immediate post-war years and less serious injuries actually rose in the 1950s, particularly as a new phase of mechanisation was undertaken after 1955, the safety issue did not attract the attention which it received in the 1930s. Rockley's recommendations were ignored for a remarkably long time in a sector owned by the state which had appointed the Commission. The explanation may be found in the reduced frictions at the workplace as sub-contracting and aggressive overmen were eliminated and the NCB enjoyed favourable markets which neither the Board nor the miners exploited effectively to increase their revenues at this time. Piecework remained a vital incentive to individual effort during these years though it is clear that it was not yielding even the face productivity that was possible with a new generation of power loaders. From their different perspectives, Coal Board, managers, unions and miners converged on the view that the traditional structure of supervision was no longer adequate to meet their various expectations in the changed conditions of the modern nationalised industry.

Finally, it is worth emphasising the contrasting experiences of British and European coalmining in these decades. As the essay by Werner Abelshauser shows, even regions with a powerful history of conflict and socialist engagement could provide a basis for cooperation between employers, labour and the state. There was no necessary reason for the high degree of politicisation of the safety issue in the British industry, though the fact that it remained an area of contention reflects the deeper problems of workplace and industrial relations in the middle decades of the twentieth century. The present essay has argued that the degree to which supervisors were drawn into these struggles would indicate a profound fissure between the mentalities which persisted in the workplace and those institutions responsible for building legitimacy in politics and society. As Abelshauser's research and the Swedish discussion of the LKAB mining venture would suggest, it was not the principle of state ownership but the practices of bargaining and consensus over goals which was to prove the critical factor in the post-war years.

Notes

* I wish to acknowledge financial support from the British Academy and the Australian Studies Centre in the completion of research on which this paper is largely based. I am grateful to John Goldthorpe, Boris Schedvin and Barry Supple for encouragement during the research.

1. R. Church, 'Production, employment and labour productivity in the British coalfields, 1830-1913: Some reinterpretations' *Business History*, XXXI (1989) , p11.
2. B.R. Mitchell, *Economic development of the British coal industry 1800-1914* Cambridge University Press (1984) Cambridge, pp317-19.
3. R. Church, *The History of the British Coal Industry. Volume 3, 1830-1913: Victorian pre-eminence* Oxford University Press. (1986) Oxford; Church, 'Production', pp7, 16-17.
4. Church, 'Production', pp19-20, citing Hirsch and Hausmann's work.
5. Church, *History*, pp340-43. Church suggests that blasting powder raised *overall* productivity of labour only by 5-8 per cent in the mid-nineteenth century but again acknowledges much greater impact at the coalface and also the continued widespread use of explosives before 1914.
6. Church, *History*, pp211-14, 311, 335.
7. D. Greasley, 'Fifty years of coal-mining productivity: The record of the British coal industry before 1939' *Journal of Economic History*, L (4), (1990) p880, Table 1.
8. *Report of the Royal Commission on the Coal Industry* (1925) [hereafter *Samuel Report*], Volume 1 (1926), Cmd. 2600, pp14-45.
9. *Samuel Report*, pp115-16; Church, 'Production', pp211-14, 311, 328-38.
10. Greasley, 'Fifty years', pp881-82.
11. Greasley, 'Fifty years', p892.
12. *Samuel Report*, p119; *Report of the Royal Commission on Safety in Coal Mines* [hereafter *Rockley Report*] Cmd. 5890 (1938), pp54-56.
13. Rockley Report p50; Minutes of evidence taken before the Royal Commission on Safety in Coal Mines [published separately]. HMSO (1936-37), Frazer's evidence, p320; c.f., p558.

14. B. Supple, *The History of the British Coal Industry. Volume 4: The political economy of decline* Oxford University Press (1987) Oxford, p11; R. Church, 'Employers, trade unions and the state, 1889-1987: The origins and decline of tri-partism in the British coal industry' in G.D.T. Feldman and K. Tenfelde (eds.), *Workers, Owners and Politics in Coal Mining: An international comparison of industrial relations* Berg (1989) Oxford, p16.
15. M. Dintenfass, 'Entrepreneurial failure reconsidered: The case of the interwar coal industry' *Business History Review*, 62 (1) (1988), pp2-3.
16. Dintenfass, 'Entrepreneurial failure', p7, Table 2.
17. Dintenfass, 'Entrepreneurial failure', pp8-10.
18. Dintenfass, 'Entrepreneurial failure', pp14-17.
19. T. Boyns, 'Rationalisation in the inter-war period: The case of the South Wales steam coal industry' *Business History* (1990), pp290-91, 296.
20. Ministry of Fuel and Power, *Report of the Technical Advisory Committee* [hereafter *Reid Report*] HMSO(1945), pp16-18, 29; W. Ashworth, *The history of the British coal industry: Volume 5. 1946-1982: The nationalized industry* Clarendon Press (1986) Oxford, p4. Shift output increased by 81 per cent in the Ruhr and 54 per cent in Poland. See Abelshauser essay for Ruhr developments after 1945.
21. *Reid Report*, p8, Fig.1. Reid noted that conveyed coal rose from 28 million tons in 1928 to 134 million by 1939.
22. *Reid Report*, pp13-14.
23. Greasley, 'Fifty years', pp879, 893-94.
24. Ashworth, *History*, p7.
25. Ashworth, *History*, p11.
26. Ashworth, *History*, p222.
27. R. Goffee, 'Incorporation and conflict: A case study of subcontracting in the coal industry' *Sociological Review*, 29 (3), (1981), pp475-497, for example. R.J. Waller, *The Dukeries transformed* Oxford University Press (1983) Oxford.
28. Church, *History*, pp337-38; Mitchell, *History*.
29. J.H. Pencavel, 'The distributional and efficiency effects of trade unions in Britain' *British Journal of Industrial Relations* XV, 2 (1977), pp137-156; B.T. Hirsch and W.J. Hausman, 'Labour productivity in the South Wales coal industry: Reply' *Economica* 52 (1985), pp391-394; c.f. D. Greasley, 'Wage rates and work intensity in the South Wales coalfield, 1874-1914' *Economica* 52 (1985), pp383-389, for the critique of Hirsch and Hausman. Church, 'Production', pp20-21, appears to support the view that productivity decline after 1900 was due to legislative interference with hours, citing Hirsch and Hausmann, though he also acknowledges that productivity levels *rose* after 1908.
30. Church, 'Employers', p35, citing Supple.
31. Church, 'Employers', p16.
32. Church, 'Employers', p54.
33. Q. Outram, R. Church and D. Smith, 'Theoretical orientations to miners' strikes', unpublished paper, Bochum *International Mining History Conference* Bochum (1989).
34. Church, 'Employers', pp55-57.
35. *Reid Report*, pp13-14. Reid noted at p65: 'We are satisfied that no single operation associated with coal production in Britain offers more scope for improved efficiency than that of underground transport.'
36. *Reid Report*, pp40-46, 48-49.
37. *Reid Report*, pp34-36, 113-15.
38. *Reid Report*, p107.
39. *Reid Report*, p111.
40. *Reid Report*, p112.
41. Church, 'Employers', p16.
42. *Rockley Report* (1938), Cmd. 5890. The *Minutes of Evidence* were not presented to Parliament as a command paper but published separately by the HMSO.
43. Mitchell, *Economic*, pp46-48, 326.
44. Mitchell, *Economic*, pp82-3.

45. Mitchell, *Economic*, p171.
46. Mitchell, *Economic*, p188, Table 6.1.
47. Mitchell, *Economic*, p300, Table 9.5. Fife was making strong profits in 1912-14 in contrast to the Midlothian and western districts.
48. Mitchell, *Economic*, pp89-90, for *Colliery Guardian*. Mitchell appears to underestimate the resilience of sub-contracting as an employer strategy, particularly in respect of mechanisation.
49. Church, *History*, pp352-357, 363. Church argues that geo-technical reasons precluded their use on the great bulk of thicker seams though it is not clear whether entrepreneurship is held to be rational because coalowners only introduced machines when forced to by geology or because the technology was only appropriate to these difficult conditions, c.f. p357.
50. Lanarkshire Coal Masters' Association [hereafter LCMA Mins], Glasgow University Archives. Minutes of Association: 6 August 1908-24 August 1908.
51. LCMA, Mins: 4 March 1908, 6 November 1908.
52. LCMA, Mins: 14 October 1912 - 19 December 1913.
53. LCMA Mins: 1 March 1911, 19 December 1913
54. LCMA Mins: 26 August 1907, 17 August 1908, 23 August 1911, 24 October 1911, for owners' successes in introducing clearance certificates.
55. LCMA Mins: 30 April 1913.
56. LCMA Mins: 3 February 1919, 22 September 1919
57. LCMA Mins: 9 April 1918
58. C.f. Church, 'Employers', pp15-19; also J. Zeitlin, 'From labour history to the history of industrial relations' *Economic History Review* XL, 2 (1987), pp159, 167-68.
59. Goffee, 'Incorporation', for example.
60. *Rockley Report*, pp58-59.
61. *Rockley Evidence*, pp1000, 1002.
62. *Rockley Evidence*, Q27899, 27923; Q28059; also Frazer's evidence, 10670-72. Frazer was the Divisional Inspector of Mines for Scotland. See *Rockley Report*, p58.
63. Report [by the Inspector of Mines] on and causes of...the explosions...at Bilsthorpe Colliery, 1934. Mines Department. Cmd. 4780 (1935), pp6-7, 16-17; Report [by the Chief Inspector of Mines] on the causes of...the explosion...at Grassmoor Colliery, 1933. Mines Department. Cmd.4550 (1934), pp5, 20.
64. Rockley Evidence, Q26441, 26486-87, 26666, etc.
65. Rockley Evidence, Q26837-844, 26949.
66. See also Samuel Report, p189.
67. Rockley Evidence, Mining Association of Great Britain President, Evan Williams, 31944, 31965-70, 31979-81, etc.
68. Rockley Report, pp180-81.
69. Rockley Report, p48.
70. Rockley Report, p180.
71. Rockley Evidence, Frazer's evidence, 9549: 'Some colliery managers tell me that the best deputies are not the most experienced face workers, but young men with scientific training and a certain amount of practical training who fear - to use their expression - neither God, nor the devil.'
72. Mitchell, Economic, p101.
73. Mitchell, Economic, p206, Fig. 7.6-7.7.
74. Rockley Evidence, evidence of Frowen of Deputies' Federation, Q15312.
75. Rockley Evidence, Frowen Q15547.
76. Rockley Evidence, Frazer p320; Q9128, 9144.
77. Report of a special inquiry into the working of overtime in coal mines in Scotland. Mines Department. Cmd.4959 (1935), p5.
78. Nimmo of the Fife Company was a prominent figure in the Mining Association and a member of the Reid Committee which sat during the Second World War.
79. LCMA Mins: 3 September 1918; 3 February 1919, where evidence suggested output of 14,314 tons by 117.5 men during three months in 1914 as against 12,672 and 51 men in 1918.
80. LCMA Mins: 24 April 1922, 22 September 1924, 25 October 1926.
81. LCMA Mins: 18 January 1927.

82. LCMA Mins: 22 November 1920.
83. LCMA Mins: 21 February 1921.
84. LCMA Mins: 13 December 1921-16 January 1922.
85. LCMA Mins: 15 March 1922.
86. LCMA Mins: 28 September 1920.
87. LCMA Mins: 11 January 1921.
88. LCMA Mins: 21 June 1921.
89. LCMA Mins: 27 March 1922, 24 March 1924; J.H. Goldthorpe, Unpublished research notes for D.Phil thesis, Oxford (c.1958). I am grateful to John Goldthorpe and Barry Supple for permission to read and cite these notes.
90. Rockley Evidence, Frowen Q15472.
91. Ashworth, History, p10.
92. Report of inquiry into overtime working in Scotland, Cmd. 4959, pp3-5.
93. Cmd.4959, pp8-9; c.f. Report of a special inquiry into the working of overtime in coal mines in Lancashire, Cmd.4626 (1934), p5 for less strenuous conditions of that coalfield.
94. Rockley Evidence, Jones, Q26896, 27049-52.
95. Rockley Evidence, Jones, Q28059-60.
96. Rockley Evidence, Frazer, Q10670-72.
97. Rockley Evidence, Williams of MAGB, Q33226-36227.
98. Rockley Report, p60, table II.
99. Rockley Evidence, Frazer 9970.
100. Rockley Evidence, Q9177, 9494, 9589, etc.
101. Rockley Evidence, Williams, Q31585-88, 33150.
102. Rockley Evidence, Q9762.
103. Rockley Evidence, Q9514.
104. Rockley Evidence, Q27063.
105. Rockley Report, p202; also Rockley Evidence, Q9787.
106. Rockley Evidence, Ritson of NFCO, Q19831.
107. Rockley Evidence, Q16643-45 for Sumner (of MFGB) calling for a return to the days of the 'old-fashioned collier.'
108. Reid Report, p10.
109. Reid Report, pp12-13.
110. See Reid Report, p16. For all its bold assertions and substantial influence on subsequent scholarship, the Reid Committee provides little hard evidence of the causes of productivity variation either in the UK or Europe during the interwar period.
111. Reid Report, p14.
112. Reid Report, pp106-111.
113. Reid Report, pp107, 116.
114. Ashworth, History, p76.
115. Ashworth, History, p85. By 1968 90 per cent of coal was cut and mechanically loaded.
116. Ashworth, History, p225.
117. Ashworth, History, p200.
118. Fleck Report quoted Ashworth, History, p171.
119. Ashworth, History, p233.
120. Church, 'Employers'.
121. Ashworth, History, p552.
122. Ashworth, History, pp556-57.
123. Ashworth, History, pp169-70.
124. Ashworth, History, pp168, 212.
125. Ashworth, History, pp596-97.
126. J.H. Goldthorpe, 'Technical organisation as a factor in supervisor-worker conflict. Some preliminary observations on a study made in the mining industry' British Journal of Sociology, X, 3, (1959), pp221-23.
127. Goldthorpe, 'Technical organisation', pp225-26.
128. H.J. Van Aswegan, "'Miner's Phthisis": Health politics on the gold mines of the Witwatersrand,

South Africa, 1886-1920', Unpublished paper, International Mining History Conference, Bochum (1989), pp12-13.

129. P.V. Fishback, 'Workplace safety during the Progressive Era: fatal accidents in bituminous coal mining, 1912-1923' Explorations in Economic History 23 (1986), pp275-77, passim.

130. Zeitlin, 'From labour history', pp159-61.

131. Church, 'Employers', p16.

132. Zeitlin, 'From labour history', pp182-3, for example; Church, 'Employers', pp43-44.

133. Church relies on Hugh Clegg's seminal account of the origins of the National Power Loading Agreement in this assessment. See the Wintertons' essay above, for a critical perspective.

9. Management and workplace trade unionism: Clydeside engineering, 1945-1957

Alan McKinlay

Introduction

This essay considers the dynamics of workplace trade unionism on Clydeside, one of the main regional concentrations of British engineering. Our starting point is James Hinton's study of the fate of wartime joint consultation.[1] Hinton concludes that the initial enthusiasm of British workers waned in the face of employer indifference and the post-1945 failure was testimony to Labour's impoverished political imagination. The crisis of war production and the first years of Labour government were, argues Hinton, moments at which the relationship between capital and labour, and the state and private enterprise could have been fundamentally redrawn. This conclusion is at odds with the evidence provided by Hinton on the experience of the Joint Production Committees (JPCs). A brief flurry of enthusiasm was followed by widespread apathy among engineering workers and, on Clydeside, deep-seated hostility. Nor was there any countervailing employer support for JPCs. On the contrary, employer opposition to JPCs was profound and unrelenting. Far from using JPCs to foster higher levels of trust between managers and managed, the first priority of engineering employers was neutralising the power and authority of the shop steward within the workplace. On the Clyde, disrupting shopfloor trade unionism and victimising leading union activists was immeasurably more important to engineering employers than building new consultative mechanisms. The relationship between the terminal decline of the JPC in the immediate post-war period and the war of attrition inside British engineering factories is discussed in the opening section. We then consider the impact of workplace trade unionism on authority relations within the factory in the decade after 1945.

Joint Production Committees: suppressed alternatives?

For two or three years after 1945 both engineering employers and unions recognised that there was a brief window of opportunity within which collective bargaining could be completely restructured. The impetus for restructuring came from the union side. Management-union dialogue on the shopfloor was envisaged as the primary level of a structure of planning and consultations whose regional, sectoral and national forums would deliver enhanced productivity and democratic accountability. The employers, on the other hand, regarded such initiatives not as a way of incorporating workplace trade unionism into the management process but as a fundamental challenge to managerial authority.

JPCs were introduced in 1942 in response to rising shopfloor discontent and levels of inefficiency which threatened the war effort.[2] Engineering employers obstinately refused to surrender their 'right to manage' unilaterally, the principle which lay behind two major lock-outs in the industry in 1897-98 and 1922.[3] Initially, the employers' suspicion of workplace consultative bodies was mirrored by the AEU: Jack Tanner was a lone voice on the Executive and the support of the Communist Party and unofficial shop stewards' movement further strengthened official opposition to JPCs. JPCs were endorsed by the AEU and employers on the strict understanding that they were completely separate from mainstream industrial relations. In practice, joint consultation could never sustain this separation in an industry in which piecework explicitly linked productivity and individual earnings. The real success in extending JPCs came in 1942 but this represented their high water mark. After 1942 JPCs rapidly declined in importance. On Clydeside, craft unionists and radical young shop stewards bitterly opposed having their independence compromised.[4] Only the Communist Party remained wholehearted advocates of JPCs.[5]

The key challenge facing the new Labour government of 1945 was increasing production and exports. For the TUC General Council, maximising production was critical if the government's welfare reforms were to be viable. Equally, the government's commitment to full employment removed the 'very severe "whip"' of mass unemployment as a stimulus to labour efficiency. JPCs were regarded as the most important vehicle for instilling a new productivist culture in British factories under full employment. But, as the TUC recognised, the diminished presence of JPCs in British industry in the later years of the war was compounded by employer hostility and 'a new psychological factor ... from the Trade Union point of view',

> workers in some instances see no reason why they should produce more in order to 'swell the profits of the boss'. It was quite different during the war when the production was for the Government. Now it is for private enterprise and in some cases the old attitude of 'beating the boss' has not lost its attraction.[6]

Communist Party support for JPCs extended into the post-war period.   Indeed, Communist Party support for increased production during the war was simply transferred to support for the new Labour government's production drive.[7] The Secretary of the unofficial but influential Scottish Shop Stewards' Conference announced 'it is our job to see that reactionary aims are thwarted by ensuring that production necessary for Labour to meet its commitments at home is achieved'.[8] Implicit in the support of shopfloor activists for the Attlee government was the demand for legislative backing for JPCs as the *quid pro quo* for increased productivity.

> We are not prepared to be mere 'hands' any longer.   The workers must play a positive role in the running of every industry at every level particularly by reviving the JPCs.[9]

Privately, however, Clydeside Communists admitted that there was little grassroots enthusiasm for JPCs and widespread indifference to the democratisation of industry:

> Rather a difficult position at the moment; workers have a tendency to regard the Production Committee as something which exists to spur them on to greater physical effort and, in view of the uncertain conditions in the average factory, there is inclined to be a feeling that JPCs are no longer necessary. A lot of campaigning remains to be done to make the workers value the political importance of JPCs and the constructive role they play in the current situation.[10]

In January 1948 even the concerted efforts of the influential communist group on the AEU's Clydeside district committees failed to check rank-and-file opposition to joint consultation. The Communists were unable to stem the opposition to 'half and half bodies in industry (which) do not give the working class any measure of control of the production process'. JPCs were not viewed as vehicles of industrial democracy but as 'a lever to speed up and discipline the working class'.[11]   Clarion calls by Communist activists, Labour politicians and union leaders for increased productivity were swamped by a rising swell of wage militancy.

The national-level institutions of wartime corporatism survived after 1945 but only as an empty shell.   Jack Tanner, the AEU's key negotiator, maintained his advocacy of JPCs on the national Engineering Advisory Council, a corporatist body established during the war.   Tanner was instrumental in shifting official AEU policy behind a highly regulated labour market in which levels of skill, training, and wages would be tightly controlled at national level.   In return, the employers were expected to concede an entirely new bargaining procedure which would be based on conciliation and, if that failed, binding arbitration at all levels. Finally, Tanner wanted the employers to revive JPCs in which stewards would play a leading role. Elevating the role of the steward would, Tanner argued, improve the union's disciplinary control and legitimise JPCs among a profoundly sceptical rank-and-file.[12] For four years the employers shadow-boxed with the AEU executive. Irrespective of the strategic merits of using JPCs to incorporate shop stewards, engineering employers were totally unwilling to dilute managerial prerogative. The employers' great fear was that the Labour government would strengthen and extend legislation for JPCs to cover small firms.[13] To undermine the prospect of legislative compulsion, the employers' organisation urged their members to follow one of two courses. Where JPCs were dormant they should make a token effort to resuscitate them. Their real intention was, however, implicit in their advice that 'general publicity rather than personal contact' was preferable as it was the method *least* likely to produce results. On the other hand, where there was some pressure from below for JPCs, employers were advised to hold meetings outside working hours and to ensure that stewards were outnumbered by foremen and staff.[14] The engineering employers adopted a highly defensive position towards JPCs through the life of the Attlee governments. In response to government enquiries, the EEF stressed its support for JPCs and that membership surveys demonstrated that there was no need for government intervention. In federated firms employing over three-quarters of a million workers 'some form of JPC is in operation'. Equally, small firms employing fewer than 150 workers were exempt from the JPC Agreement. 'If ... allowance is made for the large number of small producers, together with others who may have other means of contact regarded as appropriate', the Federation assured the Ministry of Labour, 'the conclusion is reached that consultative machinery is not only accepted but widely accepted'.[15]

On Clydeside, employers remained determined not to make any concessions which would prove impossible to roll back when the Attlee government eventually fell. More than this, they demonstrated a determination to revert to the managerial autocracy perfected during the inter-war depression. To the jaundiced eye of the Ministry of Labour's conciliation officer in the area, there was little the state could do to overcome employer resistance to the idea of JPCs.

> This is a very touchy matter because of the inability of so many people in industry to consider it dispassionately and without political feeling. It is a subject which excites strong emotions in the minds of the more crusty employers, whereas the Left Wingers on the workers side are running the idea hard with a view not to joint consultation but to workers' control.[16]

One of the main conclusions of the only extensive contemporary survey of JPCs in post-war manufacturing was that joint consultation was more likely to exist and be constructive where managements encouraged union membership and facilitated shop steward activity. Conversely, where employers adopted a hostile attitude towards shopfloor trade unionism this proved infertile ground for developing a productivist dialogue between managers and managed.[17]   The actions of employers, in other words, were vital in shaping the form and content of industrial relations.   There is little doubt about which camp Clydeside employers belonged to.   The main thrust of employer strategy on Clydeside was to disrupt workplace trade unionism rather than institutionalise it, to marginalise where it proved impossible to ostracise the shop steward.   Just a few months after the end of the war shop stewards on the Clyde noted the beginnings of concerted attacks on workshop trade unionism:'the gloves are now off'.[18]   Nor was this scaremongering.   The transition from war to peacetime production provided ample opportunity for discriminating against activists.   In some cases, stewards alleged that management were adopting 'scorched-earth' tactics by paying off whole departments of up to 300 workers in order to eliminate a handful of leading shop stewards.[19]

Clydeside employers anticipated that a short post-war boom would be quickly followed by recession.   Above all, the employers organisations were determined to avoid any serious short-term drift in wages and conditions.   'It is necessary to repeat that every Federated Employer is expected not to take action which would be prejudicial to his fellow Federated Employers'.[20]   Shortages of skilled manual and technical labour quickly caused divisions among the employers when wartime restrictions on labour mobility ended in early 1946.   The employers' organisation first instinct was to call for voluntary restraint and that member firms contact the previous employer prior to hiring new employees.   In the summer of 1946 the Clyde Association introduced a formal enquiry note system to check escalating labour mobility and the upward drift of wages and conditions. The enquiry note system was a dismal failure: thousands were issued but the decentralised system operated in name only.   In terms of exercising effective control over the labour market there was an inverse relationship between the Association's bluster and its effectiveness.   Those firms which did routinely make enquiries found themselves rebuffed and quickly became disenchanted with the unconstrained recruitment practices of their fellow manufacturers.   An unseemly scramble developed among federated firms as scarce labour was tempted by offers of additional holidays, relaxed overtime, loose piecework systems and bonus payments.   Employer surveys in 1947-48 and 1952 revealed alarmingly high levels of labour mobility.   At the extreme, one Govan firm employing 240 engineers reported a turnover rate of almost forty per cent of its skilled workforce in a single month in 1948.   Turnover rates of around 25 per cent per year appear to have been common in the decade to 1955.[21]   Much of this employment mobility was extremely local: engineers switching back and forth within clusters of neighbouring firms.   If anything, the local nature of this phenomena increased the tension between employers confronting an intractable dilemma both for individual firms and for the employers' organisation.   In February 1948 the local employers' association acidly commented that the same firms which complained most of 'labour poaching' and 'the indiscipline and irresolve' of their fellow employers were by no means innocent of abusing overtime and Sunday working.

> Unless [prospective employees] are assured plenty of Sunday work they will not accept engagement, stating that they can easily get Sunday work with other firms. ... the Association is very much concerned with the effect on the labour position of other members and the bad psychological effect on the workers concerned.[22]

The failure of the enquiry note system left the employers' Association without the kind of extensive database necessary to police the local labour market. Partly as a result of their failure to create even the most basic bureaucratic control mechanism, the Clyde Employers' Association did not even aspire to compile a central blacklist of union activists. Rather, they preferred to adopt a pragmatic arms length form of discrimination which also avoided the risk of compromising the integrity of the bargaining procedures. However, the Association did provide the framework necessary for systematic discrimination on the Clyde. The Association circulated printed annual directories of 'responsible officials', complete with internal extensions and home telephone numbers, in member firms to whom 'discreet enquiry' could be made. This was portrayed not as a new departure but simply as the formalisation of 'the "gentlemen's agreement" regarding the engagement of labour and dealing with the subversive element'. 'A firm', the Association coyly suggested, 'might feel inclined to give useful information, perhaps a warning, about a former employee to his new employers'.[23] Paranoia about Communist influence on the shopfloor was so strong within the Association that it urged that supporting the blacklist should take priority over even the most desperate short-term need for skilled labour .

> The question of selectivity in the engagement of workers in present circumstances is admittedly difficult; but knowing what may happen through indifference, it seems well worth while to make such efforts as may be possible to keep out these undesirables.[24]

There is no way to estimate the effectiveness of individual blacklisting. The Employers' Association had no effective sanction against firms which ignored its pleas to collective solidarity. The Association was often reduced to a helpless bystander as firms engaged in a free-for-all for skilled labour. 'There is no conflict we dislike dealing with so much as that of one member against another; these usually refer to unjustified increments and conditions which unsettle workers elsewhere, and also the sometimes thinly veiled incitement of ... manual workers and the offers to interview applicants for employment outside working hours'.[25] Employers on Clydeside were bitterly opposed not only to the principles of joint consultation but also, in many cases, to effective factory-level union organisation *per se*. There were clear limits to employer solidarity when confronted by a tight labour market which undermined their *collective* capability to enforce an effective blacklist: the employers' anti-union activities centred on the individual firm.

Management Strategy and Shopfloor Trade Unionism

The Second World War witnessed a dramatic rise in union membership, power and influence at all levels, from the shopfloor to the corridors of Whitehall. The AEU's total membership rose to over one million at the end of the war. Inside the factories of Clydeside, there was a sharp rise in the shop steward numbers but rebuilding shopfloor trade unionism was a highly uneven process. Outside a handful of factories, the inter-war depression had decimated shop steward organisation, often leaving only a rump of stewards relatively sheltered inside the craft enclave of the toolroom. In many cases, then, factory union organisation was built virtually from scratch during the war. Particularly in smaller firms with workforces of less than 150 employees, management's grudging acceptance that shop stewards had a legitimate place in collective bargaining was secured through a combination of constant rank-and-file pressure and repeated interventions by the Ministry of Labour's local officials. Throughout the war, Clydeside managers' resigned acceptance of shop stewards masked their constant search for ways to undermine the stewards' position. At most, many employers and supervisors would acknowledge the authority of a particular shop steward rather than the office itself. Managerial attempts to build personalised bargaining regimes reflected their over-riding objective: to make temporary concessions only when absolutely necessary and to ensure that these were never regarded as permanent alterations to the terrain of collective bargaining. This heavy reliance on personalised bargaining was to remain a central feature of the informal level of collective bargaining in engineering between 1945-68.[26] The dominant theme of industrial relations on wartime Clydeside was wage militancy, not workers' control or the role of the JPC in a productivist post-war settlement between capital and labour.[27]

The social history of British shopfloor trade unionism between 1945 and the *Donovan Report* of 1968 remains largely unwritten.[28] Union growth in engineering was not, however, a gradual process after 1945. In the years 1945-49 particularly, union densities varied enormously within and between factories. Equally, union membership levels, at least in part, reflected the depth and quality of shopfloor activism and were often highly volatile. Within six months a factory could easily change from high to low membership levels or vice versa. Such volatility was most commonly found in smaller firms but was not unknown even in the region's largest factories and shipyards. Indeed, shop steward organisation in this period varied independently of factory size: in large factories a single steward could represent up to one hundred workers, a constituency impossible in smaller units.[29] Less than a year after achieving 100 per cent membership among Harland and Wolff engineers the local AEU organiser noted despairingly that this had all but collapsed in some departments and had fallen by more than a third in the engineering works as a whole. Even the shop stewards were dismissed as having a limited interest in trade unionism'.[30] The key to creating - and sustaining - organisation was the arrival of an experienced activist or a young engineer prepared to stand as a shop steward. Both types of shop steward were extremely vulnerable to victimisation. Neither had seniority as a form of practical or moral protection. The new arrival had little opportunity to build a reputation or an extensive friendship network on the shopfloor before his activism brought him into conflict with management. Employers were well aware of the levels of organisation in their factories and the critical role of the steward in building and consolidating shopfloor trade unionism. Occasionally, they were disarmingly frank in describing their motives for victimisation. The manager of a major Renfrew factory described how the arrival of a union activist had 'disturbed' his 'placid' workforce. Joe Scott was transferred to outwork 'not on account of his qualifications as a fitter but to remove him from the Renfrew Factory for the time being'. This proved only a temporary respite and Scott was sacked three months later.[31] Despite a two week strike by Scott's 300 workmates he was not reinstated. Six months later local union officials were appalled at how quickly organisation had deteriorated in the factory.[32]

But there were dangers for the employers in such spoiling tactics. As William Carron, the AEU's autocratic President explained, 'workpeople ... [who] have not been organised for very long ... are not quite so well aware of the niceties of the Procedure ... as might be the case in longer established and longer organised factories'.[33] In other words, victimisation in organising factories could have unpredictable consequences in which the union leadership had limited power to order and minimal moral authority to curtail wildcat strikes. In factories where shop steward organisation was more firmly established management faced a different set of constraints. Only in exceptional cases was there a stable pattern of formal collective bargaining at factory level before 1960. However, as we have seen, even where an employer recognised a steward or convenor as a legitimate bargaining partner this was often a highly qualified form of personal recognition.[34] At most, the Clyde Employers' Association explained, 'the Shop Stewards are granted certain *privileges*'.[35] In the decade after 1945 'privileges' such as the right to hold stewards' meetings, to move between departments and to initiate negotiations with management reflected the balance of power inside individual factories. In highly unionised factories victimisation took a number of forms: from allocating a steward only poorly paid jobs, stopping his overtime, to giving him the dirtiest or most difficult jobs on the oldest, most temperamental machines. Shop stewards and supervisors waged a small scale war of attrition. In defence of an exasperated steward sacked for swearing and grabbing his foreman by the lapels an AEU official explained:

One could never expect that any human being could be subjected to that kind of pressure and pin-pricks and irritation, and even worse than that without there being some reaction.[36]

A widespread tactic was shifting stewards between departments, shifts and even factories.   Again, in an unguarded moment, one Glasgow manager warned 'insubordinate' shop stewards that this is precisely what he would do to disrupt their campaign to increase bonus earnings: 'I will disorganise you'.[37]

In Weirs of Cathcart, a factory which had played a central role in the shop stewards' movements of both world wars, managerial attempts to disorganise stewards were graphically illustrated in 1952-53.   John Sheriff had worked in Weirs for over twenty years and had acted as a steward since 1938.   The Weirs stewards had successfully campaigned for higher bonus earnings throughout the factory.   Amid rising tensions on the shopfloor, management moved Sheriff from tool room to production work.   Sheriff was placed on a Victorian grinding machine without the indicators and stops necessary for the complex job of finishing long turbine shafts with twelve different diameters along its length.   To add to Sheriff's difficulties he was immediately embroiled in bonus issues in his new department.   Inevitably, given the inherent difficulty of his job and the constant distractions, Sheriff scrapped expensive jobs and was sacked for incompetence.   The threat of a wildcat sympathy strike was only stopped by the Weirs stewards who took the case through the lengthy procedure but without success.[38]   Privately, even the employers' Association admitted that this had been a none too subtle piece of creative dismissal.   Despite this, however, there was no question of the employers' organisation supporting the AEU's claim against Weirs.   Sherrif was unemployed for nine months, despite an acute shortage of skilled labour, before being elected a full-time AEU organiser.

The most significant case of victimisation in well organised factories occurred in Rolls Royce Hillington in 1951-52.   With its ten thousand strong workforce perhaps the best organised on Clydeside, Rolls Royce was a pace-setter in terms of wages and conditions.   The stewards had consolidated their position during and after the war when they led a successful campaign to keep the factory open.   The leading stewards were highly experienced and included Communist activists acutely aware of the factory's importance in the local labour market.   Equally, during the 1947-51 national campaigns for a new wages structure, the Hillington stewards had led a variety of work to rule, overtime and piecework bans.[39]   Indeed, in the short-term it was the effectiveness of an overtime and piecework ban which led to management attempting to transfer workers between civil and military work.   However, in the medium term the Rolls Royce management were preparing the ground before expanding their workforce.   Rolls Royce, the Ministry of Labour's representative observed, had, decided on a show-down that may dispose of existing embargoes, and also to clean out their attics in anticipation of the substantial increase to their labour force which is now pending.[40]

Ironically, the two Communist stewards at the centre of the 1951 confrontation were trying to prevent a piecework ban escalating into an unofficial strike. Despite warnings from management to break up an impromptu meeting they clocked out and held the meeting outside the factory gates. They were sacked for challenging managerial authority.[41] AEU officials were anxious that Rolls Royce would be emulated by other local employers. If the Clyde employers abandoned their low-key attacks on shop stewards in favour of targeting high-profile activists, AEU officials warned, it would totally undermine constitutional authority in the region. The secret diplomacy involving the firm, union officials and state representatives hinged on how best to uphold the firm's decision without making martyrs of the sacked stewards.

> Superficially, the strikers appear to have no case, yet they seem to have persuaded some of their F[ull] T[ime] O[fficials] that the firm and the Association have a charge to answer. Either that or some FTOs, particularly those of the two Unions whose members were dismissed, find it politic to give an appearance of doing everything they can to help their dismissed members. This is particularly so in the case of the AEU whose District Organiser has a difficult District Committee which contains a majority of extremists, including one of the dismissed Shop Stewards. Against that, some of the FTOs only indirectly concerned seem to think that, on the long view, it would be better to let the case take its normal course; if negotiations after a resumption failed to produce reinstatement even that might be a blessing in disguise.[42]

The Rolls Royce stewards became the focal point of rank and file resentment against the union leadership for their failure to protect shop stewards through procedural bargaining. The AEU executive's support for the strike was belated and its motives dubious.[43] The Rolls Royce sympathy strike finally broke after six weeks. For John Boyd, the area's right-wing representative on the union's national executive, the strike had been 'a demonstration of weakness' rather than strength. 'The Shop Stewards completely overestimated the workers' solidarity; the workers were not behind the Shop Stewards. ... [The stewards] were leaders without an army'.[44] For the activists, however, the dispute had confirmed the weakness of the national officials and that there could be no redress for victimisation through official procedure: protecting the shop steward was a function of shopfloor strength, elevating the informal over the formal system of collective bargaining.

A common theme in all cases of victimisation was that they all involved a real or imagined challenge to managerial authority. Managerial authority was singular and indivisible - the employees could no more concede the union's right to challenge supervisory authority on the shopfloor than they could overturn a member firm's decision through procedure.   The challenge to managerial authority took a number of forms: from individual confrontations between stewards and foremen to a collective challenge such as the demand for a closed shop.   The question of authority, of the legitimacy of stewards as lay union officials was an implicit theme in all victimisation cases.   Occasionally, however, the contest for authority between management and steward was made explicit.   Three Thermotank stewards were sacked in 1957 for their part in convening a meeting about the workforce's ban on piecework and overtime.   For management the stewards activity constituted 'a direct and defiant challenge to the Company ... a challenge to authority and discipline ... which the firm could not possibly ignore'.[45]

The challenge to established authority stretched beyond the shopfloor.   The AEU leadership recognised that the wave of victimisation on Clydeside undermined their authority and that of procedural bargaining as a whole.   The unctuous John Boyd warned the employers of the dangers to the union, managerial and procedural authority:

> We as an Executive Council ... believe in the sanctity of our Procedure Agreement. We believe as an Executive, that we cannot permit our people to lead us; we have to lead them.   Once we give in to this type of things, we are going to have jungle warfare, and we will not have a Union at all, and we will not have a Procedure Agreement at all.[46]

For Boyd, victimisation initiated a vicious circle which enhanced the authority of militant stewards at the expense of the union leadership.   This was particularly true on Clydeside where Boyd warned,

> there is an ever-growing nucleus of Shop Stewards who have been dismissed and we do not want to develop the hardening core of suspicion and distrust. [47]

Boyd's diagnosis was correct.   Each act of victimisation, each time that procedural bargaining failed to check excessive managerial autocracy, confirmed the need for, and authority of, the shop steward as an independent force on the shopfloor.   More practically, the myriad forms of victimisation stimulated the development of unofficial funds at factory level to recompense stewards for loss of bonus and overtime earnings and, in extreme cases, as a form of victimisation benefit.   Such funds were to provide the financial basis for the growth of shop steward activity outside the factory from the late 1950s onward: from a pressure group in union elections to company-wide Combine Committees.[48]

Conclusions

British engineering employers rejected the real possibility of incorporating shop stewards in a hierarchy of bargaining institutions from the factory to the national level.   More than this, in the decade after 1945 they pursued a strategy of *ad hoc* but determined victimisation.   By the national strike of 1957 this war of attrition on the shop floor had completely undermined the authority of the union leadership and procedural bargaining.   As Hugh Clegg (1957) concluded, the 1957 national dispute, the first in engineering for over thirty years, was 'a conflict of principle' rather than 'a mere argument over a matter of shillings and pence in a boom year'.[49]   Employer strategy, in other words, was the prime stimulus in the creation of the 'second shop stewards' movement in British manufacturing which emerged in the 1960s.   This stewards' movement also articulated generational grievances: all these facets are implicit in Hugh Scanlon's Presidential address to the AEU in 1967, when he gave voice to this new generation of shopfloor activists who had no direct experience of the inter-war years and were openly contemptuous of established authority.

> The very problems you were faced with on the shopfloor and the struggles for a halfpenny and a penny an hour increase - knowing full well that fabulous amounts were being created by the very people you were representing - all of this contributed, together with the disillusionment any young chap who becomes active has with the old leadership.   They never act fast enough, are never militant enough for young people.   I think that's a good thing.[50]

Notes

1. J. Hinton, *Shop Floor Citizens: Engineering Democracy in 1940s Britain*, Edward Elgar (1994), Aldershot
2. R. Croucher , *Engineers at War, 1939-1945*, Merlin Press (1982) London, pp149-60.
3. See A. McKinlay and J. Zeitlin , 'The Meanings of Managerial Prerogative: Industrial Relations in British Engineering, 1880-1939', *Business History*, 31 (2) (1989), pp32-47.
4. Croucher, *Engineers*, pp167-74.
5. N. Fishman, *The British Communist Party and the Trade Unions 1933-45*, Scolar Press, (1995), Aldershot, pp298-313.
6. TUC, Memo to Ministry of Labour, 5 November 1946, Modern Record Centre (MRC) MSS292/225/3.
7. 'Proposals', CPGB Scottish Area 10.5.1946, information from Scottish Council, Labour Party to the Ministry of Labour, Public Record Office (PRO) LAB10/591.
8. *New Propellor*, September 1945.
9. *Metal Worker*, March 1946.
10. 'Proposals', PRO LAB10/591.
11. Glasgow District Committee Minutes (hereafter AEU GDC), 21 January 1948.   For parallels in Manchester see, L. James (1984), *Power in a Trade Union: The Role of the District Committee in the AUEW*, Cambridge University Press (1984) Cambridge, pp64-9.
12. EEF and AEU Central Conference, 30 April 1948, MRC MSS237/1/13/84.
13. EEF, General Council, 22 April 1948.
14. North West Engineering Trades Employers' Association, Circular Letter (hereafter NWETEA CL), 9 July 1948, Glasgow City Archives, TD1059/7/40.

15. Ramsay, EEF, Memo to Ministry of Labour, January 1950, MRC MSS292/225/4.
16. Chief Conciliators Weekly Report, 8 May 1948, PRO LAB10/368.
17. National Institute of Industrial Psychology (1952), *Joint Consultation in British Industry*, London: Staples Press, pp53-4, 56-7; A.Tatlow (1951), 'Joint Consultation in Nine Firms', *Yorkshire Bulletin of Economic and Social Research*, 3 (1), pp47, 50; T.Veness (1951), 'The Human Problems of the Building Industry: Joint Consultation on Building Sites', *Occupational Psychology*, 25 (2), p136.
18. *Metal Worker*, January 1946.
19. See AEU GDC, 30 January 1946, for example.
20. NWETEA CL, 8 April 1946, TD1059/7/37.
21. Calculated from NWETEA Case Papers, 'Labour Supply', 1947-53.
22. NWETEA CL, 25 February 1948, TD1059/7/37.
23. NWETEA CL, 12 August 1954, TD1059/7/46.
24. NWETEA CL, 24 June 1954, TD1059/7/46.
25. NWETEA CL, 26 December 1957, TD1059/7/49.
26. A. Marsh and E.Coker, 'Shop Steward Organisation', *British Journal of Industrial Relations*, 1 (2) (1963), p177.
27. On wartime industrial relations in Clydeside engineering see, W.W.Knox and A.McKinlay,   '"Pests to Management": Engineering Shop Stewards on Clydeside, 1939-1945', *Journal of the Scottish Labour History Society*, 24 (1995), forthcoming.
28. M. Terry, 'The Development of Shop Steward Organisation: Coventry Precision Tools, 1945-1972', in M. Terry, and P. Edwards (eds.), *Shopfloor politics and job controls: the post-war engineering industry*, Blackwell, (1988), Oxford, p26.
29. H.A. Clegg, A.J. Killick and R. Adams, *Trade Union Officers: A Study of Full-Time Officers, Branch Secretaries and Shop Stewards in British Trade Unions*, Blackwell (1961) Oxford, p152.
30. AEU GDC, Divisional Organiser's Report, 14 August 1948.
31. NWETEA CL, 10 January 1957, TD1059/7/49.
32. AEU, Paisley District Committee Minutes (hereafter AEU PDC), 17 July 1958.
33. EEF and AEU, Central Conference, 11 April 1958, MRC MSS237/1/13/110.
34. EEF and AEU, Central Conference, 8 April 1949, MRC MSS237/1/13/86 and 14 February 1952, MSS237/1/13/93.
35. NWETEA CL, 17 April 1948, TD1059/7/40, emphasis added.
36. NWETEA and AEU, Local Conference, 18 June 1952, TD1059/7/44.
37. AEU GDC, 13 December 1950.
38. NWETEA CL 2 May 1952, TD1059/7/44; EEF and AEU Central Conference, 13 November 1953, Informal and Local Conferences, 14 July, 15 October 1953, MRC MSS237/3/1/56.
39. J.Corina, *The British Experiment in Wage Restraint 1948-81*, Oxford University: unpublished D Phil thesis (1961), pp171-257; A.Tatlow, 'The Underlying Issues of the 1949-50 Engineering Wage Claim', *Manchester School*, 21 (3) (1953), pp. 258-71; A.Warner, *British Trade Unionism under a Labour Government: 1945-1951*, Columbia University: unpublished PhD thesis, (1954), pp147-55.
40. 'Memo', 15 February 1951, PRO LAB10/1023.
41. AEU Paisley DC (hereafter AEU PDC), 16 February 1951.
42. 'Memo', 26 Feburary 1951, PRO LAB10/1023.
43. 'Memo', 12 June 1951, PRO LAB10/1023.
44. AEU PDC, 6 April 1951.
45. NWETEA CL, 30 December 1957, TD1059/7/49.
46. EEF and AEU Central Conference, 10 April 1959, MRC MSS237/1/13/112.
47. EEF and AEU Central Conference, 8 March 1957, MRC MSS237/1/13/106.
48. S.Lerner and J. Marquand, 'Regional Variations in Earnings, Demand for Labour and Shop Stewards' Combine Committees in British Engineering' *Manchester School* 31 (1963), pp290-91.
49. Clegg, H. and R. Adams, *The Employers' Challenge: A Study of the National Shipbuilding and Engineering Disputes of 1957* Blackwell (1957) Oxford, p7.
50. H.Scanlon, 'The Role of Militancy: Interview with Hugh Scanlon, President of the AEU', *New Left Review*, 46, (1967), p 4.

Index

—A—

Abs, H.J., 117
Adenauer, K., 72, 109, 112
ADS (Germany), 117
advanced technology mining (ATM),
    UK, 134, 136, 137, 138, 139, 140
Advisory Council on Scientific Policy,
    34
Advisory Councils (UK), 13, 14
Agartz, V., 68, 69, 111
Agrarian Party (Sweden), 86, 89, 100
Aktiengesellschaften, 111
Amalgamated Engineering Union
    (AEU), UK, 15, 16, 24, 27, 28, 29,
    30, 46, 47, 50, 54, 55, 62, 63, 64,
    175, 176, 180, 181, 182, 183, 184,
    185, 186, 187
American High Commission (in
    Germany), 71
Anderton Shearer Loader (ASL), 132
Anglo-American Council on
    Productivity, 55, 57, 59, 60
Arbeitsgerichte Courts (Germany), 106
Arendt, W., 118
armoured flexible conveyor (AFC), 132
Ashworth, W., 163, 170, 172, 173
Attlee, C., 10, 22, 25, 26, 41, 42, 43,
    48, 49, 61, 176, 177
Ayrshire (Scotland), 154

—B—

Baird Iron and Steel Company, 154
Bamforth, K., 126
Bank of England, 26

bargaining, 30, 38, 39, 45, 47, 49, 50,
    58, 59, 63, 68, 70, 74, 81, 82, 83, 85,
    86, 87, 88, 89, 90, 91, 93, 95, 96, 98,
    100, 102, 103, 105, 109, 113, 128,
    131, 133, 134, 140, 141, 142, 145,
    146, 147, 150, 152, 155, 157, 160,
    161, 163, 164, 165, 166, 167, 168,
    175, 176, 179, 180, 181, 183, 184
Barnett, C., 3, 5, 10, 20, 21, 22, 23, 45,
    62
Basic Agreement (1938), 82, 83, 84, 87,
    103. *See also* Saltsjobaden
Batstone, E., 41, 44, 45, 60, 62
Berg, F., 117, 169
*Betriebsraete (German workers'
    representatives)*, 109
Bevan, M.A., 30, 41, 42
Bevin, E., 11, 15, 24, 48
Board of Trade, 28, 31, 48, 49, 58
Boeckler, H., 111
Boilermakers' Union (UK), 59
Bonn, 117, 121
Boyd, J., 183, 184
Brighton (TUC) Congress, 46. *See also*
    Trades Union Congress (TUC)
Britain, 25, 26, 31, 37, 39, 40, 41, 42,
    43, 44, 48, 60, 62, 64, 65, 66, 75, 97,
    103, 104, 105, 123, 127, 130, 141,
    142, 146, 149, 156, 159, 163, 170,
    171, 185
British Coal, 131, 137, 141, 142, 143,
    169. *See also* National Coal Board
British Employers' Confederation
    (BEC), 13, 24, 49, 51, 55, 58

187